PENGUIN BOOKS
RAP: THE LYRICS

JEFFERSON MORLEY has published investigative reporting, essays, and interviews in *The New Republic*, *The Nation*, *Rolling Stone*, *Spin*, the *Los Angeles Times*, *The New York Times*, the *Washington Post*, and other national publications. He has written on U.S. drug policy, national security issues, Central American politics, racial issues, and popular music. He has been the political correspondent for *Spin*. From 1987 to 1990 he was the Washington editor of *The Nation*, writing on the cocaine economy, the Iran-contra affair, and rock music in Eastern Europe. Before that he was Associate Editor at *The New Republic*, where he published cover stories on subjects ranging from the CIA to Bruce Springsteen. Morley has also worked as an editor at *Harper's* and *Foreign Policy*. A native of Minneapolis, Minnesota, he received a B.A. in American history from Yale in 1980. He lives in Takoma Park, Maryland.

LAWRENCE STANLEY is an attorney with a varied practice in entertainment and obscenity law. Formerly Director of Business Affairs for Tommy Boy Music, Inc. (which boasts such acts as Stetsasonic, De La Soul, Digital Underground, Queen Latifah, and Naughty by Nature), Mr. Stanley now represents several recording artists and, together with his wife, Hope Carr, runs *Clearance 13'8"*, a sample clearance business, negotiating publishing and master rights for numerous rap and dance groups and record labels. In addition, Mr. Stanley is an active opponent of censorship, and his activities range from representation of and consultation with defendants in criminal cases to journalism. In 1989, Mr. Stanley received the H.L. Mencken Award from the Free Press Association for his exposé in *Playboy* magazine on the sale of child pornography by the U.S. government. He has written for the *Cardozo Arts and Entertainment Law Journal*, *Art Journal*, the journal of the College Art Association, and *Playboy*, among other publications.

Rap the lyrics

Edited by Lawrence A. Stanley

with an Introduction by Jefferson Morley

Penguin Books

PENGUIN BOOKS
Published by the Penguin Group
Penguin Books USA Inc.,
375 Hudson Street, New York, New York 10014, U.S.A.
Penguin Books Ltd, 27 Wrights Lane,
London W8 5TZ, England
Penguin Books Australia Ltd, Ringwood,
Victoria, Australia
Penguin Books Canada Ltd, 10 Alcorn Avenue
Toronto, Ontario, Canada M4V 3B2
Penguin Books (N.Z.) Ltd, 182–190 Wairau Road,
Auckland 10, New Zealand

Penguin Books Ltd, Registered Offices:
Harmondsworth, Middlesex, England

First published in Penguin Books 1992

10 9 8 7 6 5 4 3 2

Library of Congress Cataloging in Publication Data
Rap: the lyrics/ edited by Lawrence A. Stanley; with an
   introduction by Jefferson Morley.
       p. cm.
   ISBN 0 14 01.4788 8
   1. Rap (Music)—Texts. 2. Afro-Americans—Songs and music—Texts.
3. Popular music—United States—Texts. I. Stanley, Lawrence A.
II. Title.
ML54.2.R3 1992 <Case>
782.42164—dc20   91–47632

Printed in the United States of America

Set in Electra
Designed by Kingsley Parker

Preface

This book is about rap. It is also about freedom of speech, since rap has become a battleground upon which an intolerant and powerful minority—most of whom happen to be white—has attempted to enforce its values against a disenfranchised and largely powerless minority—most of whom happen to be black. This is, of course, not to say that rap is the only focus for zealots who strive to make America a land of middle-class conformity. Heavy metal and post-punk rock, visual depictions of the human body, and the rights of sexual minorities have all come under heavy fire from fanatical religious groups, the so-called moral majority, and their allies in Congress and the state legislatures, all of whom would like to blame the failure of their American dream (and their version of the American family) on evil lyrics and immoral art.

Censorship is an insidious form of social control. It aims at silencing voices of dissent, whether political, social, or sexual, by stigmatizing the artist, the seller, and, in some cases, the buyer. It promotes intolerance, as well as conformity to the lowest common denominator. At its worst, censorship cuts off our access to information and deprives us of the right to engage in social dialogue and to decide for ourselves what is personally, or politically, acceptable. Charges of "obscenity" notwithstanding, censorship violates first principles, those underlying the Bill of Rights, which demand protection of the masses against the elite and of the few against the many.

For rap music, the censors have, at least until now, utterly failed in their attempt to rid the United States of sexual or violent imagery. The 2 Live Crew case in Broward County, Florida, demonstrated that the censors were out of step with American mores and values, rather than that they represented the community's best interest as they claimed. In popular culture, censorship often works in a contradictory fashion. While the strong language used by many artists whose lyrics are included in this book is seen by those artists as necessary to convey a sense of the violent and chaotic society in which they live, much of what the rappers say in their lyrics probably would not exist but for the censors. "Dirty words," because they have shock value, come, in part, as a reaction to prudishness, false piety, and a refusal to confront the most difficult questions regarding class, race, and sex. Attempts at censorship have also led to financial success. 2 Live Crew's treatment at the hands of a few politically powerful bigots made them a *cause célèbre* and landed their label a distribution deal with a major record company. NWA, whose label received a condemnatory letter from the FBI, now enjoys widespread success—one platinum and one double platinum LP in two years. As Ice T points out in his song "Freedom of Speech," the "explicit lyrics" stickers sought by the PMRC and other censors served as promotion rather than deterrence.

It is not the intention of this book to present a "politically correct" vision of rap music. While I certainly don't agree with every viewpoint being presented, it is more, not less, dialogue that we need. Political correctness, if used as a means to silence, is but another form of intolerance. Moreover, the insistence that rappers in each case serve as positive role models to their youthful listeners and deliver only positive messages is as unreasonable as it is unrealistic. This is, of course, not to say that all rap music is violent, profane, or politically incorrect. Far from it. Attempts at censorship of rap music have also obscured rap's diversity. As Jefferson Morley points out in his introduction, within rap one can find lyrics that are innocent, insightful, sensitive, utopian, orgiastic, and braggadocios. All the noise from both left and right over strong sexual or violent imagery has obscured the fact that rap, more than any other musical genre, has dissected, commented upon, and reflected back to us our culture with startling clarity. It is in the diversity and directness of rap and its unique ability to illuminate our culture that the value of this book lies.

All of the royalties from this book are being donated to The National Coalition on Censorship and other anticensorship organizations. For further information, contact Clearance 13'-8", Inc., 26 West 76th Street, 1R, New York, New York, 10023.

Acknowledgments

Special thanks to Hope Carr, my wife and partner; to Keith and Kevin Smith/Double Vision and Marc Richardson and Jon Schechter at *The Source*, who transcribed some of the most difficult lyrics and filled in words I simply could not hear; Dr. Major Funk, who allowed me unrestricted access to his record collection; Laura Hynes, who also transcribed lyrics in the early stages of this project; Rodd Houston, who advised me on the contents; and Donald Lehr and Elizabeth Berdann, who brought the manuscript to fruition. Thanks also to all the publishers, artists, songwriters, managers, lawyers, and everyone else who participated in furnishing rights or lyrics and making this possible—and on that note, regards to Alan Silber, Esq.; everyone at Tommy Boy crew (Tom Silverman, Monica Lynch, John Monroe, Bryan, Dre, Albie, Steve Knutson, Stella, Checkmaster David S. Barr, Paul Adelberg, Tom Beckerman, Mike Becce, Wayne, Jim Leventhal, Dan Hoffman, Leslie Greene, and Kathy); Julie Lipsius, Rod, and Janine (Lipservices); Ken Anderson, Micheline Wolkowicz, Elizabeth Scher (Loeb & Loeb); Daddy-O, Prince Be, Jarrett, Pos, Mase & Dove, Shock G, Atron Gregory, Dream Warriors, Latifah, Naughty By Nature, Paris, Stereo MC's, Subsonic 2; Lyor Cohen, Russell Simmons, John Scott (RUSH); David Harleston, Cathy Foley (RAL/Def Jam); Cory Robbins, Palissa Kelly, Peter Lightbody (Profile Records); Brian Turner (Priority Records); Fred Munao, Harry Getsov (Select Records); Monica Corten, Karen Decrenza (Cherry Lane Music); Ed Arrow, Steve Scott, Meryl Ginsberg, Jessica Zimmer (Warner-Chappell); Lisa Jacobs, Joan Schulman (Polygram/Island); Laura Rem (Island Records); Jon Baker (Gee Street); Ivan Berry (Beat Factory); Dave Taylor (Subsonic 2); Amy Jonas (Chrysalis); Linda Chelgren, Courtney Post (Almo-Irving); Bill Liebowitz (Mayer, Katz, Baker & Liebowitz); Brian Chin, Robert John (PWL); Peter van Bodegraven (2 Pieters/BMG); Bobby Robinson; Jon Fogarty (Minder Music); David Lucchesi (Danya Records); Doug E. Fresh; Cliff Lovette, Esq.; Mark Koren (MCA); Fred Silber, David Wolfson (EMI); Nancy Ubick (Hal Leonard); Veronica Gretton (Fiction Songs); Ricardo Frazer (Sir Mix-a-Lot); Ed Locke (NastyMix); Shelly Jacob and Jonathan Stone (Windswept Pacific); Renee Picard, Hal Webman (Next Plateau); David

Chackler (Luke's Records); Allen Jacobi, Esq.; Adam Levy (Warlock); Jorge Hinojosa, Steve Stewart (Rhyme Syndicate); Madeleine Smith (Songwriter Services); Desiree Gordy, Pat Charbonnet, Gigi (Street Knowledge); Joe Robinson (Sugar Hill); Aaron Fuchs (Tuff City); Ursula Menina (Manat, Phelps); Michael Ross, Jasmine (Varry White); Dee Gardner (Cold Chillin'); Rochelle Greenblatt (Zomba); Atron Gregory (TNT); Rick Rubin (Def America); Funkenklein (Hollywood Basic); Alex Mejia (Sway & King Tech); Ira Selsky, Esq.; Dante Ross, Nina Ritter (Elektra); Eric Greenspan, Esq.; Paul Connolly, Nick Phillips (MCA UK); and Bob George (Archive of Contemporary Music).

Jefferson Morley wants to thank Michael Kazin, Frank Owen, Bruce Schulman, Jack Shafer, and Alana Wartofsky for their suggestions, and Professor Harold Cruse for a history lesson.

Special thanks to *The Source*, the magazine of hip-hop music, culture, and politics.

And special thanks to David Stanford, our editor at Penguin, whose idea this was in the first place.

Contents

Rap Music as American History
by Jefferson Morley

The term "rap music" originated around 1976. Unlike other events and trends of that year—the celebration of the Bicentennial, the election of President Jimmy Carter, the vogue of disco, the growing glamour of cocaine, or the sight of a white mob in Boston using a pole-mounted American flag to beat a black man—the birth of rap music went unnoticed. Rap was the name given to a novel musical style then gaining popularity among young people in a few black and Hispanic neighborhoods in New York City. Disc jockeys in upper Manhattan and the South Bronx discovered they could keep a dance crowd hopping by playing catchy instrumental breaks from popular records. With two turntables and a sound mixer, DJs could switch from one record to another to create a never-ending dance groove. They could pump up the crowd by using a microphone to call out the names of people in the audience ("Sweet Pea is in the house!") or to boast about themselves. Soon a division of labor emerged. DJs concentrated on perfecting the techniques of manipulating the turntables, while the masters of ceremonies (MCs or rappers) concentrated on rapping in rhymes. DJs explored the sonic possibilities of scratching across the groove of a record. While the needle stays in the groove, it's the record that moves, causing the "scratching" sound. Lyrically, MCs competed to develop longer and more original rhymes. Live shows at playgrounds and house parties were recorded, and these cassettes circulated among young fans.

Older music professionals in the black community recognized the commercial possibilities in the enthusiasm of their children. They invited rappers into larger venues like the Audubon Ballroom in Harlem (Malcolm X, who has become a cultural hero to a generation of rappers, had been assassinated there in February 1965). In 1980, Joe and Sylvia Robinson, an r&b duo of the 1950s turned producers, released a single called "Rapper's Delight," by a group called Sugarhill Gang. Based on the irresistible hook to Chic's 1978 mega-hit "Good Times," "Rapper's Delight" became the first rap song to receive wide air play on radio stations.

"Rapper's Delight," dismissed by many as a novelty, was to rap what "Rock Around the Clock" was to rock and roll in 1954: it announced the commercial viability of a new musical tradition. Within ten years of "Rapper's Delight," rap had become one of the most popular musical styles in the world, heard everywhere from Harlem to Hollywood, from Peoria to Poland, from Compton to Kinsasha.

Rap music has deep and diverse roots in African-American life. In the fifteenth and sixteenth centuries, the societies of West Africa had a figure known as a *griot* who challenged social transgressors to listen to the will of the people. "Abusive songs against ordinary individuals [were] sometimes directly used as means of social pressure, enforcing the will of public opinion," according to David Toop, author of *Rap Attack: From African Jive to New York Hip Hop*. (Toop's book, though dated, remains the best history of rap.) It is no distortion to say that rappers are latter-day griots.

Rhythmic talking styles have always been part of African-American culture. Pigmeat Markham, a singer-comedian, did what would now be regarded as a rap act in New York City as early as 1929. Slim Galliard, a piano-playing, jive-talking hipster in the 1940s, was a rapper in all but name. (Galliard, in fact, made his last record with a rap group called the Dream Warriors shortly before his death in 1990.) In the 1950s, black radio featured "personality DJs," nighttime motormouths whose sly rhyming patter was a forerunner of modern rap. On the streets of black America there was "The Dozens," the duel of verbal wits organized around the linguistic violation of your opponent's mama. Jerry Jaye Ruffin, general manager of WEDR, a black radio station in Miami, grew up in Fort Lauderdale, Florida, in the late 1950s laughing to rhymes like "I fucked your mama on a bag of flour/She shit pancake for half an hour."

Among the black intelligentsia, there was talking jazz. In the 1960s, the Last Poets, an ensemble of ex-convicts, combined jazz and free verse to articulate popular ideas of black nationalism. In 1973 one of the Last Poets, Jalal Uridin, recording under the name Lightning Rod, put out an album called *Hustler's Convention*. A novelistic parable of card-playing, corruption, and violence backed by the jazz-funk-rock of Kool and the Gang, it would inspire many of the early rappers in New York.

And then there was Muhammad Ali, who used rhyme to convince himself, his opponents, and the world that he was invincible.

With a few words he transformed his fights into mythological confrontations in which he, the self-cast warrior of black America, prevailed through a combination of power and wit. He could "Float like a butterfly, sting like a bee." His 1973 rematch with Joe Frazier was "The Thrilla in Manila." His 1974 bout with George Foreman in Zaire was the "Rumble in the Jungle," in which he triumphed by using the clever "rope-a-dope" strategy. Ali was a fighter, entrepreneur, and rhymster all in one—a rapper just slightly ahead of his time.

Among black youth, there was the rock revolution of the 1960s. Rock and roll had originated in the electrified r&b of the late 1940s. It spread via southern radio stations and became hugely popular with the arrival of Elvis Presley. In the 1960s the Beatles, Woodstock, and a generation of white rock stars fixed rock music as a white form in the public mind. But rock had no small appeal in the black community.

By the early 1970s black artists were the cutting edge of American rock. Jimi Hendrix reinvented the electric guitar. Sly Stone added a rhythm guts to the psychedelic rock style. Stevie Wonder traded in the bubblegum pop of his childhood for a tough-minded rock-and-soul style and toured with the Rolling Stones. Artists like Curtis Mayfield, the Isley Brothers, Parliament-Funkadelic, and War sold millions of albums and played to large concert audiences. Musically, their sound was guitar-dominated, and grittier than the soul and Motown sounds that typified black music in the 1960s. Black rock was the most socially conscious and thematically ambitious popular music of its time. War's 1972 album, *The World Is a Ghetto*, and Parliament's *Mothership Connection* (1975) are forgotten classics of rock that rarely get played on classic rock stations.

Then came disco and format radio. Disco was a highly stylized dance music, popularized first by blacks and gays in the early 1970s. Disco began to cross over onto the pop charts in 1973–74 and exploded in 1976 with the movie *Saturday Night Fever*. The soundtrack album featuring music by the Bee Gees became the best-selling record of all time until Michael Jackson's *Thriller*. As the disco boom took hold, so did radio formats. Traditionally, music radio had been organized around the most popular forty songs in the country. Since the biggest hits could come from a variety of styles, Top 40 radio stations in the late 1960s might play Aretha Franklin, the Rolling Stones, and Englebert Humperdinck back to back. As the pop music audience mushroomed in the late 1960s and early 1970s, radio-station owners hired consultants to develop tightly defined play lists, or formats, that would appeal to select demographic markets. Top 40 was out, and so was free-form FM radio programming in which DJs played whatever they wanted. By 1976 two formats were coming to dominate American music radio. One was called "album-oriented rock" (AOR), aimed at white rock fans; the other was called "urban-contemporary," aimed at black r&b and soul fans.

Formats were a subtle form of musical apartheid. Music radio, which had been relatively integrated during the 1960s, became more segregated. Black rock bands, in particular, were simply frozen out, allegedly "too white" for black listeners, "too black" for white listeners. Black rock music, thriving and widely popular in 1972, was virtually unheard on the radio seven years later. AOR stations stopped playing black artists save for the occasional homage to Hendrix. Urban contemporary stations shied from music that was deemed excessively "black." The very term "urban contemporary" was designed to sell black music without calling it black. After disco flamed out in 1978, urban contemporary stations settled on a conservative formula featuring smooth male balladeers (Teddy Pendergrass and later Luther Vandross), up-tempo soul acts (the Whispers and Shalamar), women with big voices (Cheryl Lynn and Gladys Knight), and straitlaced funk bands (the Commodores and Lakeside). By the late 1970s, the diversity of the black street experience, from Pendergrass to Ali to Hendrix, was not well represented on the airwaves. Rap music filled a vacuum left by the success of urban contemporary radio.

The evolution of American race relations between 1954 and 1976 also figures in the emergence of rap music in the late 1970s. In 1954 the Supreme Court issued its ruling in the *Brown v. Board of Education* case. A black family in Topeka, Kansas, had filed a lawsuit against the local school board for maintaining separate schools for white and black children. The Court, citing sociological data that black children did better in school if they had white classmates, ruled that "separate but equal" school systems were unconstitutional. The Court's ruling contained an unexamined premise: that racial integration is the social embodiment of civil rights. If blacks were given equal rights before the law (the Court's logic went), then blacks and whites would come to mingle as naturally as blondes and brunettes. Desegregation (the abolition of legal barriers to race mixing) would lead naturally to integration (the mixing of the races). Race mixing became the measure of social progress. As black thinkers ranging from Harold Cruse to Clarence Thomas have noted, the authors of the *Brown* decision gave short shrift to the notion that there might be social value in preserving black-run public school systems or that blacks (if provided with genuine equal tax support) might prefer to run their own educational institutions.

The civil rights movement of the early 1960s deepened the confusion between racial integration and racial progress. Led by Martin Luther King, the movement aimed at applying the *Brown* decision to all aspects of life in the South. It tried to abolish what were known as Jim Crow laws, the system of mandatory racial segregation in the South. Initially resisted by white liberals, who were disturbed by King's use of civil disobedience, the civil rights movement eventually won limited acceptance from the white middle class. King's moral leadership and Lyndon Johnson's parliamentary skills forced passage of the Civil Rights Act of 1964, the Voting Rights Act of 1965, and the Fair Housing Act of 1968. This legislation was deeply controversial, for it destroyed legal segregation in the United States.

In its place, the civil rights legislation of the 1960s established race mixing as the legal measure of racial progress. The 1964 Civil Rights Act, which introduced the term "affirmative action" into American life, made the racial composition of the schools, the workplace, and public institutions *the* index of America's commitment to racial justice. The federal government was assigned the task of monitoring, encouraging, and requiring a degree of racial integration that substantial numbers of white Americans had resisted for at least 200 years.

There was often an unstated assumption built into the middle class's notion of integration: that as blacks gained their civil rights they would integrate themselves into white institutions, accept white values, and become part of the so-called American mainstream. This liberal integrationist ideal found expression in the mid-1960s in the racially neutral pop hits of Motown and in the popular movie *Guess Who's Coming to Dinner*, starring Sidney Poitier, Katharine Hepburn, and Spencer Tracy. The movie depicted an interracial romance between a white woman and a black man whose "blackest" feature was his skin color. The film, wrote professor Henry Louis Gates, Jr., in *The New York Times* in 1991, "ironically did more to fuel the death of the civil rights movement and the birth of black nationalism than any other—precisely because it suggested that the movement would achieve fulfillment in a new middle class, assimilated, desexualized, safe."

While Poitier was on screen in the liberal imagination, the Black Power movement was exploding on the streets of black America. In the summer of 1966, young black leaders like Stokely Carmichael and H. Rap Brown stunned liberals by rejecting the implicit condescension in their vision of integration. James Brown defined the popular mood with his smash hit "Say It Loud (I'm Black and I'm Proud)."

The results of the Civil Rights Act have been mixed. Blacks gained entrance to institutions previously closed to them, and the black middle class grew by about ten percent between 1960 and 1970. Since 1970 the percentage of black men classified as middle income or affluent has remained constant. Racial quotas were established by the Nixon administration to stimulate black economic development. At the same time the resistance of the white electorate to federally mandated race mixing remained entrenched, if not widespread. Late in George Bush's first term, affirmative action (or the "quota" system) was said to be the single most potent issue in American domestic politics. Over the course of twenty-five years, racial integration as a measure of racial justice had effectively polarized black and white political interests.

The ambiguous social legacy of the 1960s civil rights movement created conditions ripe for the emergence of rap. By the late 1970s, the ideals of the white liberals and the integrationist policies of the federal government were increasingly irrelevant to the poor and working classes of the black community. If these blacks lived near or attended school with whites, it usually wasn't for long. As blacks became a significant presence in neighborhoods, schools, and governmental bodies, whites tended to withdraw, citing fears of crime and disorder. The black professional class was able to move up to comfortable suburbs and private schools. But the poor and working-class blacks left behind did not benefit from affirmative-action programs at Ivy League schools and Fortune 500 corporations. They were not among the black entrepreneurial class that could take advantage of government set-aside programs for black business. If they benefited from affirmative action to gain entry to white institutions, they often found themselves ill prepared and isolated once they arrived. Legally and rhetorically, America had undergone a racial revolution in the 1960s. Socially and economically, the lot of many blacks was unchanged, if not worsening. In 1978 and 1980, a nationwide white backlash against the civil rights agenda of the 1960s elected a new generation of white conservative politicians hostile to black interests and dedicated to reducing social spending. At the same time, black institutions and neighborhoods were losing some of their most talented leaders to the newly integrated white mainstream.

The aspiring working class of the black community found itself looking at white America across a growing cultural chasm and looking down at the poorest of the black poor, with no social safety net below them. It was the children of this class that invented rap. *Rap music was the sound of black urban youth creating a musical alternative to urban contemporary radio and a socio-cultural alternative to the integrationist policies of the 1960s and the white backlash that accompanied them.*

Four young men in New York City played especially important roles in the birth of rap.

Clive Campbell, otherwise known as Kool Herc, is sometimes credited with being the first modern rapper. Born in Jamaica, Campbell moved to the United States when he was twelve years old. In the early 1970s, he pioneered the art of sampling. He would play a popular dance riff over and over again, throwing in rhymes and adding sound bytes from other records to create a new kind of dance mix. Kool Herc was reputed to have the best sound system of all the street DJs and an unbeatable collection of obscure records.

Afrika Bambaataa, a street DJ from the southeast Bronx, added a socially conscious tone to the emerging rap style. He had grown up among the street gangs of the Bronx in the early 1970s, then schooled himself in black nationalism. He organized playground shows as a means of diverting youth from the dead-end glamour of gangs. He was rap's most eclectic experimenter, mixing black dance cuts with tunes from the whitest of white rock acts, teasing his friends afterward that he had them dancing to the Monkees. "I'd like to catch people who categorize records," Bambaataa said.

• Grandmaster Flash, a DJ in the central Bronx, went beyond rhyming simple phrases to develop narrative. Combining scratching and old-fashioned singing, he would put several MCs on a single song. In his book *Hip Hop: An Illustrated History of Break Dancing,*

Rap Music, and Graffiti, Steven Hager has observed that Flash's vocal style "effectively merged the aggressive rhythms of James Brown with the language and imagery of Hustler's Convention." Flash would go on to record (with the Furious Five) one of rap's greatest hits, "The Message."

DJ Hollywood, a rapper from Harlem, was another leading innovator of rap. According to Nelson George, Hollywood had a deep, soothing voice along the lines of the old-time radio-personality DJs, but he used it for unusually fast and complex raps. While influential in the New York rap scene, DJ Hollywood never enjoyed much commercial success.

Rap was rarely heard on the radio in the late 1970s. Music programmers and record-company executives were not interested. They resembled no one so much as the record company executives of the '50s and '60s who resisted the rising popularity of rock 'n' roll. Even after "Rapper's Delight" became a big hit for Sugarhill Records in 1980, most music industry officials regarded rap as a passing fad. With a few exceptions, black and white entertainment executives alike believed that rap was "too black" to sell to a mass audience, a spectacularly mistaken judgment.

In recent years, rap has gained a deserved reputation for capturing the grimmer realities of black urban life. Yet in its early days rap was generally exuberant and upbeat. The spirit of an early rap classic like "Eighth Wonder" is flamboyant and fanciful, not violent or sexually explicit. In some ways, early rap was the heir of doo-wop, the sweet vocal style of the stoops and street corners in the 1950s. Both shared a spirit of what Nelson George called "inventive innocence."

Even in its more socially conscious forms, early rap was devoted more to uplift than to anger. Afrika Bambaataa and others saw in rap a way to educate and build community solidarity. In the Bronx in 1980, a math teacher named Daryl Aamaa Nubyahn set out to raise the political consciousness of black youth via rap. Under the name Brother D and the Collective Effort, he recorded a rap single called "How We Gonna Make the Black Nation Rise?" "Not only did [rap] help displace violence and the plague of destructive drugs like heroin," suggested David Toop, "but it also fostered an attitude of creating from limited materials."

All the while, the rap audience was growing steadily. "King Tim III," a rap performed by the Fatback Band, a veteran r&b group from Washington D.C., got wide air play. "Put the Boogie in the Body," by the Treacherous Three, was a street hit in 1980. Kurtis Blow, a DJ from Brooklyn, did a witty, hard-luck lament, "The Breaks," which was a crossover hit.

In 1980–82 rap spread from the clubs of Harlem and the Bronx to downtown clubs with a hip white clientele. Fab Five Freddie (now host of MTV's popular *Yo MTV Raps* show) was an uptown rapper who played cultural matchmaker. He introduced aspiring rappers to promoter Ruza Blue, who ran a club off Fourteenth Street called Negril where rappers and breakdancers often performed. Robert Christgau, music critic for *The Village Voice*, championed rap in the face of skepticism from white rock fans.

By 1982, the rap form was gaining in seriousness, variety, and complexity. Bambaataa's "Planet Rock," a sonic collage of dance beats, pop culture references, and rap exhortation, sold 500,000 copies. "The Message," released that same year by Grandmaster Flash and the Furious Five, was an edgy, frightening epic about the vicious cycle of ghetto life. Written by Melle Mel, "The Message" was filled with simple vivid images—"Rats in the front room / roaches in the back / junkie in the alley with a baseball bat"—and an unforgettable chorus—"Don't push me / Cause I'm close to the edge / I'm trying not to lose my head."

"The Message" advanced the vocal innovations of early rap and combined them with the sociopolitical ambitions of the black rockers who had been popular a decade earlier. "The Message" was a kind of sequel to Stevie Wonder's 1971 rock hit "Living for the City." Both were cautionary tales of getting caught up in the temptations of big-city life. Both end with a fadeout confrontation between homeboys and cops. In the mid-1980s, rappers increasingly turned to black rock for attitude and inspiration. George Clinton, the mastermind of Parliament-Funkadelic, succeeded James Brown as the most popular single source of rhythms for rap records. A George Clinton fanzine reports that more than four hundred rap records have sampled Clinton's music. Spike Lee's 1988 movie *Do the Right Thing* opens with Public Enemy's rap anthem "Fight the Power," whose title is lifted from a 1975 hit of the same name by the Isley Brothers.

By 1983–84, rap had become The Next Big Thing in the mainstream media. Along with graffiti art and breakdancing, rap was fashionable in the New York art scene. Major record labels began to sign up rap artists, without much idea of how to coax good work from them. Hollywood studios cranked out several obligatory rap movies. Mercifully, there was no *Saturday Night Fever* for rap. Hollywood's depiction of black life lacked credibility, and, unlike the disco sound of the 1970s, rap was not a black musical style that could easily be modified to suit white tastes.

Rap's popularity spread anyway. It spoke to a generation of young African-Americans, transmitting their styles, language, and attitude in ways that prime-time television, newspapers, and black (uh, urban contemporary) radio stations simply could and would not. By 1985, rap acts were ringing up sales that were staggering compared with those of just a few years before. Run-D.M.C. and Whodini, two rap acts from New York, put out albums that went gold, meaning they sold at least 500,000 copies. And it was the small, independent record labels that were reaping profits.

With the established media corporations ignoring rap, the market was wide open for entrepreneurs. The most important of these was Russell Simmons, a rapper and promoter from Queens who founded Def Jam Records. Simmons was a tastemaker interested in expanding the rap audience without alienating the blacks at its core. His main collaborator was Rick Rubin, a long-haired white record producer who saw rap as the successor to rock among alienated youth. In 1986 Rubin and Simmons oversaw Run-D.M.C.'s remake of Aerosmith's 1970s' rock hit "Walk This Way." The song's video featured the young black rappers and the aging white rockers having the time of their lives. "Walk This Way" made rap accessible to white rock fans for the first time. Simmons also discovered the Beastie Boys, the first white rap outfit, whose raucous debut album, *Licensed to Ill*, sold 4 million copies.

Two other entrepreneurs building the rap audience in the mid-1980s were Tom Silverman and Luther Campbell. Their styles could not have been more different.

Silverman was a white dance music fan from the suburbs of New York City whose fledgling label, Tommy Boy Records, scored a big hit with "Planet Rock" in 1982. Silverman put the Brooklyn rap group Stetsasonic together with Jesse Jackson in 1987 to make the anti-apartheid song *A.F.R.I.C.A.* A musical risk-taker, Silverman brought together diverse, innovative acts like Queen Latifah, Digital Underground, De La Soul, and Naughty By Nature.

Luther Campbell was an ambitious street disc jockey from the Liberty City section of Miami. In 1984 he started promoting rap shows in local college auditoriums. In 1986 he hooked up with a California rap group and, under the name 2-Live Crew, released a single called "Throw the D." The title referred to a popular fad in Miami in which young boys would get up on stage at outdoor parties, pull down their pants, and "throw their dicks" around. "Throw the D" was a local hit. Campbell followed with a female version, titled (naturally enough) "Throw the P," which was also a hit. When Campbell put out a second 2-Live Crew album in 1989, As Nasty As They Wanna Be, his brand of raunch rap was attracting white fans and the attention of legal authorities. In June 1990 Campbell and two members of 2-Live Crew were arrested on obscentiy charges. The resulting publicity helped Campbell sell another million albums, and his acquittal in October 1990 made American constitutional history.

As the 1980s wore on, rap became increasingly identified, at least among whites, with the chaos of black life in poor urban neighborhoods. NWA, short for Niggas With Attitude, exploded in 1989 with their debut album, Straight Outta Compton, as pure a dose of pop music alienation as anything since the Sex Pistols' "God Save the Queen." NWA denied that they could or should serve as "good examples" to their fans. In NWA's hit "Gangsta Gangsta," Ice Cube boasted of getting high, doing crimes, drinking malt liquor "straight out bottle, tell the truth, do I look like a role model? / To the kid looking up to me / life ain't about nothing but girls and money." Some critics said that NWA's lyrics did nothing to improve life in the ghetto, but few claimed they were inaccurate in their portrayal of it.

The reasons for the rage of the rappers are obvious. The civil rights revolution of the 1960s had enabled middle-class blacks to move out of inner-city neighborhoods. The poorer, less educated, less self-sufficient blacks who were left behind lost their most stable neighbors and their economic elite. Government-financed support systems for the urban poor were de-funded and dismantled by the Reagan administration. The white mainstream enjoyed an infusion of black workers and talent; the black community got little in return, save a holiday on Martin Luther King's birthday.

Then came crack. In 1984–85, the failure of the federal government's cocaine control policies, the prodigious efforts of Colombian producers in Medellín, and the respectable skills of Cuban-American importers in Miami had created a glut of cocaine on the streets of America. Retail drug entrepreneurs developed a new way of marketing cocaine. Smoking cocaine (freebasing) had long been popular but dangerous. Drug entrepreneurs took the danger out of freebasing by cooking cocaine into smokable crystalline rocks known as crack. Smoking delivered the cocaine high faster than snorting, and, unlike powder cocaine, crack could be sold in five- and ten-dollar packages, meaning it was within the price range of practically everybody. Potency and price made crack an instant hit on the streets or urban America in late 1985 and early 1986. The combination of integrationist policies and crack did more damage to the black community in America than anything since the imposition of Jim Crow laws in the 1870s.

But rage was not the rapper's only response. Anti-drug rap music from "White Lines (Don't Do It)," by Grandmaster Flash, and Melle Mel to Digital Underground's "The Danger Zone" provides a good deal more insight into the reality of the drug problem than the federal government's moralistic propaganda. In "The Danger Zone," rapper Shock G tells of being approached by an emaciated woman looking for five dollars to buy some more rocks. He says, "Bitch, I'd rather give a crippled crab a crutch / She said, 'Why you want to clown me?' / I said 'I don't like freaks hanging around me.' " In the same song, Shock G gave voice to the widely held view in the black community that the federal government itself is complicit in the drug trade. "I'm pulling no punches," he declared, "the government brings drugs in bunches."

Unlike many other commentators on American life, rappers are not afraid to confront the country's harshest social contradictions— including the commercial success of rap. Rappers are more aware than anyone that the black cultural style sells in white America: Air Jordans, Arsenio Hall, Spike Lee, and all that. Still, young blacks bear the brunt of the society's coercion. "And while they [the cops] treat my group like dirt," says M.C. Ren of NWA in the song "100 Miles and Runnin'," "their whole fuckin' family is wearing our t-shirts."

In *About Face: Race in Post Modern America*, Timothy Maliqualim Simone suggested that black teenage life had become a psychic Wild West, which non-blacks observe with fascination. Black youth, Simone suggests, are

a posse sent ahead to scout uncharted social and psychological do-
mains. The posse may be killed, maimed, or wounded so that the
rest of the society can occupy the social terrain that has been scouted
with relative personal safety. . . . These kids pose the limit embody-
ing both what American culture aims for and what the culture must
not become. In the same way that the deaths of real cowboys, out-
laws, adventurers and soldiers made images of these figures safe for
general consumption, elements of the street kid figure are becoming
incorporated into the general American character."

Rap music's fascination with criminality, like Hollywood's fascina-
tion with the West and with gangsters, has become a feature of
American folklore.

In matters of sex, too, rappers embody, as Simone says, "both
what American culture aims for and what the culture must not
become." American society professes to be tolerant, yet it remains
fearful of the consequences of sexual liberty. On the one hand, pro-
sex rappers like Luther Campbell exploit and explode this tension.
2-Live Crew's "Me So Horny" is a frank, funny celebration of ani-
malistic desire. On the other hand, such uninhibited expressions of
male desire are misinterpreted, in a violent, sexist society, as license
for sexual violence. The youths charged in the Central Park rape
case said they were out "wilding," a term coined from Tone-Lōc's
rap hit "Wild Thing." In fact, there is no sexual violence at all in
Tone-Lōc's song.

Women are a major presence in rap. The first female rapper to
enjoy any commercial success was Roxanne Shante, who built a
career around telling black men where to get off. In "Brothers Ain't
Shit," she says, "Remember Shante told you / drugs is not the only
thing a girl can say no to." To the disappointment of some feminists,
female rappers express a wide variety of views on the subject of the
male libido. While Shante wants to protect herself and her sisters
from exploitation, the rap group BWP (short for Bitches With Prob-
lems) prefers to smash the reputation of the Don Juans who brag
about the size of their penises and their sexual endurance while
utterly failing to satisfy basic female needs. Salt-N-Pepa, a sassy duo
from Queens who scored a big hit in 1989 with "Da Butt," pride
themselves on being able to party with anyone. When a man tries to
fondle one of them on the dance floor, they brush him off (and lead
him on), saying, "Hey, we just met / we can't do that yet."

•

In any case, the obsession of rap's critics with sexism and violence in rap has an element of bad faith. After fifteen years, rap music has a tradition that is far broader than talking about "bitches" and Uzis. There is the pop rap of Biz Markie and Jazzy Jeff and the Fresh Prince, whose teenage wise-guy routines like "Parents Just Don't Understand" and "Nightmare on My Street" have little to do with race or politics and everything to do with adolescent fun, frustation, and fantasy. It was natural that the Fresh Prince went from being a rapper to being the star of a prime-time network sitcom. Then there's the cultural militants, like Public Enemy, Brand Nubian, X-Clan, Professor Griff, and Paris. Unlike the black nationalists of the 1960s, the rap militants emphasize an agenda that is cultural, not political, promoting Afro-centrism and the preservation of black culture rather than demands for territory or reparations. The Native Tongues' style is personified by De La Soul, the Jungle Brothers, Black Sheep, and A Tribe Called Quest, artists that subvert or re-invent rap traditions, mixing whimsical and surreal lyrics, poking fun at racial stereotypes, and sampling musical sources ranging from George Clinton to Montavani to TV game shows and Quincy Jones.

There is also the Latin rap of Mellow Man Ace and Kid Frost and the wise-guy rap of 3rd Bass, the frat-boy rap of the Fat Boys, and the gangster-girl style of Yo-Yo. There is the cautionary rap of the Lifer's Group from New Jersey's Rahway Prison and the "slack" (sexually explicit) rap of Jamaica's Shabba Ranks. There are dozens of other categories and thousands of other artists. The popularity of rap, the sheer diversity of its sounds, its wealth of insights, images, and ideas, confirm that the music has long since transcended "fad" or entertain-ment and become an important part of American history.

Rappers are the heirs of the African-American musical tradition. Rap is the latest chapter in the black music tradition, which runs from the field hollers of sharecroppers in the late nineteenth century to the blues and jazz of the early twentieth century to the post–World War II styles of be-bop, r&b, and gospel to the rock, soul, and funk sounds of the 1960s and 1970s. Like the sounds that preceded it, rap interprets and shapes the experience of American life.

Rap is thus a social as well as a musical innovation. The rise of rap in the 1980s coincided with the resurgence of black nationalism in America. An unmistakably black art form, rap emerged in a decade when leading white American institutions were indifferent, if not hostile, to the concerns of many black Americans. It was no accident that the figure of Malcolm X was revived as a popular icon during the years when rap began to flourish. Malcolm had preached that blacks had to regain a communal sense of integrity and pride "by any means necessary." Rappers, whether they knew it or not, were doing exactly that.

As a new art form, a new way for people to express themselves, rap enables artists and audiences to see the world in new ways. Its influence has been felt throughout the popular arts. Rap has infused traditional r&b with new rhythms, energy, and candor, spawning "new jack swing." Rap has energized white rock and heavy-metal acts. It has inspired black filmmakers and helped convince white movie producers in Hollywood that the black feature film is a sensible commercial venture. In 1990 Hollywood produced more black films than in the previous ten years combined. Rap was the essential soundtrack of the so-called new black wave, exemplified by *Do the Right Thing* and John Singleton's *Boyz-N-the-Hood*. In fact, the new black wave probably would not have happened without the precedent of rap music.

Rap expresses a mood of renewed black cultural pride, while also serving as the means by which that pride is injected—integrated, if you will—into the multicultural society of the United States. It is a medium as well as a message. Rap is the basis of an alternative media network, the "hip-hop nation," as critic Greg Tate has dubbed it. The hip-hop nation includes the rappers and their fans, as well as the entrepreneurs, academics, and media professionals who sell, think, and talk about rap for a living. The institutions devoted to rap convey the music, the ideas, and the information that are often excluded from white-dominated (and increasingly corporate) media like TV, daily newspapers, magazines, and books. The hip-hop nation, predominantly black with a significant minority of whites (in the music industry and the media), has no pretensions of being "colorblind." When a group of black nationalist rappers held a conference in the editorial offices of *The Source*, a leading hip-hop journal, the discussion began with the obvious irony of black nationlists meeting at a magazine owned and run by two white rap fans from Harvard. The need for black-owned publications was noted and a wide-ranging discussion about their pro-black cultural agenda followed.

Rap culture and the rap audience is certainly far more racially integrated than, say, the ranks of the liberal and conservative critics who attack it. Public Enemy was criticized in *The New Republic* for allegedly peddling racial hatred. At the time, Public Enemy was on tour with Anthrax, a white heavy-metal band, playing before crowds more racially mixed than the masthead or readership of any elite journal of liberal opinion.

The fact is that the appeal of rap is rooted in values of alienation, self-assertion, and oral expression, values that are prevalent in the African-American community but that know no racial boundaries. In the summer of 1990, the DJs on Warsaw's hippest music program, *Radio Clash*, were pumping out "Fuck Tha Police," the anti-cop anthem by the rap group NWA, to a million listeners in Poland, northern Czechoslovakia, and the western Soviet Union. This entirely Caucasian audience understands the desire to throw off the heavy hand of illegitimate police authority—while the song was playing a listener called in to report an incident of police brutality. Of course, "Fuck Tha Police" was banned from the airwaves in the U.S. at the time.

In America, rap music stirs controversy because it is a repudiation of the defunct racial dogmas of the day. Its blackness, its nationalistic overtones, and its sexual candor disturb the educated middle class. The racial implications of rap offer an alternative to the liberal ideal of integrationism and the conservative idea of a "colorblind" society. Rap's mass success is not based on blacks accepting white middle-class values, or on the allegedly declining significance of race in American culture, or on the commerical exploitation of black criminality or pure black art form, but on an ideal at once more realistic and more radical: that in America blacks and whites alike will celebrate black values, instead of expecting blacks to accept white values.

As a musical style, rap is not to everyone's taste—another instance of "old ears can't hear new music." Aging baby boomers who gladly worked to catch all the nuances of "Desolation Row" or "A Whiter Shade of Pale" may be at a loss when it comes to rap: too many words going by too fast with too much slang. Newcomers to rap may well find reading the lyrics an agreeable introduction to the music. As for long-time fans and rappers who think they know their hip-hop, they may well be surprised at what they discover and rediscover.

Rap music is history in the literal sense: an account, a body of language that tells what happened and why, a combination of information and interpretation that summarizes, dramatizes, and makes comprehensible what African-Americans were doing from the late 1970s to the early 1990s. As a remarkable chapter in late-twentieth-century American history, rap music is a guide to the future of our culture.

Takoma Park, MD
January 1992

above The LaW

Livin' Like Hustlers

Let me start it off, 'cause I'm a player
Fade into part two, I'm the number-one ho layer
A mack, a player, and a pimp
Something much stronger than your average drink
Now correct me if I'm wrong, I'm like moonshine
Take a sip of my rhyme and I take over your mind
'Cause I don't think like the average thinker
Call me the nightstalker of your neighborhood headshrinker
187 is like a megablast
I take too many names, I kick too much ass
K.M.G, the number-one mack daddy
Eatin' chicken like a motherfucker, rollin' in my Caddy
With my brim cold bent to the side
I bump and slide
Go mack in the back, 187 to the side
Street Pilgrims pioneering the land
Above the law status with a gat in my hand
A mind designed like Frank Nitty
Livin' large on the mike, doin' damage for the city
The city of toners which is known as L.A.
Where the hustlers hustle and the ballers play
We got the dope beats from the homeboy Dre
And it had to be done (How?) the Ruthless way
187, what's up?, what do we do at our show
We wear black on black with the locs and the romeos
Start stepping, unload my mike weapon
We say it's fittin', you think it's hittin'
K.M.G means knowledge most greatly
Some people love me, most people hate me
In other words, I kick my gift
Do you be sleeping, K.M.G?
Nah, I don't drift
I lounge or lay 'cause suckers take advantage

Yo, what do we do?
Yo, we doin' damage
'Cause we not punks, fools, sissies, or busters
And the way that we live is
Like hustlers

Livin' like hustlers

I used to sell big *lleyo* on the block
Remember all the hardheads, getting all hard knocks
I started with Gs and then I moved to keys
And at this point my life went with ease
In other words, my pockets was thick
I didn't worry about the Feds, I was checking the mic.
Pull a swoop to Farouk, got dressed to please
Got the crib pimped out so that the bitches flee'd
I bought a ride, a white Corvette
So I can do a ghost move when it's time to jet
When I was nineteen, I was on my own
Hooked up big connections on my mobile phone
At home, or maybe on my person
To clock big Gs I'd be definitely certain
To live the lifestyle, the luxury, the freaks, the frills
Yo, you was livin' kinda large
On the real—deals was bein' made
Suckers was gettin' sprayed
In other words, we was gettin' paid
Like hustlers

Livin' like hustlers

Let me proceed 'cause I got the green light
For the numero uno 87 it must be hype
For now, let me lay the cards on the table
So you can figure out who's worried or stable
I max and tax and relax and stack Gs
Stick that to the facts, that's why I crack them with ease
Please get off the convoy, I think you're confused
When you cross, I told you you'd get tossed and you lose
Now A-b-o-v-e-L-a-w to some people now that spells trouble

But we're not a group promoting violence
But when it comes to speakin' the real, I won't be silent
Speak all reality when I'm on the mike
So you don't have to run and have a stereotype
See, see 'cause stereotypes will make you dumb
So kick back and listen, yo, to the knowledge that's brung
See the law has provided me, the K.M.G
That's complex with the style but done easily
Pitch a picture if I have to, you know why
I'm undercover doin' dirt I'm a hell of a spy
Now me, 187, is a detonator
More deadly than a hand grenade
Much harder than a fool to fade
Not a forty, not a quart or six-pack
Me, K.M.G, Total K-OSS, and Go Mack
'Cause I unload my weapon with force
Yeah, I'm never detected, I get respected
As a baller, a player, or a pimp
Yo, pass me the forty, I commence to dent
A sissy soft sucker with no title
Unplug the machine 187 is vital
Like a Beretta with a megaclip
With a silencer on it with the hollow point tip
But that is our business, on that we won't dwell
We make records for you to look, listen, and tell
Tell your ma, tell a friend, tell a fool, or a jerk
Till them K.M.G people started to put it to work
Like Hustlers

Livin' like hustlers

Another Bad Creation

Playground

Yeah, boy, it's another A.B.C. party
Comin' from the playgrounds, taking you straight back to the
    bricks. Yo Chris, tell them what it is.

Chillin', coolin' in the swings, kickin' dirt with my sneakers
Soldiers on the corner looking down at their beepers
That couldn't get a job or a nice home
So they would rather stand and wait for the pay phone
Take Jo Jo, he's the youngest
Girls jock him because he's best dressed
Red strollin' through the neighborhood
Sweatin' that brother, tryin' to see why he is livin' good
Rollin' through the park tryin' to make another hit
Little do they know that soldier's legit
I'm not saying this to put nobody down
This is what I see
At the playground, ya know?

Playground

Ah yeah, another A.B.C. smash
Now don't it make you mad, sissy
Ah come on, come on everybody and guess who's up next
Kick it

L-i-l D-a-v-e, four feet shorty of the crew
So let me get on the mike and show you what I can do
When I'm all alone
Cold rockin' on the microphone
At home playin' little Capone
Large is how I'm livin', home

Kick it D, kick it D, kick it
Bust it D, bust it D, bust it
Swing it D, swing it D, swing it

I swing my beat at the playground, ya know?

Come on y'all, little soldiers in effect
Put your hands in the air, put your hands in the air
I don't want to see nobody sittin' in their chairs
Do that, do that Roro, you up next

Well I'm Roro coming in third
Now it's about that time that I get heard
Hey none of my rhymes will never ever be served
Word to Herb, play tricks on your nerve (C'mon)
Every word I serve is real superb
And I'll be right back with part two of this funky rhyme, Gee (ha-ha)
Yeah boy
Yo Red, I don't want to flow no more, man, y'all go ahead
I'm just gonna sit back and listen to this ghetto swing
'Cause this is what I do
At the playground
You know what I'm sayin'?

Awww, yeah, A.B.C. is on the scene
Attitude is mental
Music is hip hop with a little ghetto swing
Yo Red, kick the ballistics, Gee

It's the R to the E to the D
And what you get is what you're seein'
Straight up B-boy, word to Miz
Kickin' and flippin' the rhymes for the kids
Man for the kids in the park, nice and smooth
Dave and Mark tried to bust my groove
Blew her a kiss and threw my books on the bleachers
This is when I met Aisha
Had a big fanny
Not like Annie
Gave up the puddin' for a leather and some candy

(Ah-Ah) Where'd ya meet her?
At the playground, ya know?
Playground

O.K. I guess you know by now
Mix match boost pants inside out
A fresh starter cap and a go-cart
With your name on the front, smooth
Yo Mark
Take it, Gee

It's the Mizzark chillin' in the pizzark
I got to brake 'cause my mother said be home by dizzark
But before I go
I'm goin' to flow for you one time, see
So listen to the rhyme, Gee
The East Coast family
Boyz II Men, A.B.C., B.B.D.,
Now flip the tracks, D
My mother is Nana, and my brother is Red
It's Mario Brothers 'til it's time for bed
Last but not least
I want to say peace
So we out of here
From the playground, ya know?

Afrika Bambaataa & the Soul Sonic Force

Planet Rock

Party people
Party people
Can y'all get funky?

Soul Sonic Force—can y'all get funky?
The Zulu Nation—can y'all get funky?
Yaaah!
Just hit me
Just taste the funk and hit me
Just get on down and hit me
Bambaataa's jus' gettin' so funky, now, hit me
Yaaah!
Just hit me

Just start to chase your dreams
Up out your seats, make your body sway
Socialize, get down, let your soul lead the way
Shake it now, go ladies, it's a livin' dream
Love Life Live
Come play the game, our world is free
Do what you want but scream

We know a place where the nights are hot
It is a house of funk
Females and males
Both headed all for the disco

The D.J. plays your favorite blasts
Takes you back to the past, music's magic (poof)
Bump bump bump get bump with some flash, people

Rock rock to the Planet Rock, don't stop
Rock rock to the Planet Rock, don't stop

The Soul Sonic Force—Mr. Biggs, Pow Wow, and M.C. Globe
We emphasize the show, we got ego
Make this your night, just slip it right, and by day
As the people say, live it up, shucks
No work or play, our world is free
Be what you be—be

Rock rock to the Planet Rock, don't stop
Rock rock to the Planet Rock, don't stop

You're in a place where the nights are hot
Where nature's children dance and set a chance
On this Mother Earth, which is our rock
The time has come, and work for soul, show you really got
    soul
Are you ready hump bump bump, get bump, now let's go, house

Twist and turn, then you let your body slide
You got the body rock and pop, bounce and pounce
Everybody just rock it, don't stop it
Gotta rock it, don't stop
Keep tickin' and tockin', work it all around the clock

Everybody keep rockin' and clockin' and shockin' and rockin', go
    house
Everybody say, rock it, don't stop it (*Crowd repeats*)
Well hit me, Mr. Biggs (*Crowd repeats*)
Pow Wow (*Crowd repeats*)
G-L-O-B-E (*Crowd repeats*)
The Soul Sonic Force

You gotta rock it, pop it, 'cause it's the century
There is such a place that creates such a melody
Our world is but a land of a master jam, get up and dance
It's time to chase your dreams
Up out your seats, make your body sway
Socialize, get down, let your soul lead the way
Shake it now, go ladies, it's a livin' dream
Love Life Live

Zih Zih Zih Zih Zih (*ad lib*)

Everybody say, rock it, don't stop it (*crowd repeats*)
Everybody say, shock it and pop it (*crowd repeats*)
Everybody say, ich me sun chi (*crowd repeats*)
Say, Planet Rock (*crowd repeats*)
It's the sure shot (*crowd repeats*)
Say, Planet Rock (*crowd repeats*)
It's the sure shot (*crowd repeats*)

So twist and turn, then you let your body glide
You got the body rock and pop, bounce and pounce
So hit me
Just taste the funk and hit me
Just get on down and hit me
Bambaataa's gettin' so funky, now hit me
Every piece of the world
Rate the message of the words
All men, women, boys, and girls, hey our Planet Rock is superb
Get on it
You got the groove, move (*ad lib*)
Feel the groove—feel it
Do what ya want but ya know ya got to be cool and boogie
Out on the floor, go down
Bring it low
Close to the ground
Everybody just rock it, don't stop it, gotta rock it
Don't stop
Keep tickin' and tockin'
Work it all around the clock
Everybody just rock it, don't stop it
Gotta rock it, don't stop (*repeats*)

Rob Base & D.J. Ez Rock

It Takes Two

It takes two to make a thing go right
It takes two to make it outta sight
Hit it!

I wanna rock right now
I'm Rob Base and I came to get down
I'm not internationally known
But I'm known to rock the microphone
Because I get stoopid, I mean outrageous

Stay away from me if you're contagious
'Cause I'm the winner, no, I'm not the loser
To be an M.C. is what I choose 'a
Ladies love me, girls adore me
I mean even the ones who never saw me
Like the way that I rhyme at a show
The reason why, man, I don't know
So let's go, 'cause

It takes two to make a thing go right
It takes two to make it outta sight
Hit it!

My name is Rob, I gotta real funky concept
Listen up, 'cause I'm gonna keep you in step
I got an idea
That I wanna share
You don't like it? So what, I don't care
I'm number one, the uno, I like comp
Bring all the suckers 'cause all them I'll stomp
Bold and black but I won't protect
All of my followers 'cause all I want is respect
I'm not a doctor, put them in rapture
A slick brother that can easy outfox ya
Cause I'm Rob, the last name Base, yeah
And on the mike, I'm known to be the freshest
So let's start, it shouldn't be too hard
I'm not a sucker so I don't need a bodyguard
I won't fess, wear a bulletproof vest
Don't smoke buddha, can't stand sess, yes

It takes two to make a thing go right
It takes two to make it outta sight
Hit it!

The situation that the Base is in
I'm kinda stingy that's why I don't wanna lend
A funky rhyme to a foe or a good friend
But listen up 'cause I want you to comprehend
'Cause I'm the leader, the man superior

I take care of ya and then ya get wearier
So just sit, my rhymes are not counterfeit
The record sells which makes this one a hit
It won't hurt to listen to Red Alert
Take off your shirt
Make sure it don't hit the dirt
I like the kids—the guys, the girls
I want the ducats 'cause this is Rob Base's world
I'm on a mission, ya better just listen
To my rhymes 'cause I'm all about dissin'
'Cause

It takes two to make a thing go right
It takes two to make it outta sight
Hit it!

I stand alone, don't need anyone
'Cause I'm Rob, just came to have fun
Don't need friends that act like foes
'Cause I'm Rob Base, the one who knows
About things that make ya get weary
Don't cheer me, just hear me
Out 'cause I got the clout—shout (Ho!)
Before I turn the party out
I won't stutter—
Project my voice, speak clearly
So you can be my choice
On stage or on record
Go to the Wiz and select it
Take it off the rack, if it's wack put it back
I like the Whopper, fuck the Big Mac
If you want static, so let's go
So, throw up your hands
Go for what you know
Bro', I got an ego
Yo, talkin' to me? No
Oh
'Cause Rob is in the front, EZ Rock is on the back up
We're not soft, so you better just slack up
'Cause I'm cool, calm just like a breeze

Rock the mike with the help of EZ
Rock on the set, the music plays
Only cuts the records that I say

It takes two to make a thing go right
It takes two to make it outta sight
Hit it!

All right, now, EZ Rock, now, when I count to three, I want you
    to get busy
You ready now? One, two, three, get loose now!

It takes two to make a thing go right
It takes two to make it outta sight
Hit it!

Beastie Boys
Fight for Your Right (to Party)

You wake up late for school, man you don't wanna go
You ask your mom, "Please?" but she still says, "No!"
You missed two classes and no homework
But your teacher preaches class like you're some kind of jerk

You gotta fight
For your right
To party

Your pop caught you smoking and he said, "No way!"
That hypocrite smokes two packs a day
Man, living at home is such a drag
Now your mom threw away your best porno mag (Bust it!)

You gotta fight
For your right
To party

Don't step out of this house if that's the clothes you're gonna
   wear
I'll kick you out of my home if you don't cut that hair
Your mom busted in and said, "What's that noise?"
Aw, mom you're jealous—it's the Beastie Boys!

You gotta fight
For your right
To party

Beastie Boys

Rhymin' and Stealin'

Because mutiny on the bounty's what we're all about
I'm gonna board your ship and turn it on out
No soft sucker with a parrot on his shoulder
'Cause I'm bad, gettin' bolder, cold cold gettin' colder
Terrorizing suckers on the seven seas
And if you've got a beef—you'll get capped in the knees
We got sixteen men on a dead man's chest
And I shot those suckers and I'll shoot the rest

Most illin-est b-boy, I got that feelin'
'Cause I am most ill and I'm rhymin' and stealin'

Snatchin' gold chains, vickin' pieces of eight
I got your money and your honey and the fly name plate
We got wenches on the benches and bitties with titties
Housin' all girlies from city to city
One for all and all for one
Taking out M.C.s with a big shotgun
All for one and one for all
Because the Beastie Boys have gone AWOL
Friggin' in the riggin' and cuttin' your throat
Big bitin' suckers gettin' thrown in the moat

We got maidens and wenches—man they're on the ace
Captain Bly is gonna die when we break his face

Most illin-est b-boy, I got that feelin'
'Cause I am most ill and I'm rhymin' and stealin'

Ali Baba and the forty thieves
Ali Baba and the forty thieves
Ali Baba and the forty thieves
Ali Baba and the forty thieves
Ali Baba and the forty thieves
Ali Baba and the forty thieves
Ali Baba and the forty thieves
Ali Baba and the forty thieves

Torchin' and crackin' and rhymin' and stealin'
Robbin' and rapin', bustin' two in the ceiling
I'm wheelin', I'm dealin', I'm drinkin', not thinkin'
Never cower, never shower, and I'm always stinkin'
Yo ho ho and a pint of Brass Monkey
And when my girlie shakes her hips, she sure gets funky
Skirt chasin', free basin', killin' every village
We drink and rob and rhyme and pillage

Most illin-est b-boy, I got that feelin'
'Cause I am most ill and I'm rhymin' and stealin'

I've been drinking my rum, a def son of a gun
I fought the law and I cold won
Black Beard's weak, Moby Dick's on the tip
'Cause I'll pull out the jammy and squeeze off six
My pistol is loaded—I shot Betty Crocker
Deliver Colonel Sanders down to Davey Jones's locker
Rhymin' and stealin' in a drunken state
And I'll be rockin' my rhymes all the way to Hell's gate

Most illin-est b-boy, I got that feelin'
'Cause I am most ill and I'm rhymin' and stealin'

Big Daddy Kane

Another Victory

Here comes the conquerer, a brother that varies and never
    ceases
Violators, pick up the pieces
That are left behind as you're left to find
The fury of the five fingers of death are mine
Grippin' on the microphone
Recitin' poems
Give me competition of Big Daddy syndrome
Some step up, none kept up
They rap a brief moment and then shut up
Lips are sealed because all of this is real
I'm not about frontin', I tell the real deal
Of society
So how we livin', like a turkey on Thanksgivin'?
Or like Robin Givens
Not to offend, I just want you to comprehend
Every message that I send (Tell 'em)
'Cause I don't understand
I have to wonder, damn, how can this life-style be fun to man
To see a brother get paid undercover
Sellin' drugs to one another
'Cause all the glamour you get is miscellaneous
And all the product you sell is real dangerous
Like oh, lum-lum let's say, ah, poison
Destruction to all you home-boys and girls
Who like to buy and give it a try
My, they can't deny the high that's why they soon die
These are games that a fool would play today
For our own kind to decay
No sign of brotherly love
Just scavengers in search of
Another victory

Another victory

When I'm cruisin' in my Volvo, cops harass me
They never ride past me
They hound me like Lassie
One to give me a summons or a ticket, huh
I got a place for them to stick it (kick it!)
They can't understand to see a black man
Drivin' a car that costs twenty-five grand
The first thing they say is where'd ya steal her
And then they assume that I'm a drug dealer
Huh, that just makes me wanna laugh
'Cause know I'm a star and your son's got my autograph
So all the cops on the highway are gettin' me
My name ain't Keith so could you please stop sweatin' me
So I can flow on it
Go on it, so on, so on, to all the jam—Cee throw on
Reachin' the summit
As ya learn from it
A lesson, to and from yours truly so here come up
The royal majesty of the path that be
Fully prepared though they still won't last with me
So when you hope to hang or even handle
I show the meanin' of power and just cancel
Out of order
Conquer and slaughter
You're comin' up shorter
Boy, ya need more to
Compete cause the heat is deep and concrete to beat
Bring out complete, plead them with me
Or stay away—put new rhymes on layaway
Then come get this when you're ready for business
'Cause ahhh, yeah, I'm with this
Yo, Mr. Cee, what is this?
Another victory

Another victory

M.C.s and enemies I freeze at thirty-two degrees
Because they don't drop rhymes like these

———————

Competition never saw none done
So pay attention as I mention the 4-1-1
Just the other day, I heard a brother say
Taxi cabs don't even come my way
They all be afraid they won't get paid
So they zoom right past to pick up a lighter shade
And if they stop, the first thing they want
"No more than two people and the money up front"
Treatin' me like I'm some type of thug
It might sound bug, but they don't wanna get mugged
Who's in the right or wrong?
It's time to unite along
As righteous we're to walk in success and be strong
Instead of lookin' for someone to beef with
A brother like the Big Daddy Kane is peace with
Rappers of today like Kid 'n Play, hey
Even my man LL Cool J
Stetsasonic and EPMD, Public Enemy and BDP
Salt-N-Pepa, 'cause we can't sever, never
Whether whatever, we better stand together
That means unite not fight nor fussin' or cussin'
Save all the base for the pipe and start lovin'
One another cause separation is a flaw
So endure for more and stop lookin' for

Another victory

Another victory

Big Daddy Kane

R.A.W.

I'm comin' I'm comin' I'm comin' I'm comin I'm comin'
Intro, I start to go
My rhymes I'll flow, so

Get up and dance 'cause Kane says so
If you were loungin' around, it's time to get up
Pardon my expression but I'm 'a tear shit up
I appear right here and scare and dare
A mere musketeer that would dare to compare
I do declare, gettin' busy is where it's at
But what you sayin'
You wouldn't get a point for that
'Cause you're a featherweight
And your rhymes are carried light
But I drop bass just like Barry White
So how could you think that you pose a threat
You say you're rockin'—how many shows you get?
All your vocals go local on the m-i-c
Mine go a great distance like AT&T
I'm not new to this
I'm true to this
Nothin' you can do to this
Fuck around with Kane and come out black and blue for this
So, yo, go for what you know
Attemptin' to bass so I can humiliate, we can go
Rhyme for rhyme, word for word, verse to verse
Get you a nurse—too late—get you a hearse
They'll take ya to your burial ground
Because the Big Daddy Kane always throws down
Correct, I get respect
I'm out to collect
Cash money 'cause I get raw

Everybody get raw
Everybody get raw
Everybody get raw
Boy, do I hate a
I'm comin' I'm comin' I'm comin' I'm comin' I'm comin'

Here I am, r-a-w
A terrorist here to bring trouble to
Phony M.C.s I move on and seize
I just conquer and snuff another rapper with ease
'Cause I'm at my apex when others are below

Nothin' but a milliliter, I'm a kilo
Second to none
Makin' M.C.s run
So don't try to step to me
'Cause I ain't the one
I relieve rappers just like Tylenol
And they know it
So I don't see why y'all try to front
Perpetratin' a stunt
When ya know that I'll smoke ya up like a blunt
I'm genuine like Gucci
Raw like sushi
This age of rage is what rap did to me
To make me wanna create
Chaos and mayhem
Cold rock a party until the A.M.
I'll make a muscle, grab the mike and hustle
While you stand dazed and amazed
I'll bust a little rhyme with authority, superiority
And captivate the whole crowd's majority
The rhymes I use definitely amuse
Better than "Dynasty" or "Hill Street Blues"
I'm sure to score, endure for more without a flaw
'Cause I get raw

Everybody get raw
Everybody get raw
Everybody get raw
Boy, do I hate a
I'm comin' I'm comin' I'm comin' I'm comin' I'm comin'

I got a speech like a reverend
Rappers start severin'
And in my lifetime, believe I've never been
Beaten or eaten and just tooken out
Ya know, come to think about it, I keep M.C.s lookin' out
I'm real nervous when I'm at your service
Gimme gimme that title, boy, you don't deserve this
I work like a slave to become a master
And when I say a rhyme, you know that it has to

Be perfectly fitted
'Cause I'm committed
The entertainer and trainer and Kane'll get with it
I go with the flow and grow to let you know
I'll damage ya, I'm not not a amateur
But a professional, unquestionable, without doubt superb
So full of action, my name should be a verb
My voice will float on every note
When I clear my throat, "That's all" she wrote
The minute that the Kane starts to go on
Believe there's gonna be smooth sailin' so on
As I put other rappers out of their misery
Get them in a battle and make them all history
Rulin' and schoolin'
M.C.s that I'm duellin'
Watch 'em all take a fall as I sit back coolin'
On my throne with a bronze microphone
God bless the child who can hold his own
'Cause I get raw

Everybody get raw
Everybody get raw
Everybody get raw
Boy, do I hate a
I'm comin' I'm comin' I'm comin' I'm comin' I'm comin'

24–7, chillin', killin' like a villain
The meaning of raw is ready and willin'
To do whatever is clever
Take a loss, never
And the rhymes I bust
Comin' off as a must
And I come on hard
With rhymes that are odd
I rip the microphone and leave it scarred
Never smokin' or hittin' or takin' a sniff
Only crushin' M.C.s that be tryin' to trip
I get strong and titanic
Do works like a mechanic
Make M.C.s panic

They all get frantic and skeptic
Like a girl on a contraceptive
As I rock, but hey, what'd you expect?
That I'll get raw for ya
Just like a warrior
Rappin' like a samurai
And I'll be damned if I
Ever let a Fisher-Price M.C. hang
Their rhymes are toys, nothin' but ying-yang
So if we battle on the microphone
Bring your own casket and tombstone
And I'm 'a preach your funeral
Tell me who in the world
Could I ever come with more

I get raw
Raw
Raw

Big Daddy Kane

Smooth Operator

Gonna give it to ya, give it to ya, give it to you

Well excuse me, take a few minutes to mellow out
Big Daddy Kane is on the mike an' I'm 'a tell about
A minimum length of rhyme with strength and power
So listen to the man of the hour
Flowin', go to a slow tempo when ya know
Sing, ho, swing low, then yo, the show
Will go on as I perform
Transform on the stage
I got deceptive con
But I'm not animated
Like a cartoon

I'm for real, shootin' lyrics like a harpoon
Across the crowd to listeners and spectators
So let's groove with the smooth operator
Just sounds so smooth

Gonna give it to ya, give it to ya, give it to you

The B-I-G-D-A-double-D-Y-K-A-N-E
I'm good 'n' plenty
Servin' many
And any competition wishin' for an expedition
I'm straight up dissin' and dismissin', listen
Rappers act so wild
And love the profile
Frontin' hard but ain't got no style
I give nightmares to those who compete
Freddy Kruger walkin' on Kane Street
Confuse and lose
Abuse and bruise
The grooves and choose
To use my name—wrong—they pay dues
Destruction from the exterminator
But in a calm manner
'Cause I'm a smooth operator
Just just sounds so smooth
Just just sounds so smooth

Gonna give it to ya, give it to ya, give it to you

Now girls step up to this
One simple kiss and it's over miss
So tonight's dream, as high as the price seems, girlfriend
You've been scooped like ice cream
So just swing a fling, a gathering, try to cling
'Cause it's a Big Daddy thing
And I'm lovin' 'em right, word is bond
And just play Marvin Gaye and let's "get it on"
I make it real good, like Doctor Feelgood
To make sure my point is understood
That when it comes to this there's none greater

Sincerely yours, the smooth operator
Just just sounds so smooth
Just just sounds so smooth

Gonna give it to ya, give it to ya, give it to you

Now ain't that the pot callin' the kettle black
Sayin' I'm a new jack
You need to be smacked
The smooth way I say 'em and the way I display 'em
To make them sound different in the way that's diffident
Hey, I'm makin' sure every lyric is done fine
And I make one line bright as the sunshine
Attack it like Robitussin on a cough
If you know like I know, step off
Competition, I'm 'a get rid of, ya can't get a bit of
So just consider a break, a rest, vacation, hibernation
And make way for my smooth operation
I'm a smooth operator

Awwww, yeah, ya don't stop
Genuine for '89, and I still ain't half-steppin'
Peace!

Biz Markie

Just a Friend

Have you ever met a girl that you tried to date
But a year to make love she wanted you to wait
Let me tell ya a story of my situation
I was talkin' to this girl from the U.S. nation
The way that I met her was on tour at a concert
She had long hair and a short miniskirt
I just got onstage drippin', pourin' with sweat
I was walkin' through the crowd and guess who I met

I whispered in her ear, "Come to the picture booth
So I can ask you some questions to see if you are a hundred
   proof"
I asked her her name, she said blah-blah-blah
She had 9/10 pants and a very big bra
I took a couple of flicks and she was enthused
I said, "How do you like the show?" she said, "I was very
   amused"
I started throwin' bass, she started throwin' back mid-range
But when I sprung the question, she acted kind of strange
Then when I asked, "Do ya have a man," she tried to pretend
She said, "No I don't, I only have a friend"
Come on, I'm not even goin' for it
This is what I'm goin' sing

You, you got what I need but you say he's just a friend
And you say he's just a friend, oh baby
You, you got what I need but you say he's just a friend
But you say he's just a friend, oh baby
You, you got what I need but you say he's just a friend
But you say he's just a friend

So I took blah-blah's word for it at this time
I thought just havin' a friend couldn't be no crime
'Cause I have friends and that's a fact like Agnes, Agatha,
   Germaine, and Jacq
Forget about that, let's go into the story
About a girl named blah-blah-blah that adored me
So we started talkin', gettin' familiar
Spendin' a lot of time so we can build up
A relationship or some understanding
How it's gonna be in the future we was plannin'
Everything sounded so dandy and sweet
I had no idea I was in for a treat
After this was established, everything was cool
The tour was over and she went back to school
I called every day to see how she was doin'
Everytime that I called her it seemed somethin' was brewin'
I called her on my dime, picked up, and then I called again
I said, "Yo, who was that?" "Oh, he's just a friend"

Don't gimme that, don't ever gimme that
Jus' bust this

You, you got what I need but you say he's just a friend
And you say he's just a friend, oh baby
You, you got what I need, but you say he's just a friend
But you say he's just a friend, oh baby
You, you got what I need, but you say he's just a friend
But you say he's just a friend

So I came to her college on a surprise visit
To see my girl that was so exquisite
It was a school day, I knew she was there
The first semester of the school year
I went to a gate to ask where was her dorm
This guy made me fill out a visitor's form
He told me where it was and I was on my way
To see my baby doll, I was happy to say
I arrived in front of the dormitory
Yo, could you tell me where is door three?
They showed me where it was for the moment
I didn't know I was in for such an event
So I came to her room and opened the door
Oh, snap! Guess what I saw?
A fella tongue-kissin' my girl in the mouth,
I was so in shock my heart went down south
So please listen to the message that I say
Don't ever talk to a girl who says she just has a friend

Biz Markie

Pickin' Boogers

Now this may sound disgusting an' like very gross
But it's sure to have you trippin'
So y'all listen close

It's not bright as the sun or sweet like sugar
But it's rather on the bug tip and it's called Pickin' Boogers
Now what I'm emceein' might not seem kosher to you
But it's still somethin' we all have to do
So go up your nose with a finger or two
And pull out one or a crusty crew
Yo, don't try to front like it's so gloomy and gray
'Cause we all pick our boogers sometime every day
Whether out in the open or on a sneak tip
With a finger, tissue, or even a Q-Tip
Take it from the Biz Markie because I'm jokin'
And also, remember this slogan
"Hey, ma, what's for dinner?
Go up your nose and pick yourself a winner"
Pickin' Boogers
Pickin' Boogers

Let me tell you what happened on the train, man

I was coolin' one day with my partner Kane
Headed up to the rooftop, ridin' the D train
When the man sittin' next to me was so profane
He'd stick his finger up his nose, then do a drain
(You should 'a moved)
I was just about, but all of a sudden, homeboy just pulled out
A big, green, slimey—naw, I'm not even gonna say it
But it weighed a good pound if you tried to weigh it
He sat there for a while with it in his hand
So I tried to play cool like a normal man
So I laid my head back to catch a quick nap
All of a sudden he plucked it dead in my lap
Now Kane sat there laughin' like it was all a joke
But a brother like Biz Markie had almost choked
So I dug up my nose and pulled out about five
And plucked every last one of them dead in his eye
Then the man jumped up and said what's wrong with you
And wiped 'em off his face and said I can't mess with you
Like if I did somethin' that was so full of shame
But yo, you got to know the name of the game

Pickin' Boogers
Pickin' Boogers

Now let me take you trippin' down memory lane
Back in public school with my partner Kane
When I was class clown and he was my brother
Sittin' at the desk, pluckin' boogers at each other
Never do our work as we were supposed
'Cause we was too busy diggin' up our nose
And in the lunch room, we would talk about rude
God forbid the person that had to leave his food
No matter who you are, we didn't give a damn
We even put teachers down with the program
Whether it was a woman or if you're a man
We put boogers in our fingers then shake your hand
Catch anyone from anywhere
But the best part about it's catchin' Kane out there
Especially we're out playin' ball in the gym
I put boogers on the basketball and pass it to him
Now we're grown up and things have changed
But we still be playin' the Pickin' Boogers game
Just last night when Kane was gettin' ready
I slipped a little green one inside his spaghetti
Pickin' Boogers
Pickin' Boogers

Let me tell you what happened with this girl

One night at Latin Quarters, I was standin' at ease
And saw a gorgeous young lady that I wanted to skeeze
I didn't show enough that I really did want it
So, no half-steppin', I pushed up on it
Pulled out the gold cable and a knot that was fat
Had a spotlight beamin' on my Biz Markie hat
But when she stepped in the light and she got real close
I saw a teeny-weenie booger on the tip of her nose
She was dressed real def and her body was hook
But that dried-up booger just ruined the look
I wanted to tell her about it but I couldn't be bold

So I played it off and said, "That's a cute green mole"
I was hopin' from that she would wipe it away
But she didn't do nothin', I guess she wanted it displayed
I said, "Before you get my number I don't mean to dis you
But write it in your hand because you're gonna need the tissue"

Biz Markie

Vapors

Can you feel it
Nothin' can save ya
For this is the season of catchin' the vapors
And since I got time, what I'm gonna do
Is tell ya how to spread it throughout my crew
Well you all know TJ Swan who sang on my records
Made the music, "Nobody Beats the Biz"
Well, check it
Back in the days before this began
He usually tried to talk to this girl named Fran
The type of female with fly Gucci wear
With big trunk jewelry and extensions in her hair
When Swan tried to kick it, she always fessed
Talkin' about "Nigger, please, you work for UPS"
Since he wasn't no type of big drug dealer
My man TJ Swan didn't appeal to her
But now he trucks gold and wears fly Valley boots
Rough leather fashions and tough silk suits
Now she stop frontin' an' wants to speak
And be comin' to all the shows
Every single weekend
To get his beeper number, she'd be beggin' please
Dyin' for the day to get skeezed

She caught the vapors
She caught the vapors

She caught the vapors
She caught the vapors

I got another partner that's calm and plain
He goes by the name of the Big Daddy Kane
A mellow type of fellow that's laid back
Back in the days, he was nothin' like that
I remember when he used to fight every day
What grown-ups would tell him he would never obey
He wore his pants hangin' down and his sneakers untied
And a rasta-type Kango tilted to the side
Around his neighborhood, people treated him bad
And said he was the worst thing his mom's ever had
They said that he will grow up to be nothin' but a hoodlum
Or either in jail or someone would shoot him
But now he's grown up, to their surprise
Big Daddy got a hit record sellin' worldwide
Now the same people that didn't like him as a child be sayin'
Can I borrow a dollar, ooh, you're a star now

They caught the vapors
They caught the vapors
They caught the vapors
They caught the vapors

Now I got a cousin by the name of Von Lee
Better known to y'all as Cutmaster Cool V
He cuts scratch, transform with finesse
. . . (cuts and scratches) . . . and all that mess
Well I remember when he first started to rock
And tried to get this job in a record shop
He was in it to win it but the boss fronted
Said, "Sorry Mr. Lee, but there's no help wanted"
Now my cousin Von still tried on and on and on
'Til the like break of dawn
To put this j-o-b in effect
But they'd look right past him and be like "next"
Now for the year of '88
Cool V is makin' dollars so my cousin's like straight
He walks into the same record shop as before

And the boss'll be like, "Von, welcome to my store"
Offerin' him a job but naw, he don't want it
Damn it feels good to see people up on it
'Cause I remember when at first they wasn't
Now guess what they caught from my cousin
The vapors

They caught the vapors
They caught the vapors
They caught the vapors

Last subject of the story is about Biz Mark
I had to work for mine to put your body in park
When I was a teenager, I wanted to be down
With a lot of M.C.-deejayin' crews in town
So in school on Nobel Street, I say "Can I be down, champ"
They said no and treated me like a wet food stamp
After gettin' rejected, I was very depressed
Sat and wrote some def doo-doo rhymes at my rest
When I used to come to parties they'd make me pay
I'd have to beg to get on the mike and rap that day
I was never into girls, I was just into my music
They acted like I wanted to keep it
Instead of tryin' to use it
But now things switched without belief
"Yo, Biz, do you remember me from Nobel Street, chief?
We used to be down back in the days"
It happens all the time and never ceases to amaze

They caught the vapors
They caught the vapors
They caught the vapors
They caught the vapors

Black Sheep

Flavor of the Month

Van dam! Let's see what kind of flavor I want
Hmm. Do I want vanilla?
Or do I want a taste of chocolate?
Naa, I want somethin' different, I want somethin' slammin'
What's the slamminest flavor out this month, let's see
Yo, Black
Hmm
What flavor are you?
Listen—

For a second I reckon I gotcha double checking
Then again, when to your needs did I beckon
Hold me only if you wanna get nekkid
Play me for the crowd only if you wanna wreck it
The name is Dres, like silk I get slick
Drop rhymes like a base-head bic flics
Constantly yes it's me, D-R-E-S, oh yes, I guess
Unless ya 'fess, you can get down to serious business with this
I never held a honey that I didn't like
I never saw a mile that I couldn't hike
I never had a spliff to make me choke
I never had a pocket that was broke
Hate no one but love only a few
Franklin, Grant and, yea, Mom-Du
I run buckwild for self or with a crew
But then again, I thought you knew
Now I hear a voice, is it what ya want
I hope it is, kid you're the
Flavor of the month

I heard ya got the fever for the flavor
I heard ya got the fever for the flavor
I heard ya got the fever for the flavor

Somebody said ya had it goin' on
I heard ya got the fever for the flavor
I heard ya got the fever for the flavor
I heard ya got the fever for the flavor
Hurry up and get a scoop before it's gone

So ya got the fever for the flavor of the other
Chocolate, sarsaparilla or is it ya like another
Flavor in my socks to the curly locks
Black sheep rolling hard and knocking peons out the box
Never have I ever never ever felt much better
Did the whole nine on the tenth, I was no wetter
Ready and I'm eager, eager as a beaver
On the radio and good ta go says your receiver
Not ta be the boldest or the oldest nor the wackest
Neither am I neatest or the newest or the blackest
Just a brown fellow
Who's not afraid of Jell-o
To the people of the world, I would like to say good day
Had to wait awhile, but the while has been waited
Never gave up hope in myself nor debated
Didn't shed a tear when I wasn't picked
'Cause I got a cone now, wanna lick?

I heard ya got the fever for the flavor
I heard ya got the fever for the flavor
I heard ya got the fever for the flavor
Somebody said ya had it goin' on
I heard ya got the fever for the flavor
I heard ya got the fever for the flavor
I heard ya got the fever for the flavor
Hurry up and get a scoop before it's gone

Now I catch a number when before I caught a glare
Now I give a pound when before I gave a stare
Now I guess I kinda got it going on
I get a wake-up call on the norm
I used to try to push a demo, now I have a coup
That's a bit more than a little but then not quite a few
Funny how they find ya when they told ya, "Get lost"

Tell me why you're gritting when you have no dental floss
Wasn't my loss, thought you were the boss
Ya never knew how much the sherbet cost
Forget it I never sweat it, your girl will give me play, I'll wet it
It only happens yes because you let it
Now everybody wants to play my phone
I see 'em with a spoon, I see 'em with a cone
Ya never knew I knew it but I knew ya would pursue it
Hurry up and get a scoop before it's gone

I heard ya got the fever for the flavor
I heard ya got the fever for the flavor
I heard ya got the fever for the flavor
Somebody said ya had it goin' on
I heard ya got the fever for the flavor
I heard ya got the fever for the flavor
I heard ya got the fever for the flavor
Hurry up and get a scoop before it's gone

blondie

Rapture

Toe to toe
Dancing very close
Body breathing
Almost comatose
Wall to wall
People hypnotized
And they're stepping lightly
Hang each night
In rapture

Back to back
Sacroiliac
Spineless movement

And a wild attack
Face to face
Sightless solitude
And it's finger popping
Twenty-four-hour shopping
In rapture

Fab Five Freddy told me everybody's fly
D.J. spinnin', I said, "My, my"
Flash is fast
Flash is cool
François, ce n'est pas
Flache mon doux
And you don't stop, sure shot
Go out to the parking lot
And get in your car and drive real far
And you drive all night
And then you see a light
And it comes right down
And it lands on the ground
And out comes the man from Mars
And you try to run
But he's got a gun
And he shoots you dead
And he eats your head
And then you're in the man from Mars
You go out at night, eating cars
You eat Cadillacs, Lincolns, too
Mercuries and Subaru
And you don't stop, you keep on eating cars
Then when there's no more cars
You go out at night and eat up bars
Where the people meet
Face to face, dance cheek to cheek
One to one, man to man
Dance toe to toe
Don't move too slow
'Cause the man from Mars
Is through with cars
He's eating bars

Yeah, wall to wall
Door to door
Hall to hall
He's gonna eat 'em all
Rapture, be pure
Take a tour
Through the sewer
Don't strain your brain
Paint a train
You'll be singin' in the rain
I said, "Don't stop, do punk rock"

Well now you see
What you wanna be
Just have your party on T.V.
'Cause the man from Mars
Won't eat up bars
Where the T.V.'s on
And now he's gone back up to space
Where he won't have a hassle with the human race
And you hip hop
And you don't stop
Just blast off
A sure shot
'Cause the man from Mars
Stopped eatin' cars
And eatin' bars
And now he only eats guitars
Get up

kurtis Blow

The Breaks

Clap your hands, everybody
If you got what it takes
'Cause I'm Kurtis Blow and I want you to know
That these are the breaks!

Brakes on a bus, brakes on a car
Breaks to make you a superstar
Breaks to win and breaks to lose
But these here breaks will rock your shoes
And these are the breaks
Break it up, break it up, break it up!

If your woman steps out with another man
(That's the breaks, that's the breaks)
And she runs off with him to Japan
And the IRS says they want to chat
And you can't explain why you claimed your cat
And Ma Bell sends you a whopping bill
With eighteen phone calls to Brazil
And you borrowed money from the mob
And yesterday you lost your job
Well, these are the breaks
Break it up, break it up, break it up!

Throw your hands up in the sky
And wave 'em 'round from side to side
And if you deserve a break tonight
Somebody say alright!
(All right) Say ho-oo!
(Ho-oo!) And you don't stop
Keep on, somebody scream!
(Owwwww!) Break down!

Breaks on a stage, breaks on a screen
Breaks to make your wallet lean
Breaks run cold and breaks run hot
Some folks got 'em and some have not
But these are the breaks
Break it up, break it up, break it up!
Break down!

To the girl in brown, stop messing around
(Break it up, break it up!)
To the guy in blue, whatcha gonna do?
To the girl in green, don't be so mean
And the guy in red, say what I said
Break down!

Brakes on a plane, brakes on a train
Breaks to make you go insane
Breaks in love, breaks in war
But we got the breaks to get you on the floor
And these are the breaks
Break it up, break it up, break it up!
Break down! Yo!

Just do it, just do it, just do it, do it, do it!
Just do it, just do it, just do it, do it, do it!
Just do it, just do it, just do it, do it, do it!
Just do it, just do it, just do it, do it, do it!

You say last week you met the perfect guy
(That's the breaks, that's the breaks)
And he promised you the stars in the sky
He said his Cadillac was gold
But he didn't say it was ten years old
He took you out to the Red Coach grill
But he forgot the cash and you paid the bill
And he told you the story of his life
But he forgot the part about . . . his wife! Huh! Huh!
Well, these are the breaks!
Break it up, break it up, break it up!
Break down!

Boogie Down productions

House Niggas

Let me see, let me see
How should I start
If I say stop the violence, I won't chart
Maybe I should write some songs like Mozart
'Cause many people don't believe rap is an art
Wake up, shake up, hypocrite look alive
Blastmaster KRS-One will revive
Four or five million still deprived
When out to survive, wake up and realize
Some people say I am a rap missionary
Some people say I am a walking dictionary
Some people say I am truly legendary
But what I am is simply a black revolutionary

I write rhymes on plain stationery
Mary, Mary, quite contrary
Doesn't make sense in my vocabulary
Uncle Tom house niggas—too scary
So they can't be around—I don't do this
For every Jesus, there must be a Judas
It's the concept of the house nigga, field nigga
The house nigga will sell you up the river
So to mess up, he'll look bigger
And when ya beat under a rock, he'll slither
But I'll grab the tail of the house nigga
Pull the trigger and his head I'll deliver
To the court of righteous people
Black, white, or Indian, we're all equal
So all ya racist codes I'll decode, explode
And eat you like apple pie à la mode
On a hot day, don't bring me no hamhocks
'Cause round the clock, I'll kick their buttocks
All afternoon in the classroom

In the living room
In the bathroom
In the swimming pool
On a footstool
Then I'll stop—nope, April fools!
Whip out the baseball bat and somehow
Punch your racist butt to Moscow
Ya know what I'm sayin'?

Are there any—are there any intelligent people in the house?
What can I say, o ye of little faith
To think that KRS-One has surely been erased
What a waste
My finger points at the face of the human race
They're confused and misplaced
My words are subliminal
Sometimes metaphysical
I teach, not preach
You want a challenge? I'll start dissin' you
I go philosophical by topical
Hearin' the call, ignorant, hot tropical
Ya want a palm tree and nice dope shade?
Only if the universal law is obeyed
Which is "know thyself" for better mental health
Yet so many rappers are preoccupied with wealth
On my shelf I got titles
Other artists want belts and idols
World cups from seminars and conventions
Competition and not to mention
The award shows for pimps and hoes
And every other hypocrite that flaunt their clothes
KRS knows, so he just grows
Always sayin' somethin' different from the average Joe's
So I confront them with the biggest chain
But it doesn't rate albums—I believe it is the brain
So I'll remain free while you reign, I'm lovin' it
You be the king and I'll overthrow your government
Send your crew to Berlin or Dublin
I'll out-think 'em, chump 'em, and shrink 'em
Down to ya size, despite the cries

In the face of intelligence, ignorance dies
Dear, it's simple edutainment
Rap needed a teacher, so I became it
Rough and ready, the beats are very steady
With lyrics sharp as a machete
Clap, there's another house nigga's neck
Another soft Uncle Tom crew is in check
Ego wrecked and rhymes corrected
By KRS-One, produced and directed.

Boogie Down productions

Illegal Business

Cocaine business controls America
Ganja business controls America
KRS-One come to start some hysteria
Illegal business controls America

One afternoon around eleven o'clock
It was freezing cold
He was standing on the block
Sellin' cheeba
Mixin' dimes
Sayin' a rhyme
Just to pass the time
The cops passed by
But he stayed calm
'Cause the leather trench coat
Was keepin' him warm
But this time they walked by real slowly
He thought to himself
They look like they know me
They drove away

But he didn't stay
He jumped in the cab
And he paid his tab
But guess who he saw
When he hit the block
It was the same cop car
The same two cops
They jumped out quick
They pulled a gun
They said, "Don't try to fight
And don't try to run
Cooperate and we will be your friend
Noncooperation will be your end"
He jumped in the car
And while they rode
They ran down the list of things he owed
They said you owe us some money
You owe us some product
'Cause you could be right
In the river tied up
He thought for a second and he said
"What is this?
You want me to pay you
To stay in business?"
They said, "That's right, or you go to prison
'Cause nobody out there is really gonna listen
To a hood," so he said, "Good
I'll pay you off for the whole neighborhood"
Because

Cocaine business controls America
Ganja business controls America
KRS-One come to start some hysteria
Illegal business controls America
(What can we get for sixty-three cents?)

A guy named Jack is selling crack
The community doesn't want him back
He sells at work

He sells in schools
He's not stupid, the cops are the fools
'Cause everyone else
Seems to go to jail
But when it comes to Jack
The cops just fail.
They can't arrest him
They cannot stop him.
'Cause even in jail
The bail unlocks him
So here is the deal
And here is the facts
If you ever wonder why
They can't stop crack
The police department
Is like a crew
It does whatever they want to do
In society you have illegal and legal
We need both to make things equal
So legal is tobacco
Illegal is speed
Legal is aspirin
Illegal is weed
Crack is illegal, cause they cannot stop ya
But cocaine is legal if its owned by a doctor
Everything you do in private is illegal
Everything's legal if the government can see you
Don't get me wrong
America is a great place to live
But listen to the knowledge I give

Cocaine business controls America
Ganja business controls America
KRS-One come to start some hysteria
Illegal business controls America

Illegal business controls America
What can we get for sixty-three cents?
What can we get for sixty-three cents?
What can we get for sixty-three cents?

KRS-One comes to start some hysteria
What what what what
What can we get for sixty-three cents

Cocaine business controls America
Ganja business controls America
KRS-One come to start some hysteria
Illegal business controls America

Yeah, illegal business controls America
(What can we get for sixty-three cents?)
Yeah, KRS-One comes to start some hysteria
(What can we get for sixty-three cents?)
Yeah, BDP takin' over America
(What can we get for sixty-three cents?)
Ganja business controls America
(What can we get for sixty-three cents?)
Cocaine, sensi, aspirin, coffee, morphine, sugar, tobacco
Got to go
(What what what what can we get?)
Illegal business controls America
(What what what can we get?)
Yeaaah (what what what what)
Ganja business controls America
(What what what can we get for sixty-three cents?)
Yeaaah, cocaine business controls America
(What what what what can we get?)
Illegal business controls America

Boogie Down productions

Jimmy

What's up, Doc?
What's goin' on in here? (Hope up!)
The J, the I, the M, the M, the Y, the J, the I, the M

It's Jimmy (come again)
It's Jimmy (word up)
The J, the I, the M, the M, the Y, the J, the I, the M
It's Jimmy (I can't hear you!)
It's Jimmy

Here we go
Here is a message
To the super hos
Just keep in mind
When Jimmy grows
It grows and grows and grows
So let it
But keep in mind about the epidemic
When Jimmy releases
Boy, it pleases
But what do you do about all these diseases?
Jimmy is Jimmy
No matter what
So take care of Jimmy
'Cause you know what's up
'Cause now in winter
AIDS attacks
So run out and get your Jimmy hats
It costs so little for a pack of three
They're Jimmy hats for the winter attack
Good for a present
Great for lovers
Demonstrated by the Jungle Brothers
Protect your Jimmy
And keep it fresh
They're Jimmy hats by KRS
So remember
You're never too old (what?)
Jimmy is wearing a hat
Remember, you're never too bold
Jimmy is wearing a hat (come again?)
Do me a favor
Wear your hat
So Jimmy (I'm tryin' to tell ya)

You have the opportunity to come back
Well Red Alert is now in BDP
Teachin' you all about Jimbrowski
I don't want to hear that you're not with it
Turn around and see your butt in a clinic
Having doctors
Just poke at Jimmy
Let me express now
What's in me
Too many people take too many risks
Too many people I see get dissed
Jimmy hats are now in style
'Cause you can't trust a big butt
And a smile
Some are dry
And some lubricated
Many companies' makes are out-dated
So all you super hos
Wear your hat
'Cause drippin' Jimmy's
Is straight up wack
Keepin' in mind about Jimbrowski
Jimmy hats by BDP
The J, the I, the M, the M, the Y, the J, the I (Don't roll it off
    now!)
It's Jimmy (Keep it on)
The J, the I, the M, the M, the Y, the J, the I (hold that)
It's Jimmy (I told you it fits)
So remember, you're never too old
Jimmy is wearin' a hat (I told you it fits)
Remember, you're never too bold
Jimmy is wearin' a hat (we can't do this)
Do me a favor
Wear your hat
So Jimmy
You have the opportunity to come back

boo-yaa Tribe

New Funky Nation

This rhyme is mine and I lived it to give it
So that the New Funky Nation can get with it
Understand the plan that's programmed
For all nations to slam this jam
One nation under a groove was the first move
So now it's time to get with the New
Funky Nation the new formation
Turn up that bass for more connection
We must get along in order to live long
So keep bumpin' that Boo-Yaa song
So maybe then you can understand the game
The gangsta draws out the picture to frame
In your mind you think, understand, and learn
You play with fire, you're gonna burn
Gangsta know 'cause I been through
Always lookin' for somethin' to get into
This into that, into my pocket I pulls out a gat
'Cause I'm a hardhead and I'm down
This is one M.C. that don't be fuckin' around
Takin' care of the issue is what I get into
So now it's your time to step to
This jam to be craved for the new generation
Here, this is for the New Funky Nation

It could be better (It could be better)
The New Funky Nation (New Funky Nation)
It could be better (It could be better)

Another nation I'm pimpin', lyric clip clippin'
The bomb is tickin' while the hour glass is drippin'
Wastin' time at the scene of a crime
It was your rhyme that put M.C.s in line or on queue
I can rock a cue in pool, put your ass on quiet

Send your ass back to old school
Step back while I reach for the rack
Grab my brim and tilt it back
I gots to funk this 'cause I invented it
Another message from the gangsta who's sendin' it
Let it be a lesson for those who don't know
Boo-Yaa soldiers packs the "O"
Tell them who's "O"
One mobsta bass who can funk a show
Hang a M.C. off the edge of a cliff and let him go
We can get to, do it, play Russian Roulette
Show us a trigger and we'll pull it
No time to waste once upon the mike
So whatcha think, Ridd? This is for the nation's delight
All together, we must come as one
Turn up the drums, jealous can't get none
Of Godfather, K.O.D., E.K.A.
Roscoe, the Ridd, and "O" makes the other *tre*
So here is your invitation, this is for the New Funky Nation

And it could be better (It could be better)
The New Funky Nation (New Funky Nation)
It could be better (It could be better)

We must go on
'Cause the New Funky Nation is ready and armed
Straight from the funk farm
Yes, we know you can't get with it
But I see your head can move to it
So let's face it
This is for the nation to taste
"O" bring in the new funky bass
Lights, camera, murder
It was the Riddler who put it together
Understand my demands, another funk band
Pulled you down like quicksand
Don't let it fool you, damn
Another goddamn preview
I have the message to give to the people
And it's about this new funky tempo

They gots to have it, break the old habits
Or another nation will sneak up and grab it
Realizing the nation I'm facin'
But we must go on
The New Funky Nation has just been reborn
Bring on the funky horns, we're ready to go
Is the New Funky Nation ready to go?
Yes, we're ready to roll, so now you know
Life has their limitations
Here, this is for the New Funky Nation

I pledge allegiance to the funk
Of the United Funky Nations
And to the public for which it stands
The new nation is now in our hands
Individuals with liberty and funk for all

Bw*p*

Two Minute Brother

Is this all you got?
One minute and you go pop?
You's a big disgrace!
I oughta mush you all in your face!
Tellin' me lies, you were a real good lover
You a two-minute brother

I hate guys who talk a lot a shit
How they last long and got good dicks
Talkin' shit, "I am the best lover"
They all two-minute brothers

Now I know you can't be talking to me, baby, 'cause ya know I'm
    swingin' long ALL night long, know what I'm saying? I turn
    you over into stupid pussy

See, I'm the type of bitch that loves to be fucked
Trim, taut, stuffed, and sucked
Up in my ass, deep down in my throat
We could get busy but Jimmy must wear a raincoat
He said, "God damn, that shit sounds dope
Look no further, ho, I'm the pope
Like religion, nasty or nice
Ya got to give me some pussy
Like a sacrifice
I got the full nine stretchin' out to twelve
Like a burnt offering, we're goin' straight to hell
'Cause I'm 'a pump you up
Cold split your clit
And let ya come in my mouth while ya suck my dick
And then I'm gonna turn ya over
Belly-up, bitch, and lick that ass right where you shit"

Well, needless to say, I took him back to my house
Took a quick shower, rinsed out my mouth
My starvin' ass, my shit wet as hell
I had to do the right thing—take a Massingail's
We lay back cool and drink a Hennessy
When he said
"Buford is ready to enter thee"
Lift 'em up, spread 'em out
Hold up, somethin' wrong
Buford was only three inches long
Now I'm pissed and I'm ready to bitch
But my cunt's so horny, I don't give a shit
'Cause I'm one nasty-assed bitch
And I, I need something up in my clit
I only got half and yes I'm still ticked
But ah what the hell, Buford, go for it
Uhhh! Ohh Ohh Ohh Ah-Ah, I'm thru!

Is this all I get?
Is this supposed to be good dick?
Damn! You said you was a good lover
But you's a two-minute brother
Nigga—I ain't even bust a sweat

Not to mention, I ain't came yet
I was about to be cool for what would have happened
But his shit shriveled up like a Vienna sausage
Now I'm hot, I got an attitude
It's time for dinner, I'm servin' seafood
On yo' knees, motherfucker, let your tongue stroke
Push up on that bitch until it hit my throat
And ladies beware of them talkative brothers
Chances are, they're two-minute motherfuckers!

"Damn! Maybe your shit broke! I know ya can't be talkin' about
    me. 'Cause shit! Man, I was so far up in that ass, I was out
    your back! I don't know what you're talkin' about baby, 'cause
    if my dick wasn't good, then why was you howlin', huh?
    Why was you howlin'?"
I was hollerin' to keep from laughin' in yo' face
"Not all the time"

Go ahead girl, go ahead girl, kick it
Go ahead girl, just kick that shit
Go ahead girl, just kick that shit
Go ahead girl, just kick that shit
Go ahead girl, just kick that shit
Yeaaaaaah, girl

Most of us girls pursue it and do it
And I'm the type of freak that throws my back into it
But here's the type of man that we can't stand
One who always holds his thing in his hand
Talkin' about it all the time
Lyin' and sayin' it's about size nine
Always got his hands between his legs
You know the kind—the one who always begs
The one who claims to be the real good lover
Usually, he's a two-minute brother

Go ahead girl, go ahead girl, kick it
Go ahead girl, just kick that shit
Go ahead girl, just kick that shit
Go ahead girl, just kick that shit

Go ahead girl, just kick that shit
Go ahead girl, just kick that shit
Go ahead girl, just kick that shit

BWP in effect once again, for all you females across America for
all those too-short, two-inched, foul-mouthed, mellow-assed
shit, two-minute brothers

C.p.0.

Ballad of a Menace

This is the ballad of a menace
Not to be confused with that of apprentice
I'm in this to be number one
When I step upon and walk the streets
Stalk the meek like that of a predator
Blow the brains out the head of my competitor

I'm a product of your sins
Though you say I never heard of ya
A killer, a dope dealer, gangsta
Murderer, merciless maniac
Monarch of manipulation
Primary focus of your local police station

I roll cold in my 'lac
Pumpin' sounds that I gained doin' a jack move
As I groove to gangsta melody
Passin' crack to a nine-year-old
And I've been told
Pimpin' hos is a felony

But I'm not a doctor or lawyer
I wasn't made to be
Ever lucifearic because I get paid to be
There ain't no rehabilitating me

Pull a gat on your grandmother
Then take her social security

The boundary lines of my jurisdiction
Expand from day to day
Ruler of all I survey and with that load up my gat
Then I pack so I can bust on the suckas that you replenish
This is the ballad of a menace

I'm a menace
I'm a me-me-menace
I'm a me—   I'm a me—
I'm a menace to society
I'm a menace
I'm a menace to society

This is the ballad of a menace
Ren will finish and diminish
All the suckas that thought they could flow like me that was in
    this
Society wishes for my death or my downfall
But they playin' theirself as if they were
Playin' some round ball
'Cause I'm terrorizin'
The territory I'm steppin' on
Endangerin' citizens while I'm keepin' my weapon on
Might hit like a psycho
'Cause to me it was fittable
I just got word, the ruthless villain was critical

Let's get it straight
The ones that want some can come with that
Illiterate muthafuckas, I make you look dumb with that
Stumble and fumble 'cause I'm 'a crush till you crumble
So you can stutter and stutter
But keep it down to a mumble

M.C. Ren is never taken as a sucka
In other words, I'm a bad muthafucka
So next time I walk the streets you should know

To lock your doors and close your windows
And if you was thinkin' that protection can stop me
It takes a continent full of niggas to drop me
And for me to be vicious, yo it's valid
While I'm conductin' and producin' the ballad of a muthafuckin'
    menace

I'm a menace
I'm a me-me-menace
I'm a me—   I'm a me—
I'm a menace to society
I'm a menace
I'm a menace to society

I come out bustin' like a gauge
Nobody's safe when I'm enraged
Sacrifice the suckas and weak muthafuckas
They run in fear
I'm the minister of misery
Answer the knock at your door and open to A.K. delivery

Best known for being unsympathetic when I pick 'em
'Cause sympathy is for the pathetic and to the victim
Kill one and kill another, mercy my only incapacity
Started by killin' my own mother
Maniacal madman, son of Mephisto
Bound to go to hell since I was an embryo

The criminal, cold standin' in gangsta pose
Steppin' with Ren the villain
Slappin' up all the hos
Your mother, your sister, your daughter, your wife
And if you was reincarnated
I would snatch your second life
In it for the money
Down for me, myself, and I, you see, and fuck the community
I know in conclusion that death is my destiny
But fuck it, 'cause shootin' muthafuckas is left in me
So write my malevolent epitaph, put it in the book of Guinness
And title it . . . The Ballad of a Menace

I'm a menace
I'm a me-me-menace
I'm a me—   I'm a me—
I'm a menace to society
I'm a menace
I'm a menace to society

Chubb Rock

Ya Bad Chubbs

This is an introduction
To music that just be pumpin'
While hits just be dippin'
The intention is for humpin' the floor
Shinin' the wood with your jeans
If it's denim, don't worry
It's hip hop, don't hem 'em
Money earnin' concernin'
I'll be teachin' and learnin'
Gettin' hot from my rhymes and my looks
Not from bourbon
No solution, no remedy
No cure like a deodorant
Yo, you have to be sure
That if you talk up or walk up into my face
That wouldn't become a big public disgrace
'Cause I'll ban you, burn you up, and tan you
Treat you like the elephant
And man you will be hocked and locked in a jar with a lid
Hångin' on a wall in Michael Jackson's crib
'Cause I'm bad, in fact I'm a thriller
I drink milk, that's why I'm a top biller
Like a funeral home, I'll make a killing
I'm not Giz even though I'm still chillin'
Guys say I'm scary, girls say I'm cuddly

Rough like bark but dark and lovely
This ain't no game and I'm no toy
And like Anita Baker, I'll bring you joy
With my word when I open my mouth
Ask Oliver North to go and break south
A homo is a no-no but you know I'll smack a faggot
Boy, you got to see me, I'm rich like Jimmy Swaggart
I'm a loon and ya know, comin' soon
A rhyme kicked to this Popeye tune
This is hip hop with a little be-bop
And I won't flop 'cause I can't stop
I will mop up the slop and then go to the top
'Cause I'm not Robocop, I'm Chubb Rock

I'm Chubb Rock risin' and I'll break your leg
And I'm more than a forty ounce, I'm more like a keg
And I'm the big dipper, rippin' like Jack the Ripper
And if you want the proof, the proof is in my liquor
So you knew it and you blew it, let's get to it
Gonna run you over with a rhyme that's like a big Buick
And since you think you're slender, I'll slap you with a fender
And bind you up, wind you up, and grind you up in a blender
And then I'll serve you with coffee and cake
Oh damn, I should've had a V-8, oh well
I'll put you on a plate so it looks a little neater
You're a tramp, so I'll sprinkle salt and pepper
And paprika on your face, like mace
So you can taste immediately
Just like the base that went up your nose previously
So it seems you're too zooed to battle
Word's up chump, acne bump, skidaddle
You're a nine, I'm a ten
Victory is mine again, this Bud's for me
So here, take a Heineken
With your self-esteem, you will never redeem
Like Martin Luther King, you have a dream
That maybe you will beat me, maybe defeat me
But you're too illiterate, so I won't consider it
Weak is the word and the rhyme is identical
This is not the late show

And I'm not Arsénio Hall
But quite tall with the gall
And I have magic and I can play ball
And guys won't boo this, girls will just screw this
It's ludicrous but we can do this
'Cause you're new to this, Brutus
I'm so smooth that I'm the smoothest
I'm not handsome but I am the cutest you ever had
That's why I'm so glad that I'm so good I'm bad

Crash Crew

On the Radio

Crash Crew rocking on the radio
It's no good to be quitting, not to be stopping
Keep moving, just keep on rocking
This music just stays on your mind
It'll rock you each and every time
We're on the mike and it's rocking
It sounds so good your hands will start clapping
When we finish rocking on the radio
We go by the name of the mighty crash
And we got a melody that will sure enough smash
You should hear what's going down with a great big splash
We're pulling all the tricks from out the stash
Reggie Reg, P. Stro, G-Man, Shoo Bee
And a brother by the name of E.K. Mike C.
If don't you ever in your mind, so keep your fantasy
Because he's the whole of the lot D.J. Darryl C.
We're rocking you down with the musical way
Ah with the rhythm nation all to come you say
It makes you follow with us to the musical flow
As we beginning to rock you on the radio
Now that we got your attention
There's something that you all should know

Reggie Reg is rocking on the radio
Now I receive a phone call from a reliable source
And he was talking too fast and I got lost
I asked him to explain what I was talking about
My man was too excited, he begin to shout
I finally figured out what homeboy was saying
You never guess what the radio's playing
I turned my stereo on and what do you know
Reggie Reg is rocking on the radio

P. Stro is rocking on the radio
I have powers that are only mind
I'll make a blind man walk a straight line
I mated queens, I beat up kings
I have twenty gold chains and five gold rings
I stole for gold, I walk around
I could even bench press three hundred pounds
His name is P. Stro and you could call him a pro
I'll be rocking on the radio

Mike C. is rocking on the radio
Oh well, that is all, my talent is a gift from God
The fine sense of though it shouldn't be
Because I'm a man that's strong is where I belong
You're guaranteed to get dissed if you tell me I'm wrong
Your mind is crunched as I take you to lunch
With my high-powered rap, I knock you out like a punch
No time to explain because it really don't matter
I'm E.K. Mike C. and I will serve you on a platter

G-Man is rocking on the radio
G-Man but other rappers can address me as Thor
The rhyme is my poem, the mike is my sword
In an M.C. job, I've never been best
Because the rap that I pop goes uncontested
Like a lethal weapon, the rap will move
Set your butt on fire with the heat in your face
So don't you get out of line
You better stay in your place
'Cause if you don't, I'm gonna dis your face

Shoo Bee is rocking on the radio
Well, I'm M.C. Shoo Bee, the M.C. supreme
Be rocking on the mike with the gangster show
I been rocking at parties since seventeen
I said I walk around town in designer jeans
And as you know that state as a fact
And I'm the only M.C. who got it like that
And I'm M.C. Shoo Bee and I want you to know
He's telling his story on the radio
It's no good to be quitting, not to be stopping
Keep moving, just keep on rocking
This music just stays on your mind
It'll rock you each and every time
We're on the mike and it's rocking
It's so good, your hands will start clapping
And when we finish rocking at the show
We will be rocking on the radio

It's no good to be quitting, not to be stopping
Keep moving, just keep on rocking
This music just stays on your mind
It'll rock you each and every time
We're on the mike and it's rocking
It's so good, your hands will start clapping
And when we finish rocking at the show
We will be rocking on the radio

cypress Hill
How I Could Just Kill a Man

Hey, don't miss out on what you're passing
You're missing the hootah of the funky buddha
Eluder of your fucked-up styles, I get wicked
So come on as Cypress starts to kick it

'Cause we're like the outlaws stridin' while suckers are hidin'
Jump behind the bush when you see me drivin' by!
Hanging out the window with my magnum taking out some
    puto's
Acting kind of loco I'm just another local
Kid from the street getting paid from my vocals

Here is something you can't understand
"How I could just kill a man"

Here is something you can't understand
"How I could just kill a man"
Here is something you can't understand
"How I could just kill a man"
Here is something you can't understand
"How I could just kill a man"
Here is something you can't understand

I'm ignoring all the dumb shit
Yo, because nothing is coming from it
I'm not gonna waste no time fuckin' around my gat straight
    humming
Hummin' coming at ya! Yeah, ya know I had to gat ya!
Time for some action just a fraction of friction
I got the clearance to run the interference
Into your satellite shining a battle light
Sen got the gat and I know that he'll gat you right
Here's an example just a little sample
"How I could just kill a man"
One-Time tried to come in my home, take my chrome
I said, "Yo, it's on"
Take cover son or you're assed-out
How do you like my chrome then I watched the rookie pass out
Didn't have to blast out but I did anyway
That young punk had to pay!
So I just killed a man

Here is something you can't understand
"How I could just kill a man"

Here is something you can't understand
"How I could just kill a man"
Here is something you can't understand
"How I could just kill a man"
Here is something you can't understand
"How I could just kill a man"
Here is something you can't understand

It's gonna be a long time before I finish
One of the many missions that I had to establish
To lite my spliff ignite you with insight so if you ain't down,
    bullshit
Say some punk tried to get you for your auto,
Would call the one-time and play the role model?
No! I think you'll play like a thug
Next you hear the shot of a magnum slug
Humming coming at ya!
Yeah, ya know I'm gonna gat ya
How do you know where I'm at when you haven't been where
    I've been?
Understand where I'm coming from
When you're up on the hill in your big home
I'm out here risking my dome
Just for a bucket or a fast ducat
Just to stay alive
Yo, I got to say "fuck it"

Here is something you can't understand
"How I could just kill a man"

Here is something you can't understand
"How I could just kill a man"
Here is something you can't understand
"How I could just kill a man"
Here is something you can't understand
"How I could just kill a man"
Here is something you can't understand

D Nice

A Few Dollars More

I grew up in the city where everything is rough
Where everywhere I turn, I seen somebody gettin bust'
Plus everywhere I look
All I could see is a crackhead or a goddamned crook
Runnin' around with a pistol or a blade
Stickin' up—in other words, gettin' paid
But I chose not to follow those ways
'Cause the only place you headin' is to jail or the grave
But on the other hand
I know a man named Stan
Who in the future had plans
To be successful on his quest to
Take his moms and pops out the ghetto
But that plan was soon to be crushed
When one day he realized he must
Get a better job to pay for his schoolin'
While his friends would sit around just coolin'
He applied for a job in the system
And everywhere he looked, everybody would dis him
He doesn't have any type of skill
And life is not all games, it's real
He took a long walk down the street
Tryin' to think of a way to make his ends meet, huh
So he could buy the fly things he adored

And all Stan wanted to make was a few dollars more

As he walked home, he thought to himself
Now what am I supposed to do to get wealth
He felt that his life was worthless
Then he ran into his man named Curtis
Now Curtis, he's the type that stops and brags
About all the things he's got

Drivin' a Saab with a black ragtop
Come to find out Curt's workin' for the cops
He told Stan there's a job that's open
Makin' it all sound good, just hopin' he would take it
Yup, and like a big dummy
Stan said "Freak it, yo, I need the money"
Curt took Stan to meet his boss
Officer Sims, a sergeant on the force
He gave him a gun and Stan began
His new career as a damn hit man
His boss really liked his work
And gave the boot to his partner Curt
He didn't realize what he was in for

And all Stan wanted to make was a few dollars more

A few dollars more is what he started to make
Now he's drivin' around a Saab, with a house upstate
He got gold and diamond rings
Crazy girls and all those glamorous things
But one day this life-style end
When one afternoon while hangin' with a friend
Sittin' in the park, drinkin' quarts of beer
And somebody said "Throw your hands in the air,
It's a stick-up" and put the gun to his head
And said, "Make another move and you're dead"
Now Stan had to make his choice
He paused and said I recognize that voice
Huh, where have I heard this
Now he remember, it's his man named Curtis
Curtis is mad and felt he'd been robbed
'Cause Stan is drivin' around in his Saab
He looked at Stan and said, "I can't believe him,
Now it's time for me to get even"
Stan made a move real quick
Curt jumped back and said, "Yo, that's it"
Shot him in the back of his head with a nine
Reached in his pocket, grabbed his cash and then dashed
Now here lies the man on the side
The same way he lived was the same way he died

He never knew what he had in store

And all Stan wanted to make was a few dollars more.

dana Dane
A Little Bit of Dane Tonight

No one knows, but I've been here for a while
I've been sitting in the back, playing a low profile
Then, like expected, well, my name would be paged
"Would the rapper Dana Dane please come to the stage?"
Well, I slid my seat back still cool, relaxed
Stood up on my feet and gave a tilt to my hat
To the front I walked, yeah, still unnoticed
Up on the stage all the eyes would be focused
Then from the left, two girlies caught their breath
And said, "There goes the Dane and he sure looks fresh."
Now a posse clocked me saying they could rock me
Mad 'cause the girlies called and they flocked me
But that didn't phase me, they must have been crazy
Forget about the guys, see I came for the ladies
And to grab the mike right, hold it tight like
Recite a hype type rhyme that I'd write
And if I may or if I might
Give a little bit of myself tonight

Just a little bit of Dane tonight
Makes you feel all right
Just a little Dana rocking you tonight
Makes you want to hold on tight

Now mike in hand and the people cheered me
1-2-1-2, Can everyone hear me?

Yeah, so let the party begin
As Clark cuts the record like a swordsman
To a worldwide rhythm that I'm sportin'
Dropped on point by producer Fresh Gordon
I came here to share my lyrical flair
Dana Dane forever rap extraordinaire
Now girls tossed their numbers and they cried my name
Saying "He's the dude," and "We love Dana Dane"
I couldn't resist, yeah, I blew them a kiss
"That was for me—no it wasn't for you"
Hey, no need to fight, so I blew them another
A fella on the side said, "Stop the mother"
But I told him "Don't mess with me
You know who the best will be
Listen to the radio
Your mother requested me
See, I've got a style, a talent, I'm gifted
Those who rift, well, it's time you get lifted
But I didn't come here to fuss or to fight
But to give a little bit of myself tonight"

Just a little bit of Dane tonight
Makes you feel all right
Just a little Dana rocking you tonight
Makes you want to hold on tight

Well, well, well, the party's heated now
There's no reason for you to be seated now
Guys, girls, do the latest dance moves
Those who can't dance, well bob out the smooth groove
I drop lines and I'll straight up wreck the shop
Is it R&B or cold hard hip hop?
It doesn't really matter, just have a good time
You better get yours, 'cause I'm sure to get mine
You never thought the Dane would be this large again, my brother
Bring it on up, I'll sign your album cover
But hold your girl, 'cause I think she's jockin' me
Can't you tell by the way that she's clockin' me
Well, at least she's got the right idea

And we can get busy when I'm finished here
'Cause she knows how to get things done right
Just get a little bit of Dane tonight

Just a little bit of Dane tonight
Makes you feel all right
Just a little Dana rocking you tonight
Makes you want to hold on tight

De La Soul

Ghetto Thang

Mary had a little lamb, that's a fib
She had two twins, though, and one crib
Now she's only fourteen; what a start
But this effect is found common in these parts
Now life in this world can be such a bitch
And dreams are often torn and shattered and hard to stitch
Negative the attitude that runs the show
When the stage is the g-h-e-t-t-o
Which is the one to blame when bullets blow
Either Peter, Jane, or John or Joe
But Joe can't shoot a gun, he's always drunk
And Peter's pimpin' Jane and John's a punk
Infested are the halls, also the brain
Daddy's broken down from ghetto pains
Mommy's flyin' high, the truth is shown
The kids are all alone 'cause it's just a Ghetto Thang

It's just a ghetto thang (Word)
It's just a ghetto thang (Word)

Who ranks the baddest brother, the one to rule
This title was sought by the coolest fool

Define "coolest fool" easy, the one who needs
Attention in the largest span and loves to lead
Always found at the jams, but never dance
Just provoke violence due to one glance
The future plays no matter, just the present flow
When the greeting place is the g-h-e-t-t-o
Lies are pointed strong into your skull
Deep within your brain against the wall
To hide or just erase a glowin' note
Of how they use the ghetto as a scapegoat
Truth from Trugoy's mouth is here to scar
Those who blame the "G" for all bazaars
So open up your vents and record well
'Cause this is where we stand for the true tell
Ghetto gain to ghetto name from ghetto way
Now there could be some ghetto gangs and ghetto play
If ghetto thing could have its way and get arranged
Then there must be some ghetto love and ghetto change
Though confident they keep it kept, we know for fact
They lie like ghettos form 'cause people lack
To see that they must all get out the ghetto hole
The truth they never told
'Cause it's just a ghetto thang

It's just a ghetto thang (Word)
It's just a ghetto thang (Word)

Do people really wish when they blow
Out the cake candles and if so
Is it for the sunken truth which could arise
From out the characters in which the ghetto hides
Roses in the ranks supply no shown relief
Granted it's planted by no shown belief
Kill and feed off your own brother man
Has quickly been adopted as the master plan
Posses of our people has yet to provoke
Freedom or death, to them it's just a joke
What causes this defect, I don't know
Maybe it's the g-h-e-t-t-o

It's just a ghetto thang (Word)
It's just a ghetto thang (Word)

Standin' in the rain is nothin' felt
When problems hold more value but never dealt with
Buildings crumblin' to the ground, impact noise is silent sound
But who's the one to say this life is wrong
When ghetto life is chosen strong
We seem to be mislead about our dreams
'Cause dreams ain't what is seen
When it's just a ghetto thang

De La SoUL

Me Myself and I

Mirror, mirror on the wall
Tell me, mirror, what is wrong
Can it be my De La clothes
Or is it just my De La song
What I do ain't make believe
People say I sit and try
But when it comes to being De La
It's just me myself and I
It's just me myself and I
It's just me myself and I
It's just me myself and I

Now ya tease my Plug One style
And my Plug One spectacles
You say Plug One and Two are hippies
No we're not, that's pure plug bull
Always pushin' that we formed an image
There's no need to lie
When it comes to being Plug One

It's just me myself and I
It's just me myself and I
It's just me myself and I
It's just me myself and I

Proud, I'm proud of what I am
Poems I speak, the Plug Two type
Please, oh please, let Plug Two be himself
Not what you read or write
Right is wrong when hype is written on the soul
De La, that is
Style is surely our own thing
Not the false disguise of showbiz
De La Soul is from the soul
And this fact I can't deny
Strictly from the Dan called Stuckie
And from me myself and I
It's just me myself and I
It's just me myself and I
It's just me myself and I

Glory Glory Hallelu
Glory for Plug One and Two
But that Glory's been denied
By Kcids and gooky eyes
People think they dis my person
By stating I'm darkly packed
I know this, so I point at Q-tip and he states
"Black is Black"
Mirror mirror on the wall
Shovel chestnuts in my path
Let's keep all nuts with the nuts
So I don't get an aftermath
But if I do, I'll calmly punch them
In the fourth day of July
'Cuz they tried to mess with third degree
That's me myself and I
It's just me myself and I
It's just me myself and I
It's just me myself and I

De La Soul

Millie Pulled a Pistol on Santa

"If you will suck my soul
I will lick your funky emotions"

This is the stylin' for a title that sounds silly
But nothin' silly about triflin' times of Millie
Millie, a Brooklyn Queen—originally from Philly
Complete with that accent that made her sound hilly-billy
Around this time, the slammin' joint was Milk is Chillin'
But even cooler was my social worker Dillon
Yeah, I had a social worker 'cuz I had some troubles
Anyone who'd riff on me, I'd pop their dome like bubbles
He'd bring me to his crib to watch my favorite races
That's how his daughter Millie become one of my favorite
    faces
She had the curves that made you wanna take chances
I mean on her, man, I'd love to make advances
I guess her father must 'a got the same feelin'
I mean, actually findin' his own daughter Millie appealing
At the time no one knew but it was a shame
That Millie became a victim of the touchy-touchy game

Yo Millie, what's the problem, lately you've been buggin'
On your dukie earrings, someone must be tuggin'
You were a dancer who could always be found clubbin'
Now you're world renowned with the frown you're luggin'
Come to think your face look stink when Dill's around you
He's your father—what done happen—did he ground you?
You shouldn't flip on him 'cuz Dill is really cool
Matter of fact, the coolest elder in the school
He hooked up a trip to bring us all the Lacey
He volunteered to play old Santa Claus at Macy's
Child, ya got the best of pops anyone could have
Dillon's cool, super hip, you should be glad

Yeah, it seemed that Santa's ways were parallel with Dillon
But when Millie and him got him, he was more of a villain
While she slept in he crept inside her bedroom
And he would toss and then would force her to give him head
    room
Millie tried real hard to let this hell not happen
But when she'd fuss, he would just commence to slappin'
(Yo Dillon man, Millie's been out of school for a week, man,
    what's the deal?)
I guess he was givin' Millie's bruises time to heal
Of course he told us she was sick and we believed him
And at the department store as Santa we would see 'em
And as he smiled, his own child was at home plottin'
How off the face of this earth she was gonna knock him
When I got home, I found she had tried to call me
My machine had kicked to her hey how ya doin' (sorry)
I tried to call the honey but her line was busy
I guess I'll head to Macy's and bug out on Dillon
I received a call from Misses Sick herself
I asked her how was she recoverin' her health
She said that what she had to ask would make it seem minute
She wanted to talk serious, I said, "go ahead—shoot"
She claimed I hit the combo dead upon the missal
Wanted to know if I could get a loaded pistol
That ain't a problem but why would Millie need one
She said she wanted her pops Dillon to heed one
Ran some style about him pushin' on her privates
Look honey, I don't care if you kick five fits
There's no way that you can prove to me that Dill's flip
He might breathe a blunt but ya jeans he wouldn't rip
You're just mad he's your overseer at school
No need to play him out like he's someone cruel
She kicked that she would go get it from somewhere else
Yeah, whatever you say, go for ya self

Macy's department store, the scene for Santa's kisses
And all the little brats demandin' all of their wishes
Time passes by as I wait for my younger brother
He ask his wish, I waste no time to return him back to Mother

As I'm jettin', Millie floats in like a zombie
I ask her what's her problem, all she says is "Where is he?"
I give a point, she pulls a pistol, people screamin'
She shouts to Dill he's off to hell cuz he's a demon
None of the kids could understand what was the cause
All they could see was a girl holdin' a pistol on Claus
Dillon pleaded mercy, said he didn't mean to
Do all the things that her mind could do nothing but cling to
Millie bucked him and with the quickness it was over

De La Soul

Say No Go

Now let's get right on down to the skit
A baby is brought into a world of pits
And if it could have talked that soon
In the delivery room
It would have asked the nurse for a hit
The reason for this
The mother is a jerk
Excuse me, Junkie
Which brought the work of the old into a new life
What a way
But this what a way has been a way of today
Anyway
Push couldn't shove me to understand the path to a basehead
Consumer should erased it in the first wave
'Cause second wave forms believers
And believers will walk to it
Then even talk to it
And say
"You got the body now you want my soul"
Well, I can't have none of that
Tell 'em what to say, Mase

Say no go
Say no go
Say no go
Say no go
Say no go

Naa,
No my brother
No my sister
Try to get hip to this
Word
Word to the mother
I'll tell the truth
So bear my witness
Fly like birds of a feather
Drugs are like pleather
You don't want to wear it
No need to ask that question
Just don't mention you know what the answer is
Now I never fancied Nancy
But the statement she made
Held a plate of weight
I even stressed it to Wade
Did he take any heed?
Naaa, the boy was hooked
You could phrase the word "base"
And the kid just shook
In his fashion class
Once "A"
Now an "F"
The rock rules him now
The only designs left
Were once clothes made for Oshkosh
Has converted to nothing but stonewashed
Now hopping in a barrel
Is a barrel of fun
But don't hop in if you want to be down, son
'Cause that could mean down and out as an action
What does it lead to?
Dum de dum dum

People say what have I done
For all my years
My tears show my hard-earned work
I heard shovin' is worse than pushin'
But I'd rather know a shover than a pusher
'Cause a pusher's a jerk

Say no go
Say no go
Say no go
Say no go
Say no go

Believe it or not
The plot forms a fee
More than charity
But the cost doesn't coincide
With the ride of insanity
Is it a chant that slant the soul to fill for it
I know it's the border that flaunts the order
To kill for it
Standin'
Schemin' on a young one
Thinkin' this time
Eight-ball for a cool pool player
Racked it all
Tried to break
Miscued got beat by the boy in blue
Next day you're out by the spot once more
Lookin' hard for a crack in the hole
I asked, "what's the fix?"
For the ill stuff
Word to the Dero
The answer should've been "no"
Run me a score from the Funky Four
Plus One More ("It's the joint")
Rewind that back
This is the age for a new stage of fiend
Watch how the zombies scream, "It's the crack"
Plain is plain, it should explain it from the start

Behind the ideals of crankin' up the heart
Now the base claims shot over every part

Say no go
Say no go
Say no go
Say no go
Don't even think about it
Say no go (*to fade*)

Def Jef

Black to the Future

As-Salaam-Alaikum, Black Man, time to make a stand
Time to wake up and
Time to make a plan and band
Together like China
We need to find a
Better form of unity
Then we'll be
In the right path, on the right track
Dark or light black
Don't let 'em tell you it's wrong to
Fight back (Come on!)
But the enemy is not your brother
It's that other motherfucker
The one that baited, robbed, and degraded you
And he don't like to see you've made it through
The bullshit that came with
Being a brother man
Stolen from the motherland
Placed in another land
Four-hundred-and-some odd years ago
'Til about the time we wore Afros

We've come so far
So fast from what they call the past
But that just passed
And we're the last in line for justice
What's this?
New man that ain't gonna work
Yo, bust this, Black
To the Future
Back to the past
History is a mystery 'cause it has
All the info
You need to know
Where you're from
Why'd you come and
That'll tell you where you're going

(We gotta unite, we gotta work together in unity and harmony)

Black to the Future

Black to the Future, what a funky concept
A poet with soul brothers and sisters—let's step
Together in sync and think about the outcome
We know where we're going 'cause we know where we came from
A united state of mind but not the kind
That the United States government fakes (nope)
They don't practice what they preach
Maybe they don't believe in those false beliefs themselves
And I can tell 'cause they look scared
To see us coming up 'cause they're not prepared
For a new breed of leaders, eager and fired up
And tired of the lies you feed us, so we just
Got together like one nation under a groove
Getting down and the funk of it can move
And start a movement of self-improvement
And before you know it, you went

Black to the Future

I grab the mike with a kung fu grip
So it don't slip and come in on a positive Black tip
Hip all my brothers and sisters to the real deal
With unity and knowledge I feel we'll
Uprise, who knows what lies ahead
But you can't see if you're living with your shut eyes
So realize, united we stand, divided we fall
Provided we all heed the call
Coming from the Muslim or the Rastaman
Two forms of a positive Blackman
W.E.B. Du Bois and Booker T.
King and X, Farrakhan and Jesse
Men with means that differ
But their goals were equal
To uplift Afrikan people
Through violence or nonviolence, I don't care
As long as we get there we're (Where?)

Black to the Future

digital Underground

Doowutchyalike

Oooh I see guys and girls dancing
Oooh I see guys and girls dancing

Now as the record spins around, you recognize this sound?
Well it's the Underground—you know that we're down
With wutchyalike, with wutchalike
And though we're usually on the serious tip, check it out
Tonight we're gonna flip and trip and let it all hang out
Tonight we're gonna say what we like
'Cause yo yo, we wanna know how many people in the flow
Would like to just let yourselves go and doowutchyalike
Yeah? well tonight's your night

Just eat food, try not to be crude or rude, kill the attitude
Chill the serious mood and doowutchyalike and doowutchyalike
Everybody doowutchyalike (I see guys & girls dancin')

Yeah, doowutchyalike (I see guys & girls dancin')
Just doowutchyalike (I see guys & girls dancin')
Yo, gowhereyalike (I see guys & girls dancin')

Now rich, poor, higher, lower, upper middle class
Let's all get together and have a few laughs and dowhatwelike
And dowhatwelike
And since you came here you've gotta show and prove
And do that dance until it don't move
Doowutchyalike, sometimes I bite
Now if you're hungry, get yourself something to eat
And if you're dirty, then go take a bath
Messed up the line? Nope, sometimes I don't rhyme
Help yourself to a cracker with a spread of cheddar cheese
Have a neckbone, you don't have to say please, eatwutchyalike
Yo, smellhowyalike
Everybody doowutchyalike (I see guys & girls dancin')
Doowutchyalike (I see guys & girls dancin')
Yo, Doowutchyalike, you know what I'm sayin'? (I see guys &
    girls dancin')
Whatever you'd like to do
Talk howyalike (I see guys & girls dancin')

Just act a fool
It's ok if you drool
'Cause everybody's gonna strip and jump in the pool
And doowhatwelike and doowhatwelike
Homegirls, for once forget you got class
See a guy you like, just grab him in the biscuits
And doowutchyalike
Now red, white, tan, black, yellow, or brown
It really doesn't matter
We can all get down and doowhatwelike and doowhatwelike
From a pink-skinned Yankee
To a blue-black Southerner
Ditch-digger or a governor

Just doowutchyalike, look howyalike
Now don't ya know, we're gettin' busy, can't be corrected
Shakespeare had to be def
I say what I like
Like I said, sometimes we bite
Even though ya don't think it's right
Yo, I like to bite
Just havin' fun y'all and if you think that it's wrong
Ya got to admit it's a new type of song
Doowutchyalike (I see guys & girls dancin')
Yeah, Doowutchyalike (I see guys & girls dancin')
Yo, go where ya like (I see guys & girls dancin')
Dowhoyalike (I see guys & girls dancin')
Alright, here we go y'all
Doowutchyalike,
Talkhowyalike,
(I feel like a nice big bowl of cereal with icy cold milk)
Drinkwutchyalike
(Come on fellas, we're gonna crack the champagne)
Grabwhoyalike
Feelwhatyalike
Eatwutchyalike
Scratchwhereyalike (I wanna take my shoes off)
Itchifyalike (and kick up my heels)
Daddy, can I go outside?
Gowhereyalike, kid

A brief announcement to all radio D.J.s:
If this record is currently being played at your station, we will
    provide the following time for you to announce your station
    identification. We'd also like to add that we've now reached
    the three-and-a-half minute mark on this song.
Radio stations may begin your fade here. For those that would
    like help, we will start your fade for you.

digital Underground

Packet Man

'Scuse me trooper, will you be needin' any packets today?
Yo B, don't be pullin' on my jacket, okay?
Cool, just tryin' to get your attention
So you can take a look at this invention
Now peep these
I got some more in my jacket
Man, what are these, condoms?
Uh-huh, sex packets
It's like a pill, you can either chew it up
Or like an Alka Seltzer, dissolve it in a cup
And get this, see the girl on the cover?
You black out, and she becomes your lover
You're trippin'
No I'm serious, these are authentic
Yeah? Well I don't take hallucinogenics
Wrong again, my man, this is way more real
But since you know everything
I'll make someone else a deal

Yeah, he's the packet man (the packet man)
Packets, got them packets
Yeah, he's the packet man (the packet man)
Packets
Yeah, he's the packet man (the packet man)
Packets, who needs packets?
Yeah, he's the packet man (the packet man)
Got them packets

Well now you got me curious
I'm kinda thinkin' about buyin' it
Three for ten dollars, it can't hurt to try it
Well what exactly do I get?
Well read what it says, look at the picture

Bet it says Chinese girl, age seventeen, waist twenty-four, hips
    thirty-three
Hmmm, this one here says young black virgin
Man, this is crazy, I'm gonna have to splurge and get me a few of
    these things
How long do they last?
Well it depends, let's see
These cheap ones here are ten minutes
But these are extra power
They last about a half an hour
And these here sell for 'bout forty
'Cause you get two girls
Yeah, it says orgy
Right, and if you're married it's no big deal
You're not cheatin' at all, you're just poppin' a pill
And if your wife's got a headache and wants to hit the sack
It's cool, take a packet, fool
Biochemically compacted sexual affection
Now here, take a look at my selection

Yeah, he's the packet man (the packet man)
Packets, got them packets
Yeah, he's the packet man (the packet man)
Packets
Yeah, he's the packet man (the packet man)
Packets, who needs packets?
Yeah, he's the packet man (the packet man)
Got them packets

Ok, I want these two boxes of three, and gimme blond here
And that one that said orgy
And by the way, I need somethin' for my woman
Sure, I got guy packets
Cool, gimme some of 'em
Now lemme tell ya how to take it
Either sit or lie down, and you really should be naked
Otherwise you're gonna mess up your clothes
Know what I mean? This is more than just a dream
It's very realistic and it's gonna blow your mind
So be careful—only take one at a time

And never take one behind the wheel
You'll black out and hit a pole
Cool, let's make the deal
These are forty, these are eighty, and this one here's ten
Just gimme a hundred dollars, I'll call it even
But don't pull your money out yet, see
There's one or two narcs in this area that sweat me
Over here
Yeah, this looks kinda cool
Twenty, forty, sixty, eighty, hundred, Schmoov
Here's my number, in case you need to reach me again
And remember, you need to be as safe as you can
There's only one thing safer than using your hand
Dial that beeper number and call the packet man

Yeah, he's the packet man (the packet man)
Packets, got them packets
Yeah, he's the packet man (the packet man)
Packets
Yeah, he's the packet man (the packet man)
Packets, who needs packets?
Yeah, he's the packet man (the packet man)
Got them packets

Man, that was cool, wasn't it?
Man, my god man, that was like nothing I ever had in my life
I tried to tell you, partner
Man, it was like she was really in the room with me, you know
   what I mean?
Man, I'm 'a make a killin'
Just listen, listen, listen
I need a couple more man, I'm kinda tapped right now
But I tell you what, you just hook me up wit' some
I'll straighten you out Tuesday
Ah, man, I can't front you nothin' man
I'm sorry, but I just don't, I can't handle it
Come on man, I'm good for it
I'm sorry partner, you know what I'm sayin'?
I just, I can't work it, man
Alright, alright, alright aahhh . . . alright see this TV right here?

Aw man, I got a (here we go man) I got enough TVs, man
It's cool man, look at it, it's brand new, man
I just paid five hundred dollars for that TV
Man, I can't have no TVs, what about her?
Man, that's my wife, man
Man, that'll work
Ya know what I'm sayin'? 'Cause I can't mess wit these things
    myself see, man, I don't get high on my own supply
I'll tell ya what—that VCR right there
Man, I, man, if I get another VCR I'm gonna hurt somebody
I can't let ya have my wife, man
Man, cut me, well alright, man, later, man
The shop's closed, man, I got to go

digital Underground

The Humpty Dance

All right, stop what you're doin'
'Cause I'm about to ruin
The image and the style that you're used to
I look funny
But yo, I'm makin' money, see
So, yo world, I hope you're ready for me
Now gather round
I'm the new fool in town
And my sound's laid down by the Underground
I'll drink up all the Hennessey you got on your shelf
So just let me introduce myself
My name is Humpty
Pronounced with a "umpty"
Yo ladies, oh how I'd like to funk thee
And all the rappers in the Top Ten
Please allow me to bump thee
I'm steppin' tall, y'all
And just like Humpty Dumpty

You're gonna fall when the stereos pump me
I like to rhyme, I like my beats funky
I'm spunky, I like my oatmeal lumpy
I'm sick with this
Straight gangster mack
Well sometimes I get ridiculous
I'll eat up all your crackers and your licorice
Yo fat girl, come here, are you ticklish?
Yeah, I called you fat
Look at me, I'm skinny
It never stopped me from gettin' busy
I'm a freak
I like the girls with the broom
I once got busy in a Burger King bathroom
I'm crazy
Allow me to amaze thee
They say I'm ugly but it just don't faze me
I'm still gettin' in the girls' pants
And I even got my own dance

The Humpty Dance
Here's your chance
To do the Hump
(Oh, do me baby)
Come on
Do the Humpty Hump
Come on and do the Humpty Hump
(Oh oh, do me baby)
Check it out, y'all
Do the Humpty Hump, just watch me do the Humpty Hump
(Oh oh, do me baby)
Do you know what I'm doin', doin' the Humpty Hump
(Oh oh, do me baby)
Come on, do the Humpty Hump, haah, do the Humpty Hump

People say, "Yo Humpty!
You're really funny lookin' "
That's all right 'cause I get things cookin'
You stare, you glare
You constantly try to compare me

But ya can't get near me
I'll give you more
See, and on the floor
B, all the girls, they adore me
Oh yes, ladies, I'm really bein' sincere
'Cause in the 69 my Humpty nose'll tickle your rear
My nose is big
Uh-uh, I'm not ashamed
Big like a pickle, I'm still gettin' paid
I get laid by the ladies
U know I'm in charge
Both how I'm living and my nose is large
I get stoopid
I shoot an arrow like Cupid
I'll use a word that don't mean nuthin' like "lupdid"
I sang in "Doowutchyalike" and if you missed it
I'm the one who said, "Just grab him in the biscuits"
Also told you that I like to bite
Whoa yeah, I guess it's obvious, I also like to write
All you had to do was give Humpty a chance
And now I'm gonna do my dance

The Humpty dance
Here's your chance
To do the Hump
Come on, yeah, sexy baby
Do the Humpty Hump
Do the Humpty Hump
Sexy baby, everybody
Do the Humpty Hump
C'mon and do the Humpty Hump
Do you know what we're doin', we're doin' the Humpty Hump, y'all
Do the Humpty Hump
Watch me do the Humpty Hump

Aw yeah that's the break, y'all
Let a little 'a that bass groove right here

Aw yeah, now that I've told y'all a little bit about myself
Let me tell you a little about this dance

It's real easy to do
Check it out

First I limp to the side
Like my legs was broken
Shakin' and twitchin', kinda like I was smokin'
Crazy wack funky
People say, "You look like M.C. Hammer on crack, Humpty"
That's all right 'cause my body's in motion
It's supposed to look like a fit or a convulsion
Anyone can play this game
This is my dance, y'all
Humpty Hump's my name
No two people will do it the same
You got it down
When you appear to be in pain
Humpin', funkin', jumpin'
Gig around shakin' your rump
And when the dude who jump funk
Points a finger like a stump
Tell him step off
I'm doin' the Hump

The Humpty dance
Here's your chance
To do the Hump
Everybody (Oh, do me baby)
Do the Humpty Hump
Come on and do the Humpty Hump
Oh, sexy lady
Do the Humpty Hump, do the Humpty Hump
(Oh oh, do me baby)
Do the Humpty Hump, do the Humpty Hump
We're doin', we're doin', we're doin' the Humpty Hump
(Oh oh, do me baby)
Watch me do the Humpty Hump
Do the Humpty Hump
Check it out
Black people
Do the Humpty Hump, do the Humpty Hump

Come on, white people
Do the Humpty Hump, do the Humpty Hump
Puerto Ricans
Do the Humpty Hump, just keep on doin' the Hump
Samoans
Do the Humpty Hump, do it, do the Humpty Hump
Aw yeah let's got stoopid . . .

disposable heroes of Hiphoprisy

Language of Violence

The first day of school
Was always the hardest
The first day of school
The hallway's the darkest
Like a gauntlet
The voices haunted
Walking in with his thin skin
Lowered chin
He knew the names
That they would taunt him with
Faggot, sissy, punk, queen, queer
Although he'd never had sex
In his fifteen years
And when they harassed him
It was for a reason
And when they provoked him
It became open season
For the fox and the hunter
The sparks and the thunder
That pushed the boy under
Then pillage and plunder
It kind of makes me wonder
How one can hurt another
But dehumanizing the victim

Makes things simpler
It's like breathing with a respirator
It eases the conscience of even
The most conscious
And calculating violator
Words can reduce a person to an object
Something more easy to hate
An inanimate entity
Completely disposable
No problem to obliterate

But death is the silence
In this language of violence
Death is the silence
But death is the silence
In this cycle of violence
Death is the silence

It's tough to be young
The young long to be tougher
When we pick on someone else
It might make us feel rougher
Abused by their fathers
But that was at home though
So to prove to each other
That they were not "homos"
The exclamation of the phobic fury
Executioner, judge and jury
The mob mentality
Individuality was nowhere
Dignity forgotten at
The bottom of a dumb old dare
And a numb cold stare
On the way home it was back to name-calling
Ten against one they had his back up
Against the wall and
They reveled in their laughter
As they surrounded him
But it wasn't a game
When they jumped up and grounded him

They picked up their bats
With their muscles strainin'
And they decided they were gonna
Beat this fella's brain in
With an awful powerful
Showerful an hour full of violence
Inflict the strictest
Brutality and dominance
They didn't hear him screaming
They didn't hear him pleading
They ran like cowards
And left the boy bleeding
In a pool of red
'Til all tears were shed
And his eyes quietly slid
Into the back of his head
Dead . . .

But death is the silence
In this language of violence
Death is the silence
But death is the silence
In this cycle of violence
Death is the silence

You won't see the face 'til the eyelids drop
You won't hear the screaming until it stops
You won't see the face 'til the eyelids drop
You won't hear the screaming until it stops

The boy's parents were gone
And his grandmother had raised him
She was mad she had no form
Of retaliation
The pack didn't have to worry about
Being on a hit list
But the thing they never thought about
Was that there was a witness
To this senseless crime
Right place wrong time

Tried as an adult
One of them was gonna do hard time

The first day of prison
Was always the hardest
The first day of prison
The hallway's the darkest
Like a gauntlet
The voices haunted
Faggot, sissy, punk, queen, queer
Words he used before
Had a new meaning in here
As a group of men in front of him
Laughing came near
For the first time in his life
The young bully felt fear
He'd never been on this side
Of the name-calling
Five against one they had his back up
Against the wall and
He had never questioned his own sexuality
But this group of men
Didn't hesitate their reality
With an awful powerful
Showerful an hour full of violence
Inflict the strictest
Brutality and dominance
They didn't hear him screaming
They didn't hear him pleading
They took what they wanted
And then just left him bleeding
In the corner
The giant reduced to Jack Horner

But dehumanizing the victim
Makes things simpler
It's like breathing with a respirator
It eases the conscience of even
The most conscious
And calculating violator

The power of words
Don't take it for granted
When you hear a man ranting
Don't just read the lips
Be more sublime than this
Put everything in context
Is this a tale of rough justice
In a land when there's no justice at all
Who is really the victim
Or are we all the cause, the victim of it all

But death is the silence
In this language of violence
Death is the silence
But death is the silence
In this cycle of violence
Death is the silence

DJ Quick

Born and Raised in Compton

Everybody wants to know the truth about a brother named Quik
I come from the school of tha sly, wicked, and that slick
A lotta people already know exactly where it's at
'Cause it's the home of the jackers and the crack
Compton, that's the name of the hometown
I'm goin' down in the town where my name is all around
The suckas just be havin' a fit, and that's a pity
But I ain't doin' nothin' but claimin' my city
See my lyrics I'm doublin' up and provin' to suckas that I can
    throw
I'm passin' a natural ten or four or six or eight before I go
Yes, I'm definitely free-stylin', all tha while I'm profilin'
Never a tricksta, D.J. Quiksta steals the show
So now that's how I'm livin'

I do as I please ya see, a younger brother that's up on reality
'Cause everybody knows, ya have to be stompin' if you're
Born and raised in Compton!

Born and raised in Compton

Now Compton is the place where the homeboys chill, ya see
But then I found that it wasn't no place for me
'Cause way back in the day, somebody must'a wanted me to quit
Because they broke in my house and cold stole my shit
They must have thought that I was gonna play the punk role
Just because my equipment got stole
But I ain't goin' out like no sucka-assed clown
They found they couldn't keep a dope nigga down
So here's some bass in yo face, muthafucka, silly sucka-assed
    clucka
Now you're duckin' 'cause ya can't stop a brotha like the Quiksta
Because I'm true to the game, ya lame, and things ain't ever
    gonna be the same
'Cause a nigga like tha Quik is takin' over
I really don't think I should have to explain it
Oh, yeah, I'm a dog but my name ain't Rover
And I'm tha kinda nigga that's feelin' no pain
Sometimes I have to wear the bullet-proof vest
Because I got the C.P.T. sign written across my chest
A funky dope brotha never ceases to impress
My name is D.J. Quik so you can fuck the rest
I'm comin' like this and I'm comin' directly
'Cause suckas get dain bramaged if I'm doin' damage
Quite effectively, rhythm is a battlezone and suckas have no win
'Cause I'm a veteran from the C.O.M.P.T.O.N.
Kick it!

Born and raised in Compton

Yo, check this shit out
Right about now I'd like to send a shout out to my buddy Teddy
    Bear
What's up nigga?
What's up KK? My buddy D

We got AMG mode definitely in the house
What's up Greg and Big?
Talkin' about the Armstrong pack
Straight up my muthafuckin' back
What's up Teddy?
Tracey and Courtney are gettin' busy on the board right about
    now
What's up big-faced Brian?
And my boy Pete Drag is in the house
And my girls here on the floor
And last but not least I wanna thank Chevy Blue
And we out
Peace

the d. O. C.
The Formula

High energy flowin' with the wisdom
Sense of a rich man, knowledge and the rhythm
This is what I'm using to come up with a style
So I'll interact altogether better with the crowd
Nervous for a second then the record starts spinnin'
And I fall into the state of mind of what I'd just created
Pump it like the Dr. D into the R.E. suckers ready to leap
Up on the tip when we made it
Creative so I'll never be regarded as a regular
More than just a little bit better than my competitor
You should never underestimate the fashion
I hold for the stage whether I'm coolin' or thrashin'
Clockin' the concoction created by me
When read you read E = the D.O. to the C.
Knowledge and the talent that my mother had born to her
Equals an artist that won't be worn, what is that Dre?
It's the formula

It's like a message that only I could understand
But those who want to comprehend will again
Be in the midst of the brother
Unlike another in any way
'Cause Dre don't play, say what the other say
Originality is a must whenever I bust
A funky composition, it's crush and I trust that you
Know it when you hear a funky record with potential
Me getting hype 'cause Dre rockin' the instrumental
Nothing like what you've heard before and more, never less
See I don't fess, I mean I'm like fresh if not the freshest
When I'm expressin' my thoughts on
Vinyl, you can't help but listen up and get caught on
Hooked because I cook when I pick up a pen
And begin, in the end it's dope, that's 'cause I want to win
Knowledge and the talent that my mother had born to her
Equals the DOC, what is it Dre?
Yo, that's the formula

Keepin' it dope as long as I can like imagine
Makin' each record that I do better than the last one
Take a little time, choose the topic and drop it
Release it, the science of makin' dope beats with
Rhythmic American poetry
Shipped it to stations, now many people know of me
I'm the D. into the O. and the O. into the C. and the C. into
    the period
Suckers are fearin' this
When heard, the dope style calculated by the great wait
And take just a second to get caught up in my record
New but not a kid to be worn
If somethin' gettin' torn up then I'm doin' the
Tearin', not bein' torn
Shapin' up to be one of the top vocalist lyricist
And when you hear of this
You shouldn't choke on this
Knowledge and the talent makes it valid
For me to get it patented
Dre, tellin' what I'm rappin'
The formula

In effect and I'm smooth, that's why I'm on the incline
Suckers frontin' for nothin' 'cause I'm goin' to get mine
It's in the cards and I think I might have read this
So don't lie and try to front like someone said this
Most who know thoughts served by the DOC see
That it's a mission impossible, tryin' to rock me
For an arena who'd ask me to perform for her
G.O. and easily I flow and ya know usin' the formula

Donald D

F. B. I. (Free Base Institute)

"People of the world, there's a serious problem
And it's called crack. I'm tellin' you
Stay away from it. It makes you do crazy things."

Disruption, disorder will nourish, not justify
Those that live at the F.B.I.
Look at Momma's baby comin' home high
As she watch the tears in her eyes
Crack will snatch your sister, your father, your mother, your
    brother
A whole lot of others
Situation number one that son of a gun
Look what the brother has done
He destroyed his credibility, and the trust in me
And he used to be down with the "D"
His mind is hungry for a piece of the rock
So he walks up and down the block
Fiendin', schemin'—no more is he dreamin'
His life is controlled by the force of beamin'
Scotty, he's gettin' deeper in the sauce
In other words, the brother is lost

(At the F.B.I.) Free Base Institute
That's where they go to get high

She's outta control on the A.M. stroll
24–7, her body is sold
She used to be the neighborhood fly girl
But now the base pipe has entered her world
I saw her one night in an alley, slobbin' the knob
To her, it's a full-time job
The sucker with her was lookin' for cheap sex
For fifty cents, she said I could be next
So I snatched the bitch by her nappy weave
And I said, "Girlfriend, please
You better check into a rehabilitation
'Cause you're a fuckin' crack patient!"
The bitch dissed me, swung, and missed me
Then she asked, could she kiss me?
It was the crack on full attack
That had this beautiful sister trapped

(At the F.B.I.) Free Base Institute
That's where they go to get high

I see baseheads in a state of their own
In the zone where the baseheads roam
And on the same block are the ones who sell to them
So I walked up to Money Makin' Slim
And said, "Do you consider, you're helpin' get rid of
Our brothers and sisters?" He did admit a
Touch of guilt, but I saw it in his eyes
That the brother was tellin' me lies
He said a man has to do what a man has to do
As he guzzled the old "E" brew
His point of view was if he wasn't drug dealin'
He would be out there stealin' and killin'
In a world of confusion, it's no illusion
Game of life people are losin'
Boozin', cocaine, crack abusin'
On the devil side you are choosin'

(At the F.B.I.) Free Base Institute
That's where they go to get high

I'm makin' it a point
While you smoke your joint
While you point at each other
Let my point reach you
Crack is not only a ghetto drug
It's a drug in the high-class too
Don't be fooled by the rich and famous
'Cause, see, they would try to blame this
On the people from the street
So they could keep
Out of the media but they can't sweep it
Under the rug, they caught the drug bug
And their own grave has been dug
And you read about it, a star in rehab
Now it's time for me to take a stab
At the sport figures, your idol, your hero
After the game, yo, yo, let's get a kilo
AWOL from practice, didn't show for the game
Because of the pipe and flame
Substance abuse has made another star go under
With the force of thunder

(At the F.B.I.) Free Base Institute
That's where they go to get high

Little Johnny and Tommy saw their mommy
Hittin' the pipe with her best friend Connie
She look like she suffers from malnutrition
The kids are hungry, no food in the kitchen
Their gear's been worn for a month and a half
That was the last time they had a bath
'Cause the crack has the man command
The welfare check to the dope man

(At the F.B.I.) Free Base Institute
That's where they go to get high

---

doug E. Fresh
The Greatest Entertainer

Topic: The Greatest Entertainer
Got more juice than you get in your container
But to stay fresh, as we are fresh
And leave everyone with a smile
I thought the proper thing for me to do is to come back doin' the
    beat box
Harmonica Style . . . Bust it . . . Bust it . . .

Now the proper thing for me to do is to use my style
Come out a little different and plus worthwhile
Leave the girlies with a smile
Couples down the aisle
Hip Hop troopers in single file
And you could hear the invitation
On your radio station
Before we go, we need some motorization
So ladies, you wanna rock with me?
"Yes we do!"
Chill Will, just hit me
Fellows, are you with me?
"It's only right!"
Barry Bee, get busy, come on

(Go Go Go Go Go Go Go Go Go)

The music is movin'
And homeboys is coolin'
And everything is on schedule
And I'm rulin'
The mike with one hand
Runnin' down the plan
The name of the game is to understand

Ladies first and homeboys come second
And I hope that I can recognize
The difference in the girl and the guys
'Cause some men want to be cutie pies
I'll say it again, like I said it before
"Yo, he's not the Herb"
Word to Big Bird, hops
I'm not the Herb that you're lookin' for
I'm the
Greatest Entertainer

Now I could even do the beatbox when I cough
And no, I'm not soft and I don't play golf
But yes, I rap
Like a jolly ole chap
And like a Chameleon, I'll adapt
To a phrase and make the ladies go crazy
I don't want no one to praise me
Just realize this jam is the move
And bust the groove 'cause I'm smooth
And bust the new dance called the Doug E. Fresh groove
Swing on it

Makin' rap music is our profession
There's only one chance at a first impression
But there are times with records you hear
That out of nowhere seem to catch your ear
Attention and you mention it
To your friends and they say
"That was DEF, play it for me again"
So first you try to find it
And then you rewind it
And then you say, "who could have designed this"
Growin' to know that it's only me
Chill Will and Barry Bee make G.F.C.
And I'm the, and I'm the, and I'm the, and I'm the
Greatest Entertainment

So clap your hands everybody
And if you feel good, stomp your feet

'Cause I'm 'a rock this rhyme on the solo side
And Get Fresh is gonna hold the beat
Bring it down
The time on the clock was made to tell
We be kickin' and tickin' and rockin' you well
This time, we'll rock stronger
And last much longer
Money back guaranteed, we are gonna
Show you things you never thought to see
I know I know you know because we're G.F.C.
We're gonna show you
I know it'll grab you and hold you
And if it don't like it, it'll grow on you
But then you won't know how to get away
But that's all right 'cause it's OK
And it's soothin' music and this I swear
Not 'cause it annoys to the human ear
Talented brothers with a bouncin' beat
And we learned our music from New York streets
Don't drive a blue sedan
And it's things I can't stand
I hate hearing "I can't," I know you can
Be smart, be wise, and keep stars in your eyes
And keep your mind from the killer, "GET HIGH"
My word is my sword
And I use my vocal cords
And I'm jammin' in the name of the Lord . . .
BREAK

Downtown Science

Radioactive

Sunrise, darkness fades to light
Illuminating the sky as well as the insight to see a new beginning
  and resurrect

Reminiscent of the Phoenix and recollect
Thoughts from the universe of ideas
Select lyrics to illustrate the obvious
Image, project it so everybody sees it
Off the soul, take the body, and freeze it!
Suspended animation
To the tenth degree of virtuosity, mind is free!
Risen from the prison of humanism
To reflect on innervision
And be enlightened
State of awareness heightened
To a level above and beyond
That of intelligent life
Divine, eternal as space and time
Able to transform shape and design
From liquid to gas, light to sound
To each new substance
Matter is constant
Not created or destroyed
Merely deployed
As words in a radiovoid!

RA-DI-O! RADIO
RADIOACTIVE! (RADIO) ACTIVE
RADIOACTIVE! (RADIO) ACTIVE

Words manifested disintegrate
Particles drift into atoms and separate
Developing a movement known as soundwaves
That travel at Mach One via the airspace
Hitting the microphone, makin' it vibrate
Electrical impulses start to migrate
Along the wire to enter the next phase of audio sequence
The infamous noisegate lifts, over the threshold
And into the system goes matter
Now converted to data
Knowledge is primary
Communication is digital
Language is binary
From the bit to the megabyte

Math is the mode to educate the neophyte
Science is the road to greater understanding
A complex network, always expanding
Growing by the minute
The realm of broadcast, borders are infinite
Signal is energized and read for transmit
Working its way up the tower
Several times an hour
Getting power rotation, zero static on the air
Receivers are fine tuned, reception is clear
Courtesy of fiber optics
The highs are bright, the lows kick

RA-DI-O! RADIO
RADIOACTIVE! (RADIO) ACTIVE
RADIOACTIVE! (RADIO) ACTIVE

Radioactive in the form of sonic energy
Same identity
Temporarily materializing through the speaker
Coming to the surface, eureka!
The final stage of a cycle, moving at such high speed
That by the time it's perceived
It's already happened again
Now is then
The future's ever-present
Time is of the essence
Coming in for a landing
On the FM band
With liquid crystal display
Lighting the runway
88 to 108 megahertz
Pushing solid state, state of the art
Climbing the chart
With a bullet
Radioactive to the fullest
Extent of the wavelength
Jamming the frequency
Relentlessly
To break through

And reach the world on the other side
So they can learn from errors that nullified
The last
Hit by the blast
Now all that remains is a shadow of the past

RA-DI-O! RADIO
RADIOACTIVE! (RADIO) ACTIVE
RADIOACTIVE! (RADIO) ACTIVE

Dream Warriors

My Definition of a Boombastic Jazz Style

Intro: What the funk is this?
My definition of a boombastic jazz style

Here we go, are you ready for one other?
Dream Warriors noise is new, discover old
Once again with a new blend
So telephone a friend (Yo! Dream Warriors got this new song—
    it's dope, man)
Compact disc to the prime is optimist
Fans are friends, I'm universal and cosmic
Concrete jungles abound
Stand by the speaker, you're smothered and covered up in the sound
You stand strong as you pump your fist
I'm talkin' all that jazz
Now what's my definition?

CHORUS: My definition
My definition
My definition is this
My definition
My definition
My definition

My definition is this
My definition
My definition is this
My definition

When I kick rhymes, it's often said to do damage
Skin so strong even Superman needs a hand
So bob your head, dread, as I kick the funk flow
This rhyme is subliminal, yet you don't think so
I walk with a gold cane, a gold brain, and no gold chain
Behind the truth lies there lies a parafix
In the mix is where Dream Warriors go
Define if you will but I know so
There is no definition

CHORUS

Right now I know where to flow in just like a poet
Your definition of me is definitely wrong
Why must I try to lie and field an alibi
When all you ask is just for me to be me
Replace a replaceable replacement with this
Relax relax relaxation boombastic
My name is King Lou
My name is Capital Q
Bags of mostly water search to find my definition

CHORUS

I sought beauty through the dust of strife
I sought meaning to my music addiction
Arise, awaken, we have need to reverse
A plague has befallen us, no time to rehearse
This rhyme speaks its speak, it has spoken
This rhyme will not change things, it needs to be changed in a
    hearse
You find caskets in my rhyme baskets of rhymes
Your definition can define what's my definition

CHORUS

Eazy E

We Want Eazy

"We want eazy!"
Well, clap ya hands then—come on
Clap ya hands everybody
Clap ya hands, come on, come on
Put ya hands together and clap 'em
Now can y'all say Eazy
Come on, say it

EAZ-Y
Everybody come on,
EAZ-Y . . .

People from everywhere gather around
Checkin' out the sound that Eazy is throwin' down
With some help from Ren and Dre
Makin' a way with dope style
Yo Eazy, what ya gotta say

A miracle of modern creation
Eazy E's on the set
Hyped up with the bass
And a little bit of what ya love
From a brother who's smooth like a criminal
I mean subliminal
Otherwise known as a villain
Because I'm ruthless
When I spot a sucka, I kill 'em
But most I think know not to deal with me
Yo, it's obvious, tell 'em who you came to see

EAZ-Y . . .

Yeah 'cuz this is the way I know you like it
So you won't strike it
I took it and I hyped it
And now that it's done, I know ya pleased
At how the E just duz it with ease
Just imagine a crowd screamin', a girl dreamin'
Just to get a picture of me 'n' my B-O-Y-Z
From the H-double-O-D
N.W.A., down with me
Strong 'n' I'm ragin'
Turn the page 'n'
See I'm not a son of a gun
I'm a gauge 'n'
Nuthin' can avoid this shot 'cause it's hittin'
It's so cool when you touch it, wear a mitten
I'm comin' off raw into ya speaker
Makin' the suckas on the street feel weaker
But most I think know not to deal with me
Yo, it's obvious, tell 'em who you came to see

EAZ-Y . . .

Aw, never, I'm just too clever
So, in fact, that no one can sever
A blow from a maniac and yo, I make it clear
So a register is all I hear
Money overturned, then I jet
To make another hit, for you to go and get
Record stores sold out because you love it
Another example of how Eazy duz it

EAZ-Y
We want Eazy . . . .

ed O.G. & the Bulldogs

Be a Father to Your Child

Hey, yo, be a father, if not, why bother, son
A boy can make 'em but a man can raise one
If you did it, admit it, and stick with it
Don't say it ain't yours 'cause all women are not whores
Ninety percent represent a woman that is faithful
Ladies, can I hear it? Thank you
When a girl get pregnant, her man is gonna run around
Dissin' her for nine months, when it's born he wants to come
    around
Talkin' 'bout "I'm sorry for what I did"
And all of a sudden he now wants to see his kid
She had to bear it by herself and take care of it by herself
And givin' her some money for milk won't really help
Half of the fathers with sons and daughters don't even wanna take
    'em
But it's so easy for them to make 'em
It's true, if it weren't for you then the child wouldn't exist
After a skeeze, there's responsibilities so don't resist
Be a father to your child

Be a father to your child
Be a father to your child
Be a father to your child
Be a father to your child

You see, I hate when a brother makes a child and then denies it
Thinkin' that money is the answer so he buys it
A whole bunch of gifts and a lot of presents
It's not the presents, it's the presence, and the essence
Of bein' there and showing the baby that you care
Stop sittin' like a chair and having the baby wonder where you
    are
Or who you are—fool, you are his daddy

Don't act like you ain't 'cause that really makes me mad, G
To see a mother and a baby suffer
I've had enough of brothers who don't love the
Fact that a baby brings joy into your life
You could still be called daddy if the mother's not your wife
Don't be scared, be prepared 'cause love is gonna getcha
It will always be your child, even if she ain't witcha
So don't front on your child when it's your own
'Cause if you front now, you'll regret it when it's grown
Be a father to your child

Be a father to your child
Be a father to your child
Be a father to your child
Be a father to your child

Put yourself in his position and see what you've done
But just keep in mind that you're somebody's son
How would you like it if your father was a stranger
And then tried to come into your life and tried to change tha
Way your mother raised ya—now, wouldn't that amaze ya?
To be or not to be, that is the question
When you're wrong, you're wrong, it's time to make a correction
Harassin' the mother for being with another man
But if the brother man can do it better than you can
Let him, don't sweat him, duke
Let him do the job that you couldn't do
You're claimin' you was there, but not when she needed you
And now you wanna come around for a day or two?
It's never too late to correct your mistakes
So get yourself together for your child's sake
And be a father to your child

EpMD

It's My Thing

M.C.s out there, ya better stand clear
EPMD is a world premier
From New York, straight talk
America's best
Cold Wild Long Island is where we rest
The style of the rap makes your hands clap
Take care, sucker, 'cause the lines are strapped

They mean business, no time for play
If you bite a line, they blow you away
The more you bite, your body gets hot
Don't get too cold because you might get shot
Knowin' that my rhyme's like a poisonous rat
Don't play dumb boy, you're smarter than that
It's my thing

The rhythmatic style keeps the rhymes flowin'
The friends already bitin' without you knowin'
You can't understand why your body's gettin' weaker
Then you realize it's the voice from the speaker
The mind becomes delirious
Situation serious
Don't get ill, go and get curious

Enough about that, let's get on to somethin' better
And if it gets warm, take off the hot sweater
And if you want some water, I'll get you a cup
And if you don't want it, then burn the hell up
I'm tellin' ya now, boy, you ain't jack
Talkin' that junk like Mr. T is your back
But he's not
So don't act cute
'Cause if we do, you in high pursuit
It's my thing

As the song goes on, you will notice a change
The way I throw down, the way I say my name
The mike that I'm packin' is flame resistant
So M.C.s be cool, and keep your distance
When I walk into the party, girls are screamin' at me
I park my mike in my holst' and then I yell, "Freeze"
Music please

Oh, where was I? Oh, yes
Say a def rhyme then I bum the rest
Everytime I rock a rhyme, I can tell that you like it
The emotion is strong, like the mind of a psychic
The mind is weary, floatin' like a dove
Sweatin' the thing just like if you was makin' love
Control the crowd so they can accept it
Total concentration, it's the perfect method
It's my thing

The wack I subtract
The strong I attack
The ones who got the mike and freeze, I throw back
I perfect and eject make M.C.s sweat
Take 'em off on the mike then I tell 'em "Step"
Not waiting or debating cause M.C.s keep hatin'
Play me too close like two dogs mating

Now let's get on with the rest of the lesson
I don't really like it when suckers start messin'
Tryin' to make a scene, talkin' very loud
Talkin' more junk to attract a crowd
You say you won the battle, your first mistake
You get the quietest stuff like you was at a wake
In the beginnin', ya knew ya wasn't winnin'
Now you for shame, your hair starts bendin'
Kind of upset, boy, I understand
You lost again, I won, goddamn
It's my thing

My funky fresh lyrics put you in a spirit
I speak a little louder for you suckers can't hear it

The rhymes I design are right on time
And at the crown of the mike, I flash a danger sign
'Cause I'm the thrilla of Manila, M.C. cold-killa
Drink Budweiser, cannot stand Miller
M.C.s cold-clockin' till the party's through
Then they tap me on my shoulder, say, "This Bud's for You"

To be a real M.C.
You can't be obedient
To be smooth is the main ingredient
You have to be silky like a Milky Way
To be able to make it work, you rest and play
I control the pace of the rate the rhymes goin'
How loud I project and to where they're flowin'
Slow, yes, just like they're oil
The comparison is wave like the motion of water
Smooth
It's my thing

While the record is spinnin'
Got your fly-girly grinnin'
MD is on the mike, ya know I'm only beginnin'
Rod's fresh and fresh, you never heard me fess
Scored a 110 on my M.C. test
My rhymes are stronger than Tyson
Hold an M.C. license
When I grab the mike
M.C.s get frightened

I'm dangerous
I need a cross and bones
Lounge, homeboy, you in the danger zone
What I mean by lounge, I don't mean bitin'
Huh, ya mess around and we'll be fightin'
It's all right if ya bite but don't recite
Because the rhymes are mine and that ain't right
But until then, just chill to the next episode
Donald J, yo, release the close
It's my thing

EpмD

Rampage

Slow down baby uhh
Slow down baby uhh

You can get rugged, though, hard like P
Trying to play my man but you couldn't touch me
You faggot no comp rapper on a quest
You get your head flown, boy you must be smokin' sens
So many often wonder if MDs paid
You're goddamn right, punk, stay outta my way
'Cause I clock Gs while you clock Zs
And I don't smoke crack, I smoke M.C.s
So pick up a pen, cop a squat, and take notes
A rapper suffered from bleeding, sprains and slit throats
My style deadly psychopath or schizophrenic
Rapper choke like a carburetor, freeze up, and panic
'Cause I clock pesos, don't sell *lleyo*
Another name for cocaine, mi amigo
That's Spanish terminology for friend
Now sit back and rub my bozack as I send
Bass funk with beats that thump
Kickers and amps cold lined up in my trunk
My system cranking, my headlights are blinkin'
Brother ridin' my tip, L, at the same time thinkin'
Damn, how could a brother be so nice
'Cause I'm the capital E-P twice M-D-E twice
I choose to squeeze, some choose to fight
I like to write but then again some bite
While you were bangin' on tables, I was bangin' Snow White

Yeah slow down baby

The ripper, the master, the overlordian
Playing M.C.s like a old accordion

I get the inspiration from a necessary station
Them sayin' I was vacationin'
You can't cope with your weak-ass throat
Tryin' 'a sneak a peak in while I freak the notes
Major M.C.s become minor B flats
So retire the mike, get your chains and your bats
Here's your chance to advance, gettin' your stance
I'm 'a shoot the holster off your cowboy pants
Pure entertainment, tonight's your arraignment
You're guilty, face down on the pavement
No holds barred, it's time to get scarred
You and your squad better praise the real god
The undertaker droppin' thunder on fakers
When it comes to lyrics I'm as freaky as Seka
So lay the mike down slow and careful
'Cause mine is fully loaded and I have another handful
A clip to slip in and start rippin'
Divin' and dippin' and givin' punks a whippin'
Just in case you wanna go a few rounds and so
I'm down so that you clowns will know
Me gettin' burnt or hurt won't be tolerated
I got rhymes up the (huh) forget it, I'm constipated

Yeah slow down baby

When I come around homeboy, watch your nugget
I master on the beat down, my style's rugged
When I attack the microphone, close the zone
Rap sees danger, can't roam
Security is packed and wall to wall can't fall
A rap tank is full so I can't stall
My microphone is filled with premium
Any whack M.C. that flexes, I'm creamin' 'em
Not with lotion, bust the motion, flotation
When I'm rockin' the mike I'm like coastin'
Underneath fatigue at my peak
You still seek the style 'cause yours is extra weak
New method, rip the stage at my age and get loose and kick
Like Bruce in a rage—I'm on a rampage

Yeah slow down baby
Slow down baby

Eric B. + Rakim

Follow the Leader

Follow me into a solo
Get in the flow
And you could pitch it like a photo
Music makes mellow, maintains to make
Melodies for M.C.s motivates the breaks
I'm everlastin'
I can go on for days and days
With rhyme displays that engrave deep as X-rays
I can take a phrase that's rarely heard
Flip it, now it's a daily word
I can get iller than all my killin' barb
But no alarm, Rakim'll remain calm
Self-esteem makes me super superb
The supreme before a microphone, still I fiend
This was a tape I wasn't supposed to break
I was supposed to wait, but let's motivate
I wanna see if ya keep followin' and swallowin'
Takin' and makin'
Bitin' and borrowin'
Brothers tried and others died to get the formula
But I'm 'a let you sweat, you're still in form
You're a step away from frozen
Stiff as if you're posin'
Dig into my brain as the rhyme gets chosen
So follow me or were you thinkin' you were first
Let's travel at magnificent speeds around the universe
What could ya say as the earth gets further and further away
Planets are small as balls of clay

Astray into the Milky Way
World's outta sight
Far as the eye can see, not even a satellite
Now stop and turn around and look
As ya stand in the darkness, your knowledge is took
So keep starin', soon ya suddenly see a star, ya better follow it
'Cause it's the R
This is a lesson if ya guessin' and if ya borrowin'
Hurry hurry step right up and keep followin'
The leader
Follow the leader
Keep followin'

This is a lifetime mission
Vision a prison
Alright listen
In this journey you're the journal, I'm the journalist
Am I eternal or on an eternal list
I'm about to flow long as I can possibly go
Keep ya movin' 'cause the crowd said so
Dance, cuts rip your pants
Eric B. on the blades, bleedin' to death
Call the ambulance
Pull at my weapon and start to squeeze
A magnum as a microphone, murderin' M.C.s
Let's quote a rhyme from a record I wrote
"Follow the leader"
Yeah, dope
'Cause every time I stop it seems ya stuck
Soon as ya try to step off, ya self-destruct
I came to overcome before I'm gone
By showin', improvin', and lettin' knowledge be born
Then after that I live forever, you disagree?
You say, "Never?" Then follow me
From century to century, you remember me
In history not a mystery or a memory
Call by nature, mind raised in Asia
Since you was tricked, I have to raise ya
From the cradle to the grave
But remember, you're not a slave

'Cause we was put here to be much more than that
But we concede because our mind was trapped
But I'm here to break away the chains, take away the pains
Remake the brains, rebuild my name
I guess nobody told you a little knowledge was dangerous
It can't be mixed, diluted, it can't be changed or switched
Here's a lesson, if it gets into borrowin'
Hurry hurry step right up and keep followin'
The leader

A furified freestyle lyrics of fury
My third eye make me shine like jury
You're just a rent-a-rap and your rhymes are minute-made
I'll be here when they fade to watch ya flip like a Renegade
I can't wait to break and eliminate
On every tread of a snake so stay awake
And follow and follow because the tempo's a trail
The stage is a cage
The mike is a third rail
I'm Rakim—the fiend of a microphone
I'm not him, so leave my mike alone
Soon as the beat is felt, I'm ready to go
So fasten your seatbelt 'cause I'm about to flow
No need to speed, slow down and let the leader lead
Word to daddy—indeed
The R's a rollin' stone, so I'm rollin'
Directions is told, then the rhymes are stolen
Stop buggin', a brother said, "Dig 'em," I never dug 'em
He couldn't follow the leader long enough so I drug 'em
Into danger zone, he should arrange his own
Face into space, it could erase a change of tone
There's one R in the alphabet
It's a one letter word and it's about to get
More complex from one rhyme to the next
Eric B. be easy on the flex
I been from state to state
Followers tailgate
Keep comin' but ya came too late but I wait
So back up, re-group, get a grip, come equipped
You're the next contestant, clap your hands, you wanna trip

The price is right, don't make a deal too soon
How many notes? Could ya name this tune?
Follow the leader is a title theme task
Now ya know, you don't have to ask
Rap is rhythm and poetry
Cuts create sound effects
Ya might catch up if ya follow the records he wrecks
Until the, keep eatin' and swallowin'
Ya better take a deep breath and keep followin'
The leader
Keep followin'
Follow the Leader

Eric B. + Rakim

Let the Rhythm Hit 'Em

Let the rhythm hit 'em

I'm the arsenal
I got artillery, lyrics of ammo
Rounds of rhythm
Then I'm 'a give 'em piano
Bring a bullet-proof vest
Nothin' to ricochet
Ready to aim at the brain
Now what the trigger say
Tempos triflin'
Felt like a rifle
Massage 'n' melodies
Might go right through
Simultaneously like an Uzi
Nothin' can bruise me
Lyrics let up when lady say don't lose me
So re-load quickly
And you better hit me

While I'm lettin' this fifi get wit me
You steppin' with .007
Better make it snappy
No time to do your hair, baby
Brothers are bustin' at me
Beats and bullets pass me
None on target
They want the R hit
But watch the god get
Quicker, the tongue is the trigger
'Cause I'm real fast
Let off some rhythm at 'em
Let 'em feel the blast
Penetrate at a crazy rate
This ain't no .38
Hit 'em at point blank range
And watch 'em radiate
Runnin' out of ammunition
I'm done wit' 'em
You ask me how I did 'em
I let the rhythm hit 'em

I push a power that's punishable
Better be a prisoner
The hit man is the
Brother wit' charisma
Showing you that I have
Powerful paragraphs
Followers will become leaders
But without a path
Ya mentally paralyzed
Crippled ya third eye
Rhymes are blurred
Then it occurred that you heard I
Reduced the friction with crucifixion
Let loose the mix then
Boost the piston
Eric hit 'em wit' some of that
Cut like a lumberjack
And me gettin' hit back

It won't be none of that
I'm untouchable
You see me in 3-D
When I let the rhythm hit another M.C.
Lyrics made of lead
Enters your head
Then eruptions of a mass production
Will spread when
Music is louder
Full of gunpowder
Microphone machinery
When I see a crowd of
Party people pumpin'
Their fist like this
Ya hide in the back
Thinkin' that I might miss
But the R is accurate
Plus I'm packed up with
Educated punch lines that
I have to hit
Whatever I aim at
I line 'em up
Ya body is weak, feel with pain
That time is up
You been hit with somethin'
Different, isn't it?
Rakim is gonna radiate and nothin's equivalent
Nothin' can harm me
Why try to bar me
You couldn't come around to rob with a army
You'll get wrecked by the architect
So respect 'em
I disconnect 'em, soon as I inject 'em
With radiation
Put 'em by the basement
Bust his chest open
Bash his face in
Let it split 'im
Since he brought his main man wit' 'im
He ask me how I did 'im

I let the rhythm hit 'im
Let it hit 'im

Dance floor's dangerous
Packed in like a briefcase
Rhythm with real rough rhyme
Beats with deep bass
Girls with tight pants
Maybe they might dance
Tonight if the Rs on the mike
There's a slight chance
The crowd is crucial
M.C.'s grounds are neutral
Now that you're here let me introduce you
Get ready
I'm hard to read like graffiti but steady
Science I drop is real heavy
Radiant energy, that'll be the penalty
Touch the third rail on the pain of remedy
The prescription's one every hour
Now it's a havoc
If ya need another hit from the freestyle fanatic
Attention: follow directions real close
Keep out of reach of children
Beware of overdose
Too many milligram
But what made a iller jam
My rhyme is the rhythm of thoughts
That kill a man
Ideas for the ear to fear
Might split 'im
He'll never forget 'im
He'll rest in peace wit' 'em
At least when he left he'll know what hit 'im
The last breath of the words of death
Was the rhythm

Now throw you hands in the air and yo, go
Rakim will do the rest of this slow
If I speed they know you'll blow the hell up

If I slow up, catch up, hell no
Wicked as I kicked it
Don't need to remix it
'Cause I prefixed it
Reversed and switched it
To perform to perfection
Section for section
Rhymes keep connectin'
Ya guessin' what's next an'
Blood pressure rise as ya damn near lost it
Ya hit the ground burnin' and woke up frostbitten
'Cause when I explained ya can't complain for pain
Travel through the brain hit a vein
Then remain, let it radiate
Vibes will vibrate
Why did you violate
Now I'm 'a have to let the style break
Moans now the tone is ingrown
After this here's thrown, gimme another microphone
Before I get that fifi I met
Whisper I wanna reach your intellect
Kiss her 'cause I wanna give her the most respect
So I shine and let the write reflect
Hold 'er, mold 'er, make 'er feel older
Lay her on my shoulder
Everything I told her
Makes her feel secure whenever I'm wit' 'er
And you know how I did 'er
Me and the rhythm hit 'er

Fatback band

King Tim III

All right y'all, here we go
You just clap your hands and stomp your feet
'Cause you're listenin' to the sound of the sure shot beat
I am the K-I-N-G
The T-I-M
King Tim the third
And I am him
Just me, Fatback, and the crew
We're doin' it all just for you
We're strong as an ox and tall as a tree
We can rock it so viciously
We throw the highs in your eyes
The bass in your face
We're the funk machines that rock the human race
Skate down, boogie, shot, let me see your body rock

To the break everybody
To the break everybody
Two, four, six, eight, Fatback don't you hesitate

Party people who like to groove
Now's the time to let your body move
Do it to the rhythm
And let it all hang out
Don't be jivin'
Ya got to show
What you be about

Catch it, catch it, catch it, catch the beat!
Catch it, catch it, catch it, catch the beat!
Do it to me and I'll do it to you
Do it to me and I'll do it to you

Do it to me and I'll do it to you
Do it to me and I'll do it to you

To the break
That keep the same old beat
About awhile ago and I wanted to know
Just who you been listenin' to
I am the voice of King Tim the Third
Tell you what I want you to do
A little left hand, right hand in the air
And you slam dunk like ya just don't care
You put your left leg out, the right leg in
Say the hustle is out and the rock is in
About a quarter to four, somebody was at your door
Well you wondered who it was
You started to shake and shiver
So I said it was me, yo, little old cous'
I said open the door and let me in
I'll rock ya so good, you heard bells ring
They went ring ding dang a ding a ding ding
Ring ding dang a ding a ding ding

To the break everybody . . .

Stomp your feat and ya clap your hands
'Cause you're listenin' to the sound of the Fatback band
Ain't nothin' new in what I do
'Cause I'm doin' it all just for you
I'm hotter than tea, I'm sweeter than honey
I'm not doin' it for the money
I'm sugar-coated, double-dunked
I'm sweeter than the Almond Joy
And grandma's sweet old jam
I'm the modified, the rectified, kazinctified, quadriplified
Kaput-the-fied, kazuk-ta-fied
To rock your minds, hey, all the time

To the break everybody . . .

It's on and on and on and on
Like hot-buttered on say what? the popcorn

Do it to me . . .
To the break . . .

You keep the tap in your step, the hip in your hop
You don't stop 'til you get on the mountaintop
Once you reach the top, you won't be alone
Ya got King Tim on the microphone
Just grab your partner, you start to swing
'Cause I'm well known just like Burger King
I don't sell burgers or french fries
I'm only here to make your nature rise
Just grab your partners round and round
And grab her by the butt and boogie down
Just open up your jacket and open up her bras
And dance like at the Mardi Gras
I'm a man of action, the main attraction
The girls call me the satisfaction
I'm the Romeo, the Casanova
Here tonight I'm gonna get over

To the break everybody, to the break everybody . . .

Fat **B**oys
Jailhouse Rap

In Jail
In jail
Unh-unh . . .
Unh-unh . . .

In jail, in jail, without no bail
In jail, we're in jail because we failed
In jail, in jail, without no bail
In jail, we're in jail because we failed

Now there was just one day
That I will never forget
I got jailed for something that
I'll always regret

It was twelve o'clock, midnight
And I wanted a snack
So I headed downstairs
Thought the fridge was packed
But when I opened the door
What did I see?
The back of the fridge staring right at me
I thought to myself
I could almost die
Then an image appeared
A pizza pie

So I put on Adidas
Headed out the door
As I pictured myself
Eating more and more
But the store was closed
I busted into a rage
So I went to the crib
And got my twelve-gauge
Ran back to the shop
Busted won the door
And all I saw
Was pizza galore

So I stuffed my face
I couldn't even walk
I couldn't laugh, smile
Shake, giggle, wiggle, or talk
So I fell asleep with my face in my plate

And the next thing you know
I was headed upstate

In jail, in jail, without no bail
In jail, we're in jail because we failed
In jail, in jail, without no bail
In jail, we're in jail because we failed

Well, Kool Rock is my name
Last part is "ski"
And I have the worst
Case of any M.C.
But listen to the story
'Cause it's kind of strange
When I had this sort of hunger pain
Walking down the street
With the bass of my box
With my stomach growling
Like a hungry fox
When I saw this scene
Or was it a dream?
A big restaurant sign
Called Burger King
So I went inside
Started stuffing my face
Didn't even think
About the things I ate
But when the bill came up
Boy, was I shocked
I said, "I don't pay for nothing
I'm the King of the Slops!"

In jail, in jail, without no bail
In jail, we're in jail because we failed
In jail, in jail, without no bail
In jail, we're in jail because we failed

But when our time is through
We'll rock you and you
We turn parties out

Make you scream and shout
We're not demanding
Or very outstanding
We got something unique
And in the middle he's standing
On the microphone
He rocks and shocks
Homeboys and girls
It's the Human Beat Box

Break

Now I'm sitting here alone
Looking at the wall
Just thinking about
How I took the fall
I thought I was cool
I thought I was slick
And now I'm writing
Letters of being homesick
I lost my freedom
When I heard the door slammer
And now I'm breaking rocks
With a big, heavy hammer
I used to drive the streets
With my big car
And now I look and all
I see are bars
In jail
Everyone's the same
You only survive
If you play the game
You don't have guns
And now you remember
You're your momma's son
You made her cry
And stay up all night
Coming home high
Just leaving a fight
You always made her feel

That you were better
But now you're a little boy
Just waiting for a letter

ſearleſs FouR

Rockin' It

They're here
DLB, Tito, Mike C. (hey girl, hey girl), Peso
DLB's rockin' it, rockin' it, yes he is rockin' it
Tito's rockin' it, yes he is rockin' it
Mike C.! rockin' it, yes he is rockin' it
Peso! rockin' it, yes he is rockin' it
We're all rockin' it
You should be rockin' it
Rockin' it
Rockin' it

Don't don't fight or fuss
If you want to rock with us
Our talent's with us so with us leave your trust
Get to the short train, cab, or bus
'Cause we're rockin' it, rockin' it, yes we are rockin' it
Rockin' it
Rockin' it

Yeah! Ha Ha Ha Haaaa!
You know party people, we are back again
With a sure-shot win
But we're much more better than we were back then
Back then we were a ball
But yo we got small
As long as the return is of the Fearless Four
Featuring DLB
Tito and Mike C.

And Peso and B-Bow and C-O-P
'Cause he can tell ya from the top that our crew won't stop
So let the bells jing-a-ling and let the champagne pop
Oh it's a celebration
Sort of a dedication
To all our fans throughout the nation
Who are sendin' in letters and dialin' on the cord
And for all the newcomers just gettin' on board
Who wanna rock with us and turn the party out
Well, we wanna know what the fearless is all about
Why dontcha come along with us if ya wanna scream and shout
And especially come if you have no doubt
That we're rockin' it
Rockin' it

Now, doin' it one by one
Individually will rhyme to expand the fun
So keep yourself on the launchin' pad as we blast off
We'll begin with the first and end with the fourth
As we're rockin' it, rockin' it, y'all
Rockin' it

My skills will climb when I start to rhyme
And I'll always guarantee to be on time
You're like me, you got good taste
Just look at my body
This microphone was in a super race
And I am in first place
It's anyway I am the best in the south and east, west
DLB is on top of all of the rest
When I'm rockin' it
Rockin' it

Ya know the rhymes are so bad when they come to me
I'll make you fans step forward and other rappers flee
Ask me about my skills and I reply, "top shelf"
Ha-ha-ha! To tell the truth, why, I amaze myself
Am I, am I so good? Well I really don't know
But I know that there's no other quite like Tito

When I'm rockin' it
Rockin' it

Well I'm a million-dollar boy in a million-dollar man
And if ya got it, I could get it with a wave of my hand
Got a voice so nice, never say rhymes twice
Never have to explain 'cause I'm so possessive
If ya ever wanna battle, ya better prevent
The Mighty Mike C. M.C. president
When I'm rockin' it
Rockin' it

Well let's get right down to the bottom of things
We're here to get you on the floor with the music we bring
Smurf it out, shake, bake, and rattle and roll
Dance to the jazzy rhymes of the great Peso
Comin' out like a winner from the starting gate
Endin' up like a ten, you know so great
I may be last on the line but I'm one of the best
Can't you hear my rhymes are funky fresh
When I'm rockin' it
Rockin' it
And we're rockin' it
Rockin' it
And you're rockin' it
Rockin' it

Now, even as we play
There's a new record sound goin' on today
We know your time is very precious so we won't stall
Just put some words together and tell ya all
That we're rockin' it (rockin' it y'all)
Rockin' it

It's up to you to rock a new electrical shock
Consisting of weird noises all around the clock
But of course music plays along and it's a must
So let us tell ya who does all this for us
O.C.! He stands up behind us strong

O.C.! He keeps the beat on time for so long
O.C.! He goes along—dance, rhyme, or song
O.C.! The master won't steer ya wrong
When he's rockin' it
Rockin' it

Crazy Eddie
My opinion, number-one protege
Crazy Eddie
Ain't a record that he can't play
Crazy Eddie
See him once and I know you'll say
Crazy Eddie
Hold his ground against any D.J.
When he's rockin' it
Rockin' it

Haaaaaaaaaaaaaa Yeah, yeah, yeah, yeah, yeah
Oh yeah? Oh yeah!

FunKy four + ONe morE

That's the Joint

If you're ready for this
Say you're ready for this
If you're ready for this
Say you're ready for this
Are you ready for this?
We're ready for this
Are you ready for this?
We're ready for this
Well we just can't miss
Just can't miss

Well we just can't miss
With a beat like this
It's the joint

We're gonna prove to the world
That we're for real
We're gonna prove to everybody
We know the real deal
We got golden voices and hearts of steel
We are the five M.C.s, we got to be real
We want to hear the party people yell, "Sugarhill"
So what's the deal (Sugarhill)
So what's the deal (Sugarhill)
Ooh—That's the joint
These words we say, we want y'all to hear
We're gonna make a lot of sense—we're gonna make it clear
We're gonna rock this place
We're gonna use some class
We're gonna do our best
We're gonna make it last
We got rhymes on our minds
We get rockin' in the heart
And now the things we do
And we can call it art
We're bad, we're slick, we're cool and hip
We're gonna rock this record and don't you forget
Ah, that's the joint
Uh, uh because little Rodney C. is the melody
Keith, help me rock, we're singing harmony
Because Jeff is the rhythm and Kay is the bass
Sha-Rock rock shocking the whole darn place
Now here's a little story ya got to be told
Party people in the place, you got a whole lot of soul
So when we're on the mike y'all shocking the house
And when we all get together we can turn it out
Now we're in the house as you can plainly see
Everybody say, "Get funky" (get funky)
Make money (make money) and you don't stop
Give it to us now

Funk it up, funk it up
Get funky uh, uh, uh
Let's go to work, come on
Say, "I got money and I can't jerk"
To the beat that makes you want to rap
Come on Sha-Rock, cut out the crap
Just turn on your mike and start to rap
Let everybody know you could never be the wack
You know that (and you know that)
And I know and she knows and we know that
We go what Sha-Rock
When I rap Funky Four, I could never be the wack
And we hear you Sha-Rock
She's the joint
Do it up y'all, do do it up
Sha-Rock is gonna show you how to get real rough
I'm Sha-Rock and I can't be stopped
For all the fly guys, I will hit the top
Well I can do it for the ones who are weak or strong
And I can do it for the ones who are right or wrong
Well I'm listed in the column that's classified
And I can be your nurse and I'm qualified
To talk about respect, I won't neglect
My strategy is for you to see
So don't turn away by what I say
'Cause I'm on, I'm bad when I'm talking to you
And they're four fly brothers who can do it too
The party people in the place, this is for you
So get down, get get get on down
(She's the plus one more) and I'm throwing down
She's the best female in this here town
And everybody knows that I'm golden brown
And you know
She's the joint
I can pull the young ladies with my style
I'm the kind of M.C. that makes women just shout
I'm Jazzy Jeff with the most finesse
I'm down with the five that rocks the mike the best
'Cause I move the groove and I do it cool
Now rock what you can do and I'm sure to prove

'Cause I want a young lady with a lot of finesse
And she's got to be on, she's with Jazzy Jeff
She's got to be sweet, yes fine and kind
And that's just the kind of woman I want to be mine
And you know
He's the joint
Huh huh come on, do it
To the funky sound
Get funky, get funky with the Funky Four plus One
Do it, do it—come on, girl do it, do it
Ah Lord, do it, do it
Come on get down, huh ah Lord
To the beat—you don't stop—here we go
'Cause the music got to be the sureshot
Turn, turn it out y'all
'Cause the music got to be the sureshot
Blondie in the house, cool, cool, cool, cool, coolin' out

Now what you see is what you get
You say I am bad and that you can bet
I have the quality for you and me
To all the young ladies, this is what it be
You say his name is Keith Keith as my rhymes go down
To all the young ladies, just gather around
With the rhymes I possess, the words I protest
And I could put it together, I could call it finesse
Now listen up ladies and listen up good
I'm gonna rock on the mike like I know I could
Like he know he should, like I know I would
Keith Keith—I rock the house
He's Keith Keith—I rock, shock, rock, turn it out
And you know that, and he got the finesse
To behold that
He's the joint
Ah keeping on to, to the crack of dawn
Ah party people in the place, you got to keep on
If you like the beat and you want some more
Scream it out and say Funky Four (Funky Four)
Plus one more (plus one more)
Now you don't stop

Ya say the beat goes on, this is high powered stuff
We won't stop rocking until you all get enough
Of the ooh ah, ooh ooh, ah, ah ooh ah, and don't stop
Hit it
That's the joint
And we have an obligation that we must reveal
Like a .357, we're out to kill
We're like Machine-Gun Kelly and Bonnie and Clyde
When we shock the house, we stand side by side
We're on top of the world, we're looking down
We goin' straight ahead, we're never turned around
Because we're all so close but yet so far
And to all the party people ya know who we are
Get the point
And if you don't, we want y'all to know
We're down, we rock, we're the Funky Four
Plus One
Ho! do it, get down to the
Funky sound, come on, you got to get down
Do it, Ah lord
Natell, rocking well
Rodney C. making history
Ho, I'm Jazzy Jeff
Sharlene, Kevy Kev, Keith Keith to the funky beat
Kool T, Charlie Rome, Lehman High

I was sitting in my house, watching my TV
When all of the sudden, it dawned on me
That I was all alone, just wasting my time
So I grabbed a pen and paper and wrote down a rhyme
And I thought to myself how nice it would be
To be on top, making cash money
To go on a tour all around the world
To tell a little story to all the fly girls
To sit on my throne, to command my own
To be number one on the microphone
Just telling a tale about how it's gonna be
For the Funky Four plus One M.C.s
Will be busting in, will be turning it out
Will be rocking any beat without a doubt

Just chillin', hard living in luxury
And being very proud to be an M.C.
He's the joint
Now I'm Kay Kay Rockwell, causing I'm raisin' lot of hell
And I like to make love to the deffer female
And I'm down with the crew that you want to hear
Now just walk through a door, you pose on the floor
First things you turn is hips galore
And then he move her up
And then he kisses your lip
And then he holds on tight so I never slip
And then he tongued ya down, all to the ground
So that if true love is there, it will be found
By the man you all can tell
Rockwell to the depths of hell
And every time you hear my name girl, it rings a bell
When the bell rings, it goes ding dong
Then I'm rocking and shocking to the break of dawn
Like a hot butter on a bag of popcorn
Like Rockwell, just singing ya song
You know
He's the joint

Ho ho come on, come on, get down
Let's go to work, go on girl
Say I got money and I can't jerk
Let's go to work, let's go to work
We gave a lot of parties and we got jerked
But that's all right because we be good sports
'Cause we know someday we get the big payoff
And rock the house
Ah turn, turn, turn, turn it out
Sylvia in the house, Sherl the Pearl rock the house
Blondie rock the house, Master Gee rock the house
Big Bank rock the house and wherever you are
Rock rock the house
To my mellow wonder Mike rock the house
Wherever you are, rock shock the house
To my mellow cowboy, the real McCoy rock the house, turn turn
     it out

To my mellow Melle Mel rock the house
Wherever you are, rock shock the house
To the mellow Kid Creole solid gold rock the house
To my mellow Mister Ness, down with the best
Just rock the house with the most finesse
To my mellow, to my mellow, to my mellow, to my mellow
Rahiem in all the ladies' dreams
Rock the house with the gangster lean
Sugarhill, Sugarhill, Huh!
Get, get, get, get, get get the point, get the point, get the point
That we're the joint, Huh!
Break out, rock the house, wherever you are keep coolin' out
Uptown rock the house and
Ho! downtown just cooling out
West Side gonna turn it out
And to the East Side rock the house
KC check it out, KC check it out
Ooh THAT'S THE JOINT

Gang starr

Just to Get a Rep

Stick up kids is out to tax
Stick up kids is out to tax
And this is how the story goes

Brothers are amused by others brother's reps
But the thing they know best is where the gun is kept
'Cause in the night, you'll feel fright
And at the sight of a 4–5th, I guess you just might
Wanna do a dance or two
'Cause they could maybe bust you for self or with a crew
No matter is you or your brother's a star
He could pop you in check without a getaway car

And some might say that he's a dummy
But he's stickin' you and takin' all of your money
It's a daily operation
He might be loose in the park or lurkin' at the train station
Mad brothers know his name
So he thinks he got a little fame
From the stick-up game
And while we're blamin' society
He's at a party with his man
They got their eye on the gold chain
That the next man's wearin'
It looks big
But they ain't starin'
Just thinkin' of a way and when to get the brother
They'll be long gone before the kid recovers
And back around the way, he'll have the chain on his neck
Claimin' respect
Just to get a rep

Ten brothers in a circle
Had the kid trapped—the one with the hood, he said, "We'll hurt
    you"
If you don't run out your dues and pay
Give up the Rolex watch or you won't see another day
See, they were on the attack
And one said, "Yo, you wanna make this to a homicide rap?
Make it fast so we can be on our way
Kick in the rings and everything, ok?"
The kid was nervous and flinchin'
And little shorty with the 3–8, yo', he was inchin'
Closer and closer, put the gun to his head
Shorty was down to catch a body instead
Money was scared so he panicked
Took off his link and his rings and ran frantic
But Shorty said, "Now" pulled the trigger and stepped
It was nothin'
He did it just to get a rep

The rep grows bigger, now he's known for his trigger finger
Rollin' with troops of his sons like a gangster figure

He's near the peak of his crazy career
His posse's a nightmare—mack 'n' jewels 'n' crazy gear
But as we know, the things we do come back
And Shorty's not peepin', others are schemin' to counteract
'Cause the kid that got shot didn't perish, so
He pulls up in a jeep with tinted windows
Too late, Shorty was caught in the midst
His time ran out, his number came up, and that's it
You know the rest, so don't front, the plan has been upset
Some brothers gotta go out
Just to get a rep

The GeniuS

Life of a Drug Dealer

Life of a drug dealer

There's a rumor that an old lady heard a
Kingpin hiring a hit man to murder
A federal prosecuting drug-dealing witness
But that's how it is in the business
And I'm in it, physically gaining power
Constantly counting up cash by the hour
And it feels good to be paid
Regardless of how many victims get slayed
Accomplices of mine drop like flies
But in this every day a homeboy dies
Whether shot in the body or cyanide in ya Bacardi
'Cause it's a cutthroat party
Now it's up to me to retaliate
And if I score, I'll increase the murder rate
I move on ones who double-cross
Set them up, now they suffer the loss
Of he or she who's ever on the agenda
Most likely a family member

Informants, rattle-tattle-telling snakes
Get shot up, brutalized and thrown in lakes
The parts of a body is found days later
The other half was done by an amputator
I'm undefeated in plenty fights
My enemies are beaten with many stripes
I'll shoot up funerals, firebomb wakes
Vehicular homicides, whatever it takes
Just to keep control of my empire
I'll set ya own mother on fire
'Cause when it comes down just to me and my money
Ain't a fucking thing funny
All those who pose a threat I'll stick them
Ya friends, ya family and innocent victims
Get caught in the midst when I'm busting of nines
But they was in the wrong place, the wrong time
Decapitated bodies found in lots
While I'm still cooking up kilos in pots
The kilos becomes bricks and the bricks becomes rocks
Then retailed on the blocks
I drive around in expensive cars
And get women who fuck like porno stars
I get them high, you know, like powder they nose
Then put 'em in the streets as my high-class hoes
I'm wild, living foul and I'm ruthless
I leave motherfuckers toothless
I had a worker who stepped on the scene lively
Then started selling my customers Ivory
Soap, counterfeit vials of cracks
I stuck 'em to death with a thousand thumbtacks
You've seen my resume, that's just the half
I'm a bad motherfucker, just like Shaft
A character played by who? Richard Roundtree
The only difference, my guns are sound-free
Silencers ring off then wisp by
Then all you hear is a last-minute cry
Of those who tried to control my territory
Not the West Side but the Bed-Stuy story
Police be giving me eye-to-eye contact
But I smile 'cause I'm putting out contracts

Now a G-Note is placed upon ya head
You say picture that alright, bang ya dead

This is the Life of a Drug Dealer

Geto Boys

Mind of a Lunatic

Paranoid sittin' in a deep sweat
Thinkin' I got to fuck somebody before the weekend
The sight of blood excites me
Shoot you in the head, sit down and watch you bleed to death
I hear the sound of your last breath
Shouldn't have been around, I went all the way left
You was in the right place with me at the wrong time
I'm a psychopath in a minute, lose my fuckin' mind
Come down, back to reality
Don't fear death 'cause I know that it's promised to me
Flashes, I get flashes of Jason
Gimme a knife, a million lives I'm wasting
The shadow of death follow me, I don't give a fuck
Pussy, play Superman, your ass'll get boxed up
Put 'em in a straitjacket, the man's sick
This is what goes on in the mind of a lunatic

Lookin' through her window now, my body is warm
She's naked and I'm a peepin' Tom
Her body's beautiful so I'm thinkin' rape
Shouldn't have had her curtains open so that's her fate
Leavin' out her house, grabbed the bitch by her mouth
Drug her back in, slammed her down on the couch
Whipped out my knife, said, "If you scream, I'm cuttin' "
Opened her legs and commenced to fuckin'
She begged me not to kill her, I gave her a rose

Then slit her throat and watched her shake till her eyes closed
Had sex with the corpse before I left her
And drew my name on the wall like *Helter Skelter*
Run for shelter, never crossed my mind
I had a gauge, a grenade, and even a nine
Dial 911 for the bitch
But cops say shit when they're fuckin' with a lunatic

I sit alone in my four-cornered room, starin' at candles
Dreamin' of people I've dismantled
I close my eyes and in the circle appears the images of
Son of bitches I've murdered
Glad bags of bodies bein' fucked up
Once I attack, I'm like a pit on a rage that's goin' for guts
Boys used to die when I'm full of that fry
I be ebbin' when I'm high, I say fuck it, just let the bullets fly
Like I said before, Scarface is my identity
I'm a homicidal maniac with suicidal tendencies
I'm on the violent tip so you'll get a grip
And bitch comes equipped ain't takin' no shit 'cause here comes

My girl's gettin' skinny, she's strung out on coke
So I went to her mother's house, said, "Cut out her throat"
Her grandma was standin' there creamin'
As she reached for the tele, I put the blade on granny's ass
Went to the back and grabbed a shovel
Now granny's on her way to meet the devil
Pulled out my .38 and aimed at the bitch
A cop says, "Freeze, motherfucker," bitch, suck my dick
No sheriff's gonna take me on a road
Dark as fuck and let his pistol explode
Fuck that 'cause I ain't's to die
So I reloaded my Uzi and fired up another fry
It's got me crazy as fuck
Ragin' psychotic, full of that angel's dust
The cops had the place surrounded
Hunted for a way to get out, I found it
Innocent bystanders watchin', set an example
I popped one

Let me go, goddamnit, scot free
Or all of these motherfuckers comin' with me
All of a sudden, the shit got silent
I remember wakin' up and in an asylum
Bein' treated like a troubled kid
My shirt was all bloody and both of my wrists was split
Think this harsh, this ain't as harsh as it gets
No tellin' what's being thought of in the mind of a lunatic

November 1, 1966
A damn fool was born with the mind of a lunatic
I should've been killed
But sister fucked around and let me live
Now I developed a criminal behavior
Fuck with me and I'll slay ya ass
But you recognition shit
Your dental records couldn't prove your identity, bitch
I beg your pardon on talkin' to Borden
You'll never find the motherfucker so save your milk cartons
Cross the line, your ass is mine
I don't give a fuck if you're nine or ninety-nine
Blind, crippled, or crazy don't faze me
Your funky ass will be pushin' up daisies
You wanna know what makes me click
My psychiatrist said I got the mind of a lunatic

I ain't got it all, so don't fuck with me
Unless your ass wanna be made history
I'll blow your motherfuckin' house up
And if your wife and kids are inside
They're fucked
I don't give a fuck who I slay
Don't let me get a hold to some E & J
'Cause when the shit hit the fan
I'll stab your ass quicker than a Mexican
The nightmares I leave you with on the scene
Will make Freddy bitch ass look like a wet dream
This is fact not fictional, son of a bitch
I got the mind of a lunatic

goldMoney

Mnniiggaahh

(Yo mamma was a nigga)
Nigga
(Yo mamma was a nigga)
Nigga

Yeah, I'm a nigga
But that is just the way that I choose to act
It ain't got nothin' to do with bein' black
"All niggas are black"
Shut up, fool, how ya figure?
'Cause where I'm from there's a lot of white niggas
Like the one who likes to stick his tongue out
At a girl when he meets 'er
Take 'er out for beer and a pizza
Keep pourin' that liquor down her throat
'Til you think she's had enough
Take 'er to the house, the first he wants is muff, so tell me
That ain't what a so-called nigga would do
So what's the difference between me and you
So to the brothers, the next time they throw that little word at
    you
You look at 'em in the eye and call them niggas too

(Yo mamma was a nigga)
Nigga
(Yo mamma was a nigga)
Nigga

Now it's a simple fact that gang-bangin' leaves niggas dead
So what's the difference between the Crips, the Bloods, and the
    Skinheads
Or the KKK 'cause the way they play

Is blowin' niggas off the U.S.A.
They say a nigga just wants to get over, that's the name of the
    game
So I guess we're the same
'Cause the president be slingin' 'caine
Ya say that brothers get addicted to seed
But even Bush and Quayle smoke weed
'Cause they niggas

(Yo mamma was a nigga)
Nigga
(Yo mamma was a nigga)
Nigga

I got a white bitch
She got a ass like a jigaboo
So I guess you can call her nigga too
Made her turn a trick in the bushes just to get my money
So now she's known to everybody as a jungle bunny
I got a Mexican bitch
She got hips like a nigga
Lips like a nigga
Sucks dicks like a nigga
Turns tricks like a nigga
Brings her money to a nigga
Who pimps her like a nigga
When I beat her like a nigga
She limps like a nigga
To the stroll like a nigga
Play the role like a nigga
Cause she's hoin' for a nigga
Everyday for a nigga
Doin' the most for a nigga
Or gettin' roasted like a nigga

Niggarace!
Niggarace!
Niggarace!
Niggarace!

Grandmaster Flash
and the Furious Five

Superrappin'

It was a party night, everybody was breakin'
The highs were screamin' and the bass was shakin'
And it won't be long till everybody know when that
Flash was on the beat box goin' that
Flash was on the beat box goin' that
Flash was on the beat box goin'
and / and / and / and
Sha na na

Italian, Caucasian, Japanese, Spanish, Indian, Negro, and
     Vietnamese
M.C.s, disc jockeys to all the fly kids and the young ladies
Introducin' the crew ya got to see to believe
We're one, two, three, four, five M.C.s
I'm Melle Mel and I rock it so well
And I'm Mr. Ness because I rocks the best
Rahiem in all the ladies' dreams
And I'm Cowboy to make ya jump for joy
I'm Creole—solid gold
The Kid Creole playin' the role
Dig this

We're the Furious Five plus Grandmaster Flash
Givin' you a blast and sho' 'nuff class
So to prove to ya all that we're second to none
We're gonna make five M.C.s sound like one
Ya gotta dip did dive, so-so-socialize
Clean out your ears then open your eyes
And then pay at the door as a donation

To hear the best sounds in creation
He's a disco dream of a mean machine
And when it comes to size, ya see what we mean

Ya see his name is not found in the hall of fame but he'll shock
And amaze ya and make ya feel shame
He takes a lime from a lemon
From a lemon to lime
He cuts the beat in half the time
And as sure as three times two is six
Ya say Flash is the King of the quick mix
We're five M.C.s and we're on our own
And we're the most well known on the microphone
And we throw down hard and we aim to please
With finesse to impress all the young ladies
We got rhymes galore and that's a fact
And if the satisfaction's guaranteed to cause a heart attack
We are the best as you can see
So eliminate the possibility
That to be an E-M-C-E-E
Is not a threat to society
Say step-by-step
Stride by stride
I know the fly young lady would like to ride
If mama say this, "Young ladies"
If mama say this, "Young ladies"
If mama say to breakdown and dull my grill
I will drive up in a new Seville
If my Seville break down, I take it all back
I will dull my grill in a new Cadillac
If my Cadillac break down, it's just too much
I will shock your mind in a new star Stutz
And if a Stutz break down, I make another choice
I will dull my grill in a new Rolls Royce
And if a Royce break down, I'll be out in the rain
And then forget it, forget it, forget it, forget it, forget it
Huh, take the train
Take the train, take the train
Can't, won't, don't, stop rockin' to the rhythm
'Cause I get down, 'cause I get down, 'cause I get down

---

146 SUPERRAPPIN'

Ladies who don't know my name
And you fellers who don't know my game
Yes I'm called the Prince of Soul
But others call me the Kid Creole
The M.C. delight, young ladies bite
When on the mike and I rock the house right
I'm the dedicated prince, heart of solid gold
Rockin' to the rhythm while I'm bringin' the roll
A cool calm piece of the master plan
It takes a sucker's man to try to jump my hand
And the things I do and what I say
Affect a lot of people in the strangest way
Makes them clap their hands and say "all right"
3–0 to the broad daylight
It's the Nazz, my mellow, what he look like
With ya on the mike

Let's 'a rock y'all, 'a let's rock the house
Because the Furious Five are gonna turn it out
So young ladies if ya think ya heard
Ya heard the best rap, ya heard the best word
This is true that we got to fuss
Because it can't be the best unless it came from us
There's five of us and we take no stuff
We comin' through the city, we're comin' through rough
We number one ain't nothin' you can do
And if ya wanna get down, we'll rock ya too
So free-formin' y'all, ya don't stop
Come on, come on and let the see 'a rock rock
Cowboy, they say ya from the Bronx
So why don't ya rock the beat and add a little spunk

Yes yes, y'all and ya don't stop
'A come on fly girls, I wanna hit the top
I am the Cowboy C-O-W-B-O-Y
Why the man so bad that ya can't deny
Ya better watch your woman 'cause I'll tell ya why
'Cause I'm Cowbody, I might give her a try
The call me K P
The young ladies' relief

Known as the man of romance to make ya dance
Can any of ya ladies stand a chance?
I'm Cowboy and I'm shockin' the house ya say
Ya say one, two, one more is three
And Melle Mel, come on, watcha got for me?

To the hip hop, a hip hop, a don't stop, don't stop that body rock
Just get up off ya seat, get ready to clap
Because Melle Mel is startin' here to rap
Ever since the time at my very first party
I felt I could make myself somebody
It was something in my heart from the very start
I could see myself at the top of the chart
Rappin' on the mike, makin' cold cold cash
With a jock spinnin' for me called D.J. Flash
Signin' autographs for the young and old
Wearin' big time silver and solid gold
My name on the radio and in the magazine
My picture on the TV screen
It ain't like that yet but—huh—you'll see
I got potential and you will agree
I'm comin' up and I gotta step above the rest
'Cause I'm usin' that ladder they call success
Ya say it 1–2–3–4–5–6–7
Rap like hell and make it sound like heaven
A 7–6–5–4–3–2–1 a come-on Rahiem come and get some!

Yes yes y'all, ya don't stop, come on, come on, huh
I wanna hit the top
I'm a one of a kind, a man supreme
I know I'm in all of the ladies' dreams
I'm the R-A-H and the I-E-M
I put the wiggle in your butt if ya tell me when
I'm a son of a gun with a hell of a fire
Got to mess around and take ya' all higher
My clientele climb the great big boost
I'm the give it all and a turn it loose, huh
All you fly girls that don't know my game
Come up and talk to me and we'll tell ya all the same
When ya wake up in the night in a hell of a dream

Ya know ya been possessed by the voice of Rahiem
In all the ladies' dreams
And makin' more currency than any M.C.
And if the dream will turn to reality
And Melle Mel'll be makin' money
Mr. Ness, make make ya money
Rahiem, make ya money
Cowboy, make make ya money
Creole, make ya money
D.J. Flash, make make ya money
Hit it

Take your time and you will agree
That black girl got good security
So when ya walk through the door, just do me a favor
Be sure to be on your best behavior
Young man, what do you wanna do
When the party is through
And a young lady wanna go home with you
Ya search your pocket, ya soon aware
That ya don't have enough for cab fare
So ya say to yourself what a mistake you made
Your heart start pumpin' right on Kool-Aid
When she walks to you and she starts to say
"Call one-double-o, get down with O.J.
And you pave the way.

Grandmaster Flash
and the Furious Five

The Message

It's like a jungle sometimes, it makes me wonder
How I keep from going under
It's like a jungle sometimes, it makes me wonder
How I keep from going under

Broken glass everywhere
People pissing on the stairs
You know they just don't care
I can't take the smell, can't take the noise
Got no money to move out, I guess I got no choice
Rats in the front room, roaches in the back
Junkies in the alley with a baseball bat
I tried to get away but I couldn't get far
'Cause the man with the tow truck repossessed my car

Don't push me 'cause I'm close to the edge
I'm trying not to lose my head
Ah huh huh huh huh
It's like a jungle sometimes, it makes me wonder
How I keep from going under

Standing on the front stoop, hanging out the window
Watching all the cars go by, roaring as the breezes blow
Crazy lady, living in a bag
Eating outta garbage pails, used to be a fag hag
Says she danced the tango, skip the light fandango
Was zircon princess seemed to lost her senses
Down at the peep show, watching all the creeps so
She could tell the story to the girls back home

She went to the city and got social security
She had to get a pension, she couldn't make it on her own

Don't push me 'cause I'm close to the edge
I'm trying not to lose my head
Ah huh huh huh huh
It's like a jungle sometimes, it makes me wonder
How I keep from going under
Huh ah huh huh huh
It's like a jungle sometimes, it makes me wonder
How I keep from going under

My brother's doing bad, stole my mother's TV
Says she watches too much, it's just not healthy
"All My Children" in the daytime, "Dallas" at night
Can't even see the game or the Sugar Ray fight
The bill collectors, they ring my phone
And scare my wife when I'm not home
Got a bum education, double-digit inflation
Can't train to the job, there's a strike at the station
Neon King Kong, standing on my back
Can't stop to turn around, broke my sacroiliac
A mid-range migraine, cancered membrane
Sometimes I think I'm going insane
I swear, I might hijack a plane

Don't push me 'cause I'm close to the edge
I'm trying not to lose my head
It's like a jungle sometimes, it makes me wonder
How I keep from going under

My son said, "Daddy, I don't want to go to school
'Cause the teacher's a jerk, he must think I'm a fool
And all the kids smoke reefer, I think it'd be cheaper
If I just got a job, learned to be a street sweeper
Dance to the beat, shuffle my feet
Wear a shirt and tie and run with the creeps
'Cause it's all about money, ain't a damn thing funny
You got to have a con in this land of milk and honey"

They pushed that girl in front of the train
Took her to the doctor, sewed her arm on again
Stabbed that man right in his heart
Gave him a transplant for a brand new start
I can't walk through the park 'cause it's crazy after dark
Keep my hand on my gun
'Cause they got me on the run
I feel like a outlaw
Broke my last glass jaw
Hear them say, "You want some more?"
Livin' on a seesaw

Don't push me 'cause I'm close to the edge
I'm trying not to lose my head
Say what?
It's like a jungle sometimes, it makes me wonder
How I keep from going under

A child is born with no state of mind
Blind to the ways of mankind
God is smiling on you but he's frowning too
Because only God knows what you go through
You grow in the ghetto, living second rate
And your eyes will sing a song of deep hate
The place that you play and where you stay
Looks like one great big alleyway
You'll admire all the number book-takers
Thugs, pimps, and pushers and the big money makers
Driving big cars, spending twenties and tens
And you wanna grow up to be just like them, huh
Smugglers, scramblers, burglars, gamblers
Pickpockets, peddlers, even panhandlers
You say, "I'm cool, huh, I'm no fool"
But then you wind up dropping out of high school
Now you're unemployed, all nonvoid
Walking 'round like you're Pretty Boy Floyd
Turned stick-up kid but look what you done did
Got sent up for a eight-year bid
Now your manhood is took and you're a Maytag
Spend the next two years as a undercover fag

Being used and abused to serve like hell
'Til one day you was found hung dead in the cell
It was plain to see that your life was lost
You was cold and your body swung back and forth
But now your eyes sing the sad sad song
Of how ya lived so fast and died so young

So don't push me 'cause I'm close to the edge
I'm trying not to lose my head
Ah huh huh huh huh
It's like a jungle sometimes, it makes me wonder
How I keep from going under

(Dialogue)
Yo, Mel, you see that girl man?
Yeah, man
Cowboy
Yo! That sound like Cowboy, man
That's cool
Yo! What's up money?
Yo!
Hey, where's Creole and Rahiem at, man?
They upstairs cooling out
So, what's up for tonight y'all?
Yo! We could go down to Fever, man
Let's go check out June Bug, man
Hey yo! You know that girl Betty?
Yeah, man
Her moms got robbed, man
What?
Not again?
She got hurt real bad
When this happen? When this happen?
(Tires squeal)
Everybody freeze! Don't nobody move nothing, y'all know what
    this is
Get 'em up!
What?
Get 'em up!
Man, we down with Grandmaster Flash and the Furious Five

What's that? A gang?
No!
Look, shut up! I don't want to hear your mouth
'Scuse me, Officer, Officer, what's the problem?
You the problem, you the problem
You ain't got to push me, man
Get in the car! Get in the car! Get in the godda—
Get in the car!

Grandmaster melle Mel

White Lines

Fun baby
Freeze!
Rock!
Bass!
White lines (Vision dreams of passion)
Going through my mind (And all the while I think of you)
High rise (A very strange reaction)
Brought us to unwind (The more I see, the more I do)
Something but a phenomenon baby
Telling your body to come along with white lines
Blow away
Blow! rockin'! blow!

Ticket to ride
White line highway
Tell all your friends, they can go my way
Pay your toll, sell your soul
Pound for pound, cost more than gold
The longer you stay, the more you pay
My white lines go a long way
Either up your nose or through your vein
With nothing to gain except killing your brain

Freeze! rock! freeze! rock!
Freeze! rock! freeze! rock!
Blow—higher baby
Get higher baby, get higher baby
And don't ever come down—free base

Rang dang diggah dee dang dee dang
Rang dang diggah dee dang dee dang
Rang dang diggah dee dang dee dang
Diggah dee dang dee dang diggah dee dang dee dang

Pipe line
Pure as the driven snow
Connected to my mind
And now I'm having fun, baby
High rise
It's getting kind of low
'Cause it makes you feel so nice
I need some one-on-one, baby
Don't let it blow your mind away, baby
And go into your little hideaway
'Cause white lines blow away
Blow! rockin'! blow!

A million magic crystals
Painted pure and white
A multimillion dollars
Almost overnight
Twice as sweet as sugar
Twice as bitter as salt
And if you get hooked, baby
It's nobody else's fault
So don't do it
Freeze! rock! freeze! rock!
Freeze! rock! freeze! rock!
Blow!
Higher baby, get higher, baby
Get higher, baby and don't ever come down
Free base!

Don't you get too high
Don't you get too high, baby
Turns you on
You really turn me on and on
Could you ever come down?
My temperature is rising
When the thrill is gone
No I don't want you to go

A street kid gets arrested, gonna do some time
He got out three years from now just to commit more crime
A business man is caught with twenty-four kilos
He's out on bail and out of jail and that's the way it goes

Cane! sugar! cane! sugar! cane!

Athletes reject it, governors correct it
Gangsters, thugs, and smugglers are thoroughly respected
The money gets divided, the women get excited
Now I'm broke and it's no joke
It's hard as hell to fight it
Don't buy it!
Freeze! rock! freeze! rock!
Freeze! rock! freeze! rock!
Blow!
Get higher, baby, get higher, girl
Get higher, baby
Come on

White line
Vision dreams of passion
Blowing through my mind
And all the while I think of you
High rise
A very strange reaction
Brought us to unwind
The more I see, the more I do
Something but a phenomenon baby
Telling your body to come along
But white lines—blow away

Little Jack Horner, sitting on the corner
With no shoes and clothes
This ain't funny but he took his money
And sniffed it up his nose

Hey, man you want to cop some blow?
Sure, what you got
Dust, flakes, or rocks
I got china white, mother pearl, ivory flakes, what you need?
Yeah, all let me check it out, man, let me get a freeze
Go ahead, man, that stuff'll kill ya
Yeah, that's, that's raw, wugh!

Don't do it! Baby, Baby!
Don't do it!

Freeze! Rock! Freeze! Rock!
Freeze! Rock! Freeze! Rock!

heavy D and the Boyz
We Got Our Own Thang

Everybody, shake your body, we don't ill, we chill at a party
Keep a groove that's sensual, three-dimensional, unquestionable
The lover is professional
Got a category, my own and I'm the president
Don't be alarmed, but I'm sewing up the resident
With my particular style, particular, extracurricular, smoother
    and trickier
Throwing on lyrics like you throw up a flapjack
You're a Chicken McNugget and I'm a Big Mac
Brainstorm soloist, have a Coca-colaist, doing very well
Because it took the right road to this
Path, make the undertake, the recordbreaker

Get up on the floor and do the Heavy D shake
Started with a pow and I'm going to end with a bang

We've got our own thang

Picture the set, girlies wet with sweat
In the corner people sitting down, they've had as much as they
     could possibly get
Here while I'm lamping, feeling like a champ and push up on a
     cutie, phone digits I'm stamping
The place was packed though, stuffed like an Oreo
Everybody broke for a Heavy D video
Pumping in stereo, people said, "Here we go," a cutie down in
     front said, "Heavy you're my hero"
Understand this, before you make a comment, because there's
     always a meaning in a Heavy D statement
In this life, I strive for improvement
Be your own guide, follow your own movement
Loving is a legend
Me, I'm legendary at it
Living on the mike makes me a rapping acrobat
Don't try to swing, because you couldn't even hang
We've got our own thang

We've got our own thang

Original, smooth criminal, dance a lot, dance a little, shuffle to
     the middle
Don't clock anybody, let them all clock you
Don't be down with anybody, let them all be down with you
Stay self-managed, self-kept, self-taught
Be your own man, don't be borrowed, don't be bought
Started with a pow and I'm going to end it with a bang
We've got our own thang

We've got our own thang

Ice CubE

Dead Homiez

Up early in the morning, dressed in black
Don't ask why 'cuz I'm down in a suit and tie
They killed a homie that I went to school with (damn)
I tell you, life ain't shit to fool with
I still hear the screams from his mother
While my nigger lay dead in the gutter (shit)
And it's getting to my temper
Why is that the only time black folks get to ride in a limo?
It makes me so mad I want to get my sawed-off
And have some bodies hauled off
But no, I pay my respects and I'm through
Hug my crew and maybe shed a tear or two
Then I wanna get blitzed
Grab my forty and then I reminisce
About a brother who had to be the one and only
So I dedicate this to my dead homie

Another homie got murdered on a shakedown
Now his mother's at the funeral, having a nervous breakdown
Two shots hit him in the face when it blasted
A framed picture and a closed casket
A single-file line about fifty cars long
All driving slow with their lights on
He got a lot of flowers and a big wreath
What good is that when you're six feet deep?
I look at his shit and gotta think to myself
I thank god for my health 'cuz nobody really ever knows
When it's going to be they family on the front row
So I take everything slow, go with the flow
Shut my motherfuckin' mouth if I don't know
'Cuz that's what pops told
But I wish he could have said it to my dead homie

I remember, we painted our names on the wall for fun
Now it's rest in peace after every one
Except me
An' I ain't the one to front
Seems like I'm viewing a body every other month
Plus I knew him when he was yay big
Pour my beer on the curb before I take a swig
But something ain't right
When there's a tragedy, that's the only time that the family is
    tight
Loving each other in a caring mood
There's lots of people and lots of food
They say, "be strong" and you're trying
How strong can you be when you see your pops crying?
So that's why Ice Cube's dressed up
Because the city is so fuckin' messed up
And everybody's so phoney
Take a little time
To think about your dead homie

Ice CubE

Who's the Mack?

Straight gangsta mack
Straight gangsta mack
Straight gangsta mack
Straight gangsta mack
Who's the mack? is it some brother in a big hat
Thinking he can get any bitch with a good rap?
Rolling in a fucked-up Lincoln
Leaning to the side
So it looks like he's sinking
Into that leopard interior
This nigga thinks every girl's inferior
To his tongue, get a dumb bitch sprung

As she's selling more butt
Don't even get a cut of the money
His name is Sonny
And he know the play
And hope to God that he don't find a runaway
That's looking to become a star
He'll have your ass in and out of every car
With every Ron and Rick, sucking every John's dick
Come short of the money, get your ass kicked
You don't like it but you still call him hunk
Last night the nigga put yo' ass in a trunk
You wanna leave but Sonny started talking fast
And it make you wanna go and sell more ass
He's getting rich, you his bitch and it's like that
Now ask yourself
Who's the mack?

Who's the mack?
It is that fool that wanna pump the gas
Give you a sad story and you give him cash?
He starts macking and macking and you sucking
Quick to say I'm down on my luck
And you give a dollar or a quarter and he's on his way
Then you see his sorry ass the next day
Are you the one getting played like a sucka?
Or do you say, "Get a job, motherfucker"?
Every day, the story gets better
He's wearing dirty pants and a funky-assed sweater
He claims he wants to get something to eat
But every day you find yourself getting beat
He gets your money and you run across the street
Don't look both ways 'cause he's in a daze
And almost get his ass hit for the crack
Now ask yourself
Who's the Mack?

Who's the Mack?
Is it that nigga in that club asking
Have you ever been in a hot tub?
I know the game so I watch it unfold

When I see the boy pinned to your earlobe
He's talking shit and you crack a smile
When he tell you that he can go buck wild
For a girl like you and make it feel good
You know it's drama but it sound real good
He started dragging and hopefully he can start tagging
The pussy so he can keep bragging
He say, "I'm 'a leave baby, can you go with me?"
You wanna do it but you feeling like a H-O-E
You grab his hand, you leave and it's over
'Cause the nigga ain't nothing but a rover
Ya knew the game and you still ended up on your back
Now ask yourself
Who's the Mack?

Macking is the game and everybody's playing
And as long as you believe what they saying
Consider them a M.A.C.K. and with no delay
They are gonna get all the play
But when it comes to me, save the drama for your momma
It's Ice Cube and you know that I'm a
Mack in my own right
When it comes to rhyme and rap 'cause all I do is kick facts
Unlike Iceberg Slimm and all of them be claimin' be P.I.M.P.
No, I'm not going out that way
I'm just a straight up N I double G A
Next time U get over on a fool
And you did the shit like real smooth
Thank Ice Cube for giving up the facts
And ask yourself
Who's the Mack?

Straight Gangsta Mack
Straight Gangsta Mack
Straight Gangsta Mack
Straight Gangsta Mack

Ice T

Freedom of Speech

Hey, yo, Ice, man, I'm workin' on this term paper for college
What's the First Amendment?

Freedom of Speech
That's some motherfuckin' bullshit
You say the wrong thing
They'll lock your ass up quick
The FCC said, "Profanity, no airplay"
They can suck my dick while I take a shit all day
Think I give a fuck about some silly bitch named Gore?
Yo, PMRC, here we go, war!
Yo, Tip, what's the matter, you ain't gettin' no dick?
You bitchin' 'bout rock and roll
That's censorship, dumb bitch
The constitution say we all got a right to speak
Say what we want, Tip, your argument is weak
Censor records, TV, school books, too?
And who decides what's right to hear, you?
Hey, PMRC, you stupid fuckin' assholes
The sticker on the record—it what makes 'em sell gold
Can't you see, you alcoholic idiots
The more you try to suppress us, the larger we get

Freedom of Speech!
Just watch what you say
Freedom of Speech!
Yeahhh, just watch what you say
Freedom of Speech!
Yeah, boy, just watch what you say
(You have the right to remain silent)

Fuck that right!
I want the right to talk

I want the right to speak
I want the right to walk where I wanna
Yell and I'm gonna
Tell and rebel every time I'm on a
Microphone on a stage cold illin'
The knowledge I drop will be heard by millions
We ain't the problems, we ain't the villains
It's the suckers deprivin' the truth from our children
You can't hide the fact, Jack
There's violence in the streets every day
Any fool can recognize that
But you try to lie and lie
And say America's some motherfuckin' apple pie
Yo, you gotta be high to believe
That you gonna change the world by a sticker on a record sleeve
'Cause once you take away my right to speak
Everybody in the world's up shit creek

Freedom of speech
Yeahhh, just watch what you say
Freedom of Speech!
Yeah, boy, just watch what you say
Freedom of Speech!
Ha-Haaa, you better watch what you say
(Explicit lyrics)
(Explicit lyrics)

Let me tell you about down South
Where a motherfucker might as well not even have a mouth
Columbus, Georgia, said they'd lock me up
If I got on the stage in my show and said "fuck"
So I thought for a minute and said "no"
I wasn't even gonna do a damn show
'Cause for me to change my words for my rhymes
Is never gonna happen, cause there's no sell-out, no mind
But I vow to get those motherfuckers one day
They even arrested Bobby Brown and Cool J
Yo, they got this comin' 'cause I'm mad and I'm gunnin'
Homeboys and there's no runnin'
I'm gonna tell you how I feel about you

No bull, no lies, no slack, just straight fact
Columbus, Georgia, you can suck my dick
You ain't nothin' but a piece of fuckin' shit on the damn map

Freedom of speech
Yeahhh, just watch you say
Freedom of speech
Yeahhh, you better watch what you say
Freedom of Speech
Just watch what you say
(Parental advisory)
(Parental advisory)

Freedom of speech, let 'em take it from me
Next they'll take it from you
Then what you gonna do?
Let 'em censor books, let 'em censor art
PMRC, this is where the witchhunt starts
You'll censor what we see, we read, we hear, we learn
The books will burn
You better think it out
We should be able to say anything
Our lungs were meant to shout
Say what we feel, yell out what's real
Even though it may not bring mass appeal
Your opinion is yours, my opinion is mine
If you don't like what I'm sayin' fine
But don't close it, always keep an open mind
A man who fails to listen is blind
We only got one right left in the world today
Let me have it, or throw the constitution away

Freedom of Speech
Yeahh, just watch what you say
Freedom of Speech
You better watch what you say
Freedom of Speech
Yeah, boy, you better watch what you say
(Explicit lyrics)

Ice T

I'm Your Pusher

"Yo, what's up, man, I need to get high, man,
I need to get hold of some big-time dope, man.
You know where I can get a key?"

I know where you can get a LP.

"LP, man? Have you went crazy?
Man, I'm talkin' about some dope, man.
I need to get high right now, man.
Why don't you hook me up with a five-oh."

I can hook you up with a twelve-inch.

"Twelve-inch, man, you done went crazy?
You don't even know what time it is.
Out here on the streets
And you don't know what time it is, man.
You's a fool."

Yo, homeboy, YOU a fool.
You don't know what time it is,
Out here messin' up your mind,
You know what I'm sayin'?
This is Ice T talkin' to you, boy.
I'm 'a tell you what time it is.

Yo, it's time for me to pump up the volume
No problem, the record's revolvin'
Evil's the mixer, I'm the rap trickster
Paparazzis on the bum rush for pictures
Ice, coolin', yo, colder than ever
Punk executioner E, pull the lever
Rotate the wax then cut an' axe the tracks

Push up the levels till the red lights max
Don't try to size up, you better wise up
To the rap criminals, we're on a rise up
We're sellin' dope till we've succeeded
Dope beats and lyrics, no beepers needed
For this drug deal, I'm the big wheel
The dope I'm sellin' ya don't smoke, ya feel!
Out on the dance floor, on my world tour
I'm sellin' dope in each and every record store
I'm the king pin when the wax spins
Crack or smack will take you to a sure end
You don't need it, just throw that stuff away
You wanna get high? Let the record play

"Oh, man, I like this dope here, man,
It's feelin' all right, boy.
What'd you say your name was, man?"

I'm yo' mommy
I'm yo' daddy
I'm that nigga in the alley
I'm the brother when you need
A true player to M.C.
You know me, I'm your friend
Your main boy, thick and thin
M.C. Ice T
I'm your pusher
I know you're lovin' this drug as it's comin' out your speaker
Bass through the bottoms, highs through the tweeters
But this base, you don't need a pipe
Just a tempo to keep you hype
Groovin' like I see you doin'
Some stupid crack would just ruin
Your natural high, why? that ain't fly!
And anyone who says it is lies
Move like I knew you would, like I knew you could
And if you ain't cracked out, then I know you should
Be able to give me a clap, to match exact with the track
And since I know that ya ain't, I expect that
Oh now this jam is lit, it's like the ultimate

People high off dope, but still physically fit
I make a million bucks, pack my dough in trucks
From sellin' dope beats, dope rhymes, dope cuts
I'll be the biggest dope dealer in history
'Cause all the fly will be high off that Ice T!

"Oh, man, you ain't never lie, man,
This dope is all right, man,
I got to get back with you, man,
Let me get your number, man."

I'm yo' mommy
I'm yo' daddy
I'm that nigga in the alley
I'm the brother when you need
A true player to M.C.
You know me, I'm your friend
Your main boy, thick and thin
M.C. Ice T
I'm your pusher
I'll bring it to boil, evil E, rock it up
You want it? I don't think you got enough
Last suckers crossed, syndicate shot 'em up
Cops found 'em in the lake bottom up
I don't play when it comes to my dope
I check my lyrics close, like with a microscope
I don't clean 'em up with no Ivory Soap
I leave 'em hard and pure, hope that you can cope
'Cause you might O.D. if you overdrive
This record, tape, or CD, because the sound I've
Created on this wax is like a chemical
And the knowledge I give makes me invincible!

"Oh, Mr. Dope Man, I'm lovin' you, man,
You got it goin' on, man
What else you got?"

I got some o' that Kool Moe Dee

"Aw, yeah, man, I want some a that, man."

Got some Doug E. Fresh

"Aw, gimme a ounce o' that, man, I want that all night long."

Got some Eric B and Rakim

"Oh, that is some real dope right there."

Got some o' that LL Cool J.

"Naw, naw, man, I don't want none o' that, man,
You can keep that, man."

Got some Boogie Down Productions, KRS-1.

"Aw, now you're talkin' man, come on."

Public Enemy

"Yeah, don't stop, don't stop."

Biz Markie

"Make the music with your mouth, Biz.
I love it."

I'm yo' mommy
I'm yo' daddy
I'm that nigga in the alley
I'm the brother when you need
A true player to M.C.
You know me, I'm your friend
Your main boy, thick and thin
M.C. Ice T
I'm your pusher
The cops don't know what to do because my dope breaks through
No matter what they do, my stuff gets to you
Kickin' on the boulevard, my tempo's hyped and hard
I don't ask, the Ice just bogarts
Sire Records puts me with Warner Brothers clout

My dope hits the streets with no doubt
Evil E adds the cut, then removes it
Iz checks for purity, and then approves it
And then you get it, try it, and like it
And if it ain't potent, we remix it and spike it
To bring you the pure dope, not a noose in a rope
'Cause if you're doin' crack, you're on death row
You're just a toy punk to mess with that junk
You want some real dope, come look in my trunk
The dope I'm sellin' is life, a hundred percent legit
So get real, fool, and try some real hit

"Word up, my brother, you got me high as a kite,
I feel good tonight. Ice T man, you all right."

I'm yo' mommy
I'm yo' daddy
I'm that nigga in the alley
I'm the brother when you need
A true player to M.C.
You know me, I'm your friend
Your main boy, thick and thin
M.C. Ice T
I'm your pusher.

JaZZy Jeff & the fresH PrinCE

Nightmare on My Street

Now I have a story that I'd like to tell
About this guy—you all know me—had me scared as hell
He comes to me at night after I crawl into bed
He's burnt up like a weeny and his name is Fred
He wears the same hat and sweater every single day
And even if it's hot outside—he wears it anyway

He's home when I'm awake but he shows up when I'm asleep
I can't believe that there's a nightmare on my street

It was a Saturday evening if I remember it right
And we had just gotten back off tour last night
So the gang and I thought that it would be groovy
If we summoned up the posse and bum-rushed the movie
I got Angie
Jeff got Tina
Ready Rock got some girl I'd never seen
In my life
That was all right though 'cause the lady was chill
Then we dipped to the theater set to ill
Buggin', cool, havin' a ball
And somethin' 'bout Elm Street was the movie we saw
The way it started was decent, ya know
Nothin' real fancy
About this homeboy named Fred and this girl named Nancy
But—word—when it was over
I said yo', that was def
And everything seemed all right when we left
But when I got home and laid down to sleep
That began the nightmare on my street!

It was burning in my room like an oven
My bed soaked with sweat
And man I was bugging
I checked the clock and it stopped at twelve-thirty
It had melted it was so darn hot
And I was thirsty
I wanted something cool to quench my thirst
I thought to myself, yo, this heat is the worst!
But when I got downstairs
I noticed something was wrong
I was home all alone but the TV was on
I thought nothing of it as I grabbed the remote
I pushed the power button and then I almost choked
When I heard this awful voice
Coming from behind
It said, "You got my favorite letter but now you must die!"

Man, I didn't even wait to see who it was
Broke inside my drawers and screamed, "So long, cous'!"
Got halfway up the block
I calmed down and stopped screaming
Then thought, "Oh, I get it, I must be dreaming"
I strolled back home with a grin on my grill
I think that since this is a dream I might as well get ill
I walked in the house, the Big Bad Fresh Prince
But Freddy killed all that noise real quick!
He grabbed me by my neck and said
"Here's what we'll do
We gotta lotta work here, me and you
The souls of your friends you and I will claim
You've got the body and I've got the brain"
I said, "Yo Fred
I think you got me all wrong
I ain't partners with nobody with nails that long
Look, I'll be honest, man, this team won't work
The girls won't be on you, Fred, your face is all burnt!"
Fred got mad and his head started steaming
But I thought, "What the hell, I'm only dreaming"
I said, "Please leave, Fred, so I can get some sleep
But give me a call and maybe we'll hang out next week"
I patted him on the shoulder and said, "Thanks for stoppin' by"
Then I opened up the door
And said, "Take care, guy!"
He got mad, threw back his arm, and slashed my shirt
I laughed at first, then thought, "Hold up, that hurt"
It wasn't a dream, man, this guy was for real
I said, "Freddy, uh, pal, there's been an awful mistake here"
No further words and then I darted upstairs
Crashed through my door then jumped on my bed
Pulled the covers up over my head
And said, "Oh please do something with Fred"
He jumped on my bed, went through the covers with his claws
Tried to get me, but my alarm went off
And then silence
It was a whole new day
I thought, "Huh, I wasn't scared of him anyway"

Until I noticed those rips in my sheets
And that was proof that there had been
A nightmare on my street

O man, I gotta call Jeff, I gotta call Jeff
Come on, come on
Come on Jeff, answer! Come on, man
Hello
Jeff, this is Prince, man
Jeff, wake up, Jeff, wake up
What do you want?
Jeff, wake up, man, listen to me, Jeff
It's three o'clock in the morning
Jeff, Jeff, would you listen to me?
What?
Listen, whatever you do, don't fall asleep
Maaan
Jeff, listen to me, don't go to sleep, Jeff
No, No, I talk to you tomorrow, I'm goin' to bed
Jeff!
Ahhhhhh! Ahhhhhh! (Ha ha ha ha ha haaaa)
Jeff! Jeff! Jeff! Jeff! Answer me, Jeff!
I'm your D.J. now, Princy! Ha ha ha ha ha ha ha haaaaa!

JaZZy Jeff & the freSH PrinCE

Parents Just Don't Understand

You know parents are the same
No matter time nor place
They don't understand that us kids
Are going to make some mistakes
So to you, all the kids all across the land
There's no need to argue
Parents just don't understand

I remember one year
My mom took me school shopping
It was me, my brother, my mom, oh, my pop, and my little
    sister
All hopped in the car
We headed downtown to the Gallery Mall
My mom started bugging with the clothes she chose
I didn't say nothing at first
I just turned up my nose
She said, "What's wrong? This shirt cost $20"
I said, "Mom, this shirt is plaid with a butterfly collar!"
The next half hour was the same old thing
My mother buying me clothes from 1963
And then she lost her mind and did the ultimate
I asked her for Adidas and she bought me Zips!
I said, "Mom, what are you doing, you're ruining my rep"
She said, "You're only sixteen, you don't have a rep yet"
I said, "Mom, let's put these clothes back, please"
She said "No, you go to school to learn not for a fashion
    show"
I said, "This isn't Sha Na Na, come on Mom, I'm not Bowzer
Mom, please put back the bell-bottom Brady Bunch trousers
But if you don't want to I can live with that but
You gotta put back the double-knit reversible slacks"
She wasn't moved—everything stayed the same
Inevitably the first day of school came
I thought I could get over, I tried to play sick
But my mom said, "No, no way, uh-uh, forget it"
There was nothing I could do, I tried to relax
I got dressed up in those ancient artifacts
And when I walked into school, it was just as I thought
The kids were cracking up laughing at the clothes Mom bought
And those who weren't laughing still had a ball
Because they were pointing and whispering
As I walked down the hall
I got home and told my Mom how my day went
She said, "If they were laughing you don't need them,
'Cause they're not good friends"
For the next six hours I tried to explain to my Mom
That I was gonna have to go through this about 200 more times

---

So to you all the kids all across the land
There's no need to argue
Parents just don't understand

Oh-kay, here's the situation
My parents went away on a week's vacation and
They left the keys to the brand new Porsche
Would they mind?
Umm, well, of course not
I'll just take it for a little spin
And maybe show it off to a couple of friends
I'll just cruise it around the neighborhood
Well, maybe I shouldn't
Yeah, of course I should
Pay attention, here's the thick of the plot
I pulled up to the corner at the end of my block
That's when I saw this beautiful girlie girl walking
I picked up my car phone to perpetrate like I was talking
You should've seen this girl's bodily dimensions
I honked my horn just to get her attention
She said, "Was that for me?"
I said, "Yeah"
She said, "Why?"
I said, "Come on and take a ride with a helluva guy"
She said, "How do I know you're not sick?
You could be some deranged lunatic"
I said, "C'mon toots—my name is the Prince—
Besides, would a lunatic have a Porsche like this?"
She agreed and we were on our way
She was looking very good and so was I, I must say—word
We hit McDonald's, pulled into the drive
We ordered two Big Macs and two large fries with Cokes
She kicked her shoes off onto the floor
She said, "Drive fast, speed turns me on"
She put her hand on my knee, I put my foot on the gas
We almost got whiplash, I took off so fast
The sun roof was open, the music was high
And this girl's hand was steadily moving up my thigh
She had opened up three buttons on her shirt so far
I guess that's why I didn't notice that police car

We're doing ninety in my Mom's new Porsche
And to make this long story short—short
When the cop pulled me over I was scared as hell
I said, "I don't have a license but I drive very well, officer"
I almost had a heart attack that day
Come to find out the girl was a twelve-year-old runaway
I was arrested, the car was impounded
There was no way for me to avoid being grounded
My parents had to come off from vacation to get me
I'd rather be in jail than to have my father hit me
My parents walked in
I got my grip, I said, "Ah, Mom, Dad, how was your trip?"
They didn't speak
I said, "I want to plead my case"
But my father just shoved me in the car by my face
That was a hard ride home, I don't know how I survived
They took turns—
One would beat me while the other one was driving
I can't believe it, I just made a mistake
Well parents are the same no matter time nor place
So to you all the kids all across the land
Take it from me
Parents just don't understand

Jungle BrotHers
Black Is Black

Now from the Tribe Called Quest
And I'm here tonight with the Jungle Brothers
And we're about to get into this thing
Called black is black is black is black

Black is black (Ah-hah, Oh baby) Black is black
Black is black is black is black

In America today
I have to regret to say
Somethin', somethin' is not right
And it deals with black and white
Tell me Michee, is it me?
Naw, it's just society
Filled with propaganda, huh?
But why do we meander, huh?
In a zone with hate for peace
All of this b.s. must cease
All I am is one black man
In a mighty big white hand
Brother brother sister sister
If you're miss or if you're mister
Listen please to this fact
Black is black is black is black

Black is black. Black is black.
Black is black is black is black
Black is black. Black is black.
Black is black is black is black

Way back when in '68
When brothers didn't have it great
They fought back with civil rights
That scarred the soul, it took your sight
The common foe you plainly see
On the streets or on TV
Segregation was the key
Vietnam was full in swing
Martin Luther had to shout
Let's get out, get out, get out
The situation sort of changed
But what really makes matters strange
Is our vote
Is well-disguised
We don't know where our fate lies
Still and all we cannot lack
The fact
Black is black is black is black

Black is black. Black is black.
Black is black is black is black
Black is black. Black is black.
Black is black is black is black

Judged by both my race and color
Don't you know we need each other
I need you and you need me
And if not now you soon will see
My light complexion has no meaning
If you think so, you're still dreaming
Wake up, wake up, wake up, wake up
There's no time for us to break up
Black is black not blue or purple
Being black is like a circle
Round and round we all will go
Where we end up I don't know
Listen to me if you will
Your fantasies will get you killed
Reality is what is real
Reality is black is black
I tried and tried to tell my people
We all are one, created equal
Before we master, we must plan
Is that so hard to understand?
Today's the day we get together
To try to change and make things better
If not, where will be tomorrow?
Drownin' in the pool of sorrow
Daylight shines but still few see
That we must fight for unity
And the picture that's fixed is black and white
Why's it both to have to fight
Uplift the race, uplift the race
See my soul and not my face
All for one and one for all
Black is black—that's right y'all

Black is black. Black is black.
Black is black is black is black

Black is black. Black is black.
Black is black is black is black

KiD 'n play

Rollin' with Kid 'n Play

Olah, Olah, hey (Olah, Olah, hey)
Rollin', rollin', rollin' with Kid 'n Play now
Olah, Olah, hey (Olah, Olah, hey)
Rollin', rollin', rollin' with Kid 'n Play now

Now, Play, I don't know what it is about this beat
That we have here but it sure is funky

Olah, Olah, hey, Olah, Olah, hey

Yo, Kid, I don't know what it is about this groove
That's here makin' us move but it sure is funky

Olah, Olah, hey

I think it's time to rap!
Shall we?
Surely?
Kid 'n Play back, rollin' strong
Dope and def
We can get funky with the best
We're just hypin' it up!
You know, just how it had to be
Just take a look around, boy
Can't you see?
Guys are bum-rushin'
Girls are just blushin'
Wiz rocks the scratch
While Hurb's on percussion

Settin' the stage so the stage can get set off
I'll bust a rhyme and a dance so just jet off
So get off because you bit off
More than you can chew
Now watch the dynamic duo do a little go-go thang
C'mon rock and swing
Ya gotta
Roll with Kid 'n Play
Now everybody say

Olah, Olah, hey (Olah, Olah, hey)
Rollin', rollin', rollin' with Kid 'n Play now
Olah, Olah, hey (Olah, Olah, hey)
Rollin', rollin', rollin' with Kid 'n Play now

Now we're the stars of stage, wax, and video
We're here to tear it up so c'mon, here we go
Pump it up, this is high-powered stuff
Kid 'n Play can't get enough
Of that Funky
Go-go-go rhythm
You wanted a dope jam
Well that's what we're givin'
We're headed for fame
Because Kid 'n Play's driven
Boy, we no game
And large is how we're livin'
We stay paid
You know the boys have got it made
See I'm the tramp
And I'm the fella with the high top fade
Gettin' down to the sounds
You know we're gonna turn it out
Roll with Kid 'n Play, everybody shout

Olah, Olah, hey (Olah, Olah, hey)
Rollin', rollin', rollin' with Kid 'n Play now
Olah, Olah, hey (Olah, Olah, hey)
Rollin', rollin', rollin' with Kid 'n Play now

I bet you ladies
Want to see
P-L-A-Y
And K-I-D
And not like the rest
Our style is def
And we present ourselves as the very best
On the microphone, we bring life to your soul
Your whole damn body we will control
So, stay calm, don't be alarmed
We're gonna relax you ladies with a deadly charm
Wanna go to work on you fellas too
Make you wanna do the things we do
'Cause when a
Kid 'n Play is in your town
You gotta
Keep rockin' to the Go-Go sound
You gotta
Keep rockin' all day, all night
'Cause we're a different delight
Dynamite on the mike
So shake it
Your butt, shake it down
We've got the best music all around
Hurb's the producer, Wiz is the D.J.
Roll with Kid 'n Play
Now everybody say

Olah, Olah, hey (Olah, Olah, hey)
Rollin', rollin', rollin' with Kid 'n Play now
Olah, Olah, hey (Olah, Olah, hey)
Rollin', rollin', rollin' with Kid 'n Play now

Kool G Rap

Talk Like Sex

"Can't you dig it Honey?"
"Rated XXX"

For the ladies, one hundred and ninety-five pounds of beef
Chinky eyes, curly hair, and gold teeth
Swingin' with this here stud, you need practice
I'm leaving floods of blood on your mattress
I'll leave you holdin' your swollen backside and rollin'
Fillin' all three holes just like bowlin'
Don't ask me what the price is
But it's more than your battery-operated devices
And I come fully equipped
With a temperature adjustment to heat up the tip
For demonstrations, watch me slam her
You'll notice the sound of steady poundin
Like a jackhammer
Once on it, ya can't cop out
I'm poundin' ya down until your eyeballs pop out
I'm not your ordinary player
Because you'll leave in a wheelchair, dear, after I lay ya
Get a grip on your headboard and hold on to it
Or get sent right through it
Bite your nipples when I lick 'em
Not gentle when I stick 'em, huh
I'll leave 'em lookin' like a rape victim
Any girl who steps to it
Ends up gettin' their stomach pumped like Rod Stewart
I do a damn good job
That's why—
Chicks are on my dick like a human shish kebab

Only nineteen and over permitted
No matter how much young girls wanna be with it

_____

You ain't ready for the bed
You still got a pussy like Isaac Hayes' head
Come back in five years
When ya grow some hairs and when you started drinkin' beers
I'm hittin' hookers by the dozen
Makin' ya wetter 'cause I fuck better than your husband
Givin' ya girl back spasms
'Cause G Rap has 'em orgasm after orgasm
Change the sheets? Ya must be kiddin'
Ya gotta change the whole box spring
I ain't bullshittin'
You get hit with hysteria
'Cause I'm 'a bury a big one inside your private area
All hell is in your tush
When Kool G Rap push pushes inside this bush
Another homegirl flinches
But I got inches for all you little wenches
The letter G is better when it comes to the letter X
An' I'm 'a talk like sex
Rated XXX

"Can't you dig it Honey?"
"Rated XXX"

Some say that I'm nasty plus
Hookers are mad because they can't outlast me
Girl, you ain't too small
'Cause I turn your crystal to one size fits all
So if you're still confused when I'm screwin'
Let me explain to you exactly what I'm doin'
Exploring your body like a biologist
Inventin' new ways just like a scientist
Taggin' my name on your buns just like a printist
While I'm hurtin' your ass just like a dentist
You're so wild I feel like I'm a zoologist
Stretchin' your shit more than a gynecologist
I'm gonna twist your ass to death, miss
And when you piss, you'll see more stars than an astrologist
G Rap is hot blooded
Freakin' horny

Far from corny
Come and jump on me
I'm not small and all, I won't break down a stall
I drive the ass up the wall
Nuts and everything are well in shape
The only thing missin' on my dick is a cape
Let's get together, honey, ya never know what's next
And I'm 'a talk like sex
Rated XXX

"Can't you dig it Honey?"
"Rated XXX"

Big girls try to squash me
But I think with my dick, honey, so come and brainwash me
Hit the sack 'cause I ain't jokin'
'Cause when I start pumpin' shit up
I leave it smokin'
So ya better hold on tight all right
'Cause my dick is a brown stick of dynamite
A stick, a trick, and it kills her
I'm probably related to Long Dong Silver
But it gets gooder and gooder
Every time I grab a hooker and I put her on my frankfurter
Kiss your breasts to your navel and then I skip
'Cause the only thing I'm lickin' is your ass with a whip
And it's a real freaky scene
I'm hittin' girls with their heads in a guillotine
Why certainly I'm squirtin'
Bust your nut and get up and wipe my dick on your curtain
Pushin' your head to the pillow
And givin' more pleasure than a double-headed dildo
A big ass gives me a hard-on
But I fuck bitches with titties like Dolly Parton
Time or place doesn't matter to me, sweety
I'll fuck you on the "A" train while I write graffiti
In a restaurant, takin' you straight to heaven
In a cab or the back of 7–11
Whether you're white and the music you like is rock
You can come and get some hip-hop cock

Consider this dick on your clitoris
But never try to flex
'Cause I'm 'a talk like sex

K₀oL m₀e dee

Go See the Doctor

(Skeezer)
But three days later, go see the doctor
(Skeezer)

I was walkin' down the street, rockin' my beat
Clappin' my hands and stompin' my feet
I saw a little lady so neat and petite
She was so sweet, yes, I wanted to meet her
So I asked this lady could I take her out
We could wine and dine and talk about
The birds and the bees and my waterbed
And you can treat me like a Buddha and
Bow your head
We continued to talk and before you knew it
We were at my house and it was time to do it
As soon as I finished, I lost my poise
Ran outside and told all my boys
I said, "Listen up fellows, come over here, bust it"
They said, "Did you get it?" I said, "Yea" they said, "How was it"
The poontang was dope and you know that I rocked her
But three days later, go see the doctor
(Skeezer)

I rocked her to the left, rocked her to the right
She felt so good, hugged me so tight, I said, "Goodnight"
Three days later
Woke up fussin', yellin', and cussin'
Drip, drip, drippin' and pus, pus, pussin'

I went to the bathroom and said, "Mama mia"
I'm 'a kill that girl next time I see her
The madder I got, the more I reminisce
Why is my thing thing burnin' like this
Well I remember the first day I saw that girl
I just couldn't wait to rock her world
I said, "Hey good lookin', what you got cookin' "
What have I done, stuck my dick in
Now I know why her ex-boyfriend Dave
Calls her Misses Microwave
'Cause she was hotter than an oven and
I had to learn the hard way
Stay in a microwave too long, you get burned
But the poontang was dope and you know that I rocked her
But three days later, go see the doctor
(Skeezer)

I went to the doctor's office
I said, "What have I got?"
He said, "Turn around boy and take this shot"
I looked at him like he was crazy and
I said, "What? Ain't nobody stickin' nuttin' in my butt"
He turned and said in a real deep voice
"Have it your way if that's your choice
And now put it down if you want me to put it
But don't blame me if it turns into a foot
Extended from the middle of your body
And the next time you see a cute hotty
You won't be able to screw
The only thing you can do is just kick her
So go take karate"
As I turned around to receive my injection
I said, "The next time I'll use some protection"
If I see another girl and I get an erection
I'm walkin' in the other direction
'Cause I don't wanna do the sick sick dance
So I'm keepin' my prick inside my pants
And if I see another girl and I know I can rock her
Before I push up, I'll make her go see the doctor
(Skeezer)

KooL moe dee

Knowledge Is King

I'm not going—I'm gone
Up up up and away and I'm on
A higher plane with a brain with a flame
Feel the fire, desire the same
Knowledge and wisdom and understandin'
Possessed by God, transferred to man in
A script or a book or a scripture that looks
Like a biblical writing
Inviting a hook
Of a song, sing along with a strong subliminal
Message divesting all men from criminal
Acts of the devil, revealed and reveled
Designed to decline the mind to a lower level
Read the holy Qu'ran or the Bible
Because it's liable to be a revival
For the weak that seek power it'll bring
Insoluble power—
Knowledge is king

Now who wants some, come git it
A battle is a test of wits and I'm wit' it
Hard beats a torch and I lit it
Set the world on fire, I did it
Now that it feels good, I'm heatin' up
I feed off knowledge, and can't eat enough
'Cause knowledge is infinite, sucker's ain't into it
Ignorance is bliss and they're kin to it
They party and dance and they don't ever glance
At a book or a look for their mind to advance
Caught in the rut, chasin' butt
Tryin' to get a dollar or a nut
Evil feeds off a source of apathy
Weak in the mind and of course you have to be

Less than a man, more like a thing
No knowledge you're nothin'
Knowledge is king

My knowledge comes from a spiritual force
Stronger than any earthly source of
Propaganda, hype, or slander
I don't believe the hype, I understand the
Media dictates the mind and rotates
The way ya think
And syncopates slow pace
Brains can't maintain
Ascertain insipid inane crass vain
Insane lame traditions
All praise fame, positions
Want be a star, drive a big car
Live bourgeois and don't know who you are
Lost in the sauce and praisin' the dollar
Whether your faith is Christ or Allah
The knowledge of God'll teach one thing
The dollar is moot
Knowledge is king

My rhymes make a weak mind anorexic
You can't hang without slang so eject it
I've selected, rhymes for records
To affect the effect of a rhyme that left it
Hangin' like a pound
That can't come down
But ya hangin' in the brain so your brain is hell-bound
Lost and found by the serpent sound
What ya don't know can't hurt—that's profound
Absurd's a better word
An ignorant fool is a real kool nerd
Your pockets are fat with an empty head
Got a little bit of fame and a name and you're brain dead
You count your dollars so ya think you're in
Ya know how to count but ya don't know when
Add history today and it'll equal the future
Repetitive mistake because the brain ain't of the future

Need knowledge to understand the concept of sacrifice
But man don't understand so we have to fight
War, killin' people we never saw before
Some don't even know what they're killin' for
Followin' rulers instead of the prophets
The wicked can rule ya but knowledge can stop it
Souls can't be controlled 'cause it's a spiritual thing
But ya got to have knowledge
Knowledge is king
Knowledge is king

LL Cool J

Big Ole Butt

I was at the mall, sippin' on a milkshake
Playin' the wall, takin' a break
Admirin' the girls with the bamboo earrings
Baby hair and bodies built to swing
That's when I seen her
Her name was Tina
Grace and poise kinda like a ballerina
I said, "How you doin', my name's Big L
Don't ask me how I'm livin', 'cause, yo, I'm living swell
But then again I'm livin' kind of foul
'Cause my girl don't know that I'm out on the prowl"
To make a long story short, I got the digits
Calls her on my car phone and paid her a visit
I was spankin' her and thankin' her, chewin' her and doin' her
Laughin' 'cause my girl didn't know that I was screwin' her
Layin' like a king on sheets of satin
That's what time it is, you know what's happenin'
She had a big ole booty, I was doin' my duty
I mean, yo, I admit that my girl's a cutie
But Tina was exotic, Earl's my witness
With the kind of legs that put stockings out of business

When I went home, I kissed my girl on the cheek
But in the back of my mind it was this big butt freak
I sat my girl down, I couldn't hold it in
And said to her with a devilish grin . . .

TINA got a big ole butt
I know I told you I'd be true
But TINA got a big ole butt
So I'm leavin' you
TINA got a big ole butt
I know I told you I'd be true
But TINA got a big ole butt
So I'm leavin' you

I went to the high school about three o'clock
To try to catch a cutie ridin' my jock
My homeboy's jeep, the system blastin'
Cold forty dogs, smilin' and laughin'
Girls all over, the kind I adore
I felt like a kid in a candy store
That's when I seen her
Her name was Brenda
She had the kind of booty that I'd always remember
I said to my man, "Stop the jeep"
She's only seventeen but, yo, don't sleep
I kicked the bass like an NFL punter
And scoped the booty like a big game hunter
I said to the girl, "Yo, you look tired
Let's go get some rest, relax by the fire"
I put the big booty on a bearskin rug
She gave me a kiss, I gave her a hug
I said to the girl, "Them young boys ain't nothin'
You want to get freaky, let me kiss your belly button"
I circled it and teased it and made her squeal
Grabbed a pack of bullets and pulled out the steel
When I was through, I wiped the sweat from my eyes
Went to the kitchen and got some sweet potato pies
Tina busted in my house while I was eatin'
You know what I said
Too bad you caught me cheatin', but . . .

BRENDA got a big ole butt
I know I told you I'd be true
But BRENDA got a big ole butt
So I'm leavin' you
BRENDA got a big ole butt
I know I told you I'd be true
But BRENDA got a big ole butt
So I'm leavin' you

I went to Red Lobster for shrimp and steak
Around the time when the waitresses are on their lunch break
I pulled in the parkin' lot and parked my car
Somebody shouted out, "I don't care who you are"
I paid it no attention, I walked inside
Because Brian had a nine and he was chillin' in the ride
I walked in the place, everybody was lookin'
And shrimp and steak wasn't the only thing cookin'
I sat down to eat, ordered my food
I said to the waitress, "I don't mean to be rude
But I'll take you on a platter"
She said, "You got a girl," I said, "It don't matter
You look like you're tastier than a pipin' hot pizza
What's your name?" She said, "My tag says Lisa"
I said, "O.K., you're smart and all that
But when you get off work, yo, I'll be back"
She looked at me and said, "Make yourself clear
L, where we going?" I said, "Right here"
She looked kind of puzzled, I said, "You'll see"
I pulled up at ten on the D.O.T.
When she walked out the door, I threw my tongue down her throat
Pushed her back inside and pulled off her coat
Laid her on the table and placed my order
And gave her a tip much bigger than a quarter
On and on to the break 'a dawn
All over the restaurant, word is born
I heard somebody coughin', I checked my watch
I couldn't believe it said nine o'clock
I grabbed my pants, put on my Kangol
Who did I see, Oh, yo, it was Brenda
Yo, she worked at Red Lobster but I didn't remember

LISA got a big ole butt
I know I told you I'd be true
But LISA got a big ole butt
So I'm leavin' you
See ya
LISA got a big ole butt
I know I told you I'd be true
But LISA got a big ole butt
So I'm leavin' you
See ya

LL Cool J

Rock the Bells

Rumor has it that you're tired of my scratchin' and drums
And of course I wanna expand to the maximum
So I inject in one more element to that of L.L.
Came up with somethin' funky called Rock the Bells
During this episode vocally I explode
My title is the king of the FM mold
See, my volume expands to consume
And my structures emote a lyrical heirloom
Vocally pulsating, I initiate gyrating
Ya must respond to my bells, there's no waiting
For the duration, there's no articulation
Receiving ovation for the bell association
The vocalization techniques I employ
The voice of my shadow could take a toy boy
The injection of bells into this beat
The result—enough energy to amputate your feet
Greater insulator microphone dominator
My name is Cool J, manipulator innovator
Connoisseur, I'm sure my percussion will excite
These bells are gonna rock all night
Rock the bells

The bells make your energy escalate
A sort of musical fury L.L. might detonate
Subject matter entitled "The Bells"
The lyrical appraisement is by L.L.
My program strains the tympanic membrane
I've been ordained the BLZ I'll flame
Paragraphs I concoct, Cut Creator's like an organist
Cool J exists as a journalist
I illuminate over any number on the Richter
My throat contracts like a boa constrictor
You're totally engulfed by the structure and the format
It's not dormant, it goes to the core, man
As you repair, you'll say I went
To torture individuals for excitement
Ambassador, the fiend of Cordor
Dialect so def, it'll rip up the floor
Ignite and excite with verbal extensions
What I'll mention will put you on pension
Makin' you tremble, nothin' resemble
The bells and if it don't
I disassemble
Hit if you bit
I go have a fit
The master impresario of lyrical wit
A hip-hop creature, concert feature
Amateur teacher, my rhymes reach ya
When I commence with excellence
It eradicates levels of pestilence
Upon a plateau
No mortal can go
Mythological characters stand below
Rock the bells

A B-boy symphony complete with bells
No classical fanatic is parallel
From the design of my lyrics many people call me
An immortalized B-boy prodigy
Eeee a misdemeanor, cleaner women I subpoena
No conjecture in my lecture, name and adversary Gina
Promoter, my tune revolves like a rotor

Whilst I decode-a the cranium of Yoda
Rehearsing steadily, growing I sing tweeter, mid-range
And woofers need guarding
The bells rip your auditory canal
Plagiarism is suicide for then I shall
Be forced to assault
Our position will halt
Upset you with words
Drink your blood like it's a malt
Opposite of illusions ·
Evidently it's true
The beat metabolism supposed to accelerate you
Hallucinating severe convulsion
Your equilibrium is took from my propulsion
I came here tonight to rock
These bells will never stop
Rock the Bells

Ya livin' on my lines side
Autographs I sign
Inferior fan—recorder of my rhyme
Perfect spectator, well I'm the dominator
You reline and refine, it and you save it for later
Swipe it as you type it
You recite it as you bite it
Then you claim it as your own to get them excited
About it as you shout it
You don't tell them how got it
And you repeat it and rock it
Multiply it, divide it, ya even sit inside it
It's L.L.'s rhyme, I know ya wanna bite
You announce, I pounce, destroy, annihilate
If you break, you'll be straight when I eliminate
You sonny like scholars and you write 'em on your collars
You'll bomb and you'll try before a million dollars
I get like a leopard, attack, ransack, disturb, cold crush
Use a line, I make 'em hush
The lovers in the taker, faker, lovers of the Lakers, simulator
Rap traitor, perfect perpetrator
To see ya as you bit the words

You'd think you never heard
The mike sings like a hummin' bird
Rock the Bells

Jack the Ripper
King Hercules
Professor of Death in the Seven Seas
Grim reaper of rhyme
Holder of the rock
Eradicating suckers all around the clock
The supreme machine
A microphone dream
My revenge is brutal when you start to scheme
I mean, you're my adversary, I enjoy the few
The Peruvian rock, cocaine or quaalude
The story, the beginning of your death is heard
But your cries are ignored by the kind of word
I'm the super insane murderer in the rain
Like a vampire goin' for your jugular vein
Exterminating crews with my manuscript
And the best thing you wrote was a bunch of bullshit
The night of the nights
You're my victim tonight
You ain't nothin' nobody so get outta any sight
Bein' crushed by the source
It's reinforced (thoughts)
Now ya feel remorse 'cause ya know who's boss
L.L. Cool J is your undertaker
Def hit-maker plus a bone-breaker
Treble terminator, bass mutilator
You can drop your drawers, I'm a rapper castrator
On the microphone you will never recoup
When I'm finished with you, boy, you'll be suckin' on soup
Music virtuoso, melodical employer
I knew you was a sucker, first time I saw ya
Roll the red carpet, royalty's arrived
Don't try to fight back 'cause you won't survive
So don't never ever in any kind of weather
Try to mess with the tall young legend in leather
L.L. servin' 'em well

The beat elevates and the scratch excels
Rock the Bells

laqllan

Imprison the President

Imprison the President
Incarcerate the Congress
Levitate the Pentagon (Now we're making progress)

A Senate seat, what a feat to beat
Four mil until you buy the seat
Illicit contributions
Political prostitution
Looking for that fix
Peddle influence until it sticks
Are they funds or are they bribes
I'm talkin' about the Keating Five
The Senators are gettin' paid off
So Lincoln won't get laid off
The banks are bankrupt
The Congress corrupt
What I don't get is the Federal bet
Two hundred billion in debt
Damn that's enough to get a nigger upset
What I'm stating is incriminating evidence
Imprison the President

Imprison the President
Incarcerate the Congress
Levitate the Pentagon (Now we're making progress)

Congress spoke, slaveowners wrote
A joke if you ask my folks
All men are created and stated equal
Then contemplated

Best-seller fiction to the people
Yo, I can't wait to read the sequel
The people tell me this is phony
Give me your testimony, homey
They had to use, abuse, a low blow
1990 and still flying Jim Crow
Using Willie Horton for the fight
Frighten whites on election night
A thousand points of light, right
The glare is bright and there's still no sight
Remember 83 in Panama?
A tip and trip from the drug czar
A summit with Bush and Noriega
Classic coke is what they gave ya
Fly 'em in via CIA
Chumped from up above as they say
Start a war, yo, what the hell for
Take him out, he won't talk no more
What I'm stating is incriminating evidence
Imprison the President

Imprison the President
Incarcerate the Congress
Levitate the Pentagon (Now we're making progress)

I dis, dismiss what I choose to lose
The attitude is funk it while I'm swinging the blues
Self-worth ain't worth shit
While I'm staring down a big black federal pit
You know Reagan can break the law
Live another day to make a score
Phony cronies steal from HUD
Iran-contra, political mud
Who can respect the legal system
When any Senator can put the fix in
Every Congressman gets his licks in
And in the White House still sits Dick Nixon
False prophets and demagogues
Living large while the people starve
Famous speeches can't do jack

When down the block you're under attack
Preach hatred, preach salvation
Fifteen secs, a media sensation
Go ahead, juice the poets of revolution
Now's the time for some hard solutions
So many answers lie in yourself
So don't go following someone else
Learn and teach your own damn evidence
Imprison the President

Imprison the President
Incarcerate the Congress
Levitate the Pentagon (Now we're making progress)

*Lea*d*ers* of the New Sch*o*o*l*

Case of the PTA

It's just another case of that old PTA

In school I wrote notes, and took quotes from Shakespeare
And other types of rhymes to show you that I care
From things like "together forever" to "you're my only one" (Only
      one)
It was special, I can say it was a loving one
You would say someone's knocking at my window (knock, knock)
Someone's ringing my bell (ding dong)
It's about two in the morning
Hey, Yo D, what the hell is going on?

It's just another case of that old PTA

But nevertheless it goes to show my potential
And even though our love was three-dimensional
One (me) two (you) three (yer pops) now what am I to do?
I had to transform into an educated lad
Going around doing chores for your dad

Playing a duck, wearing sweaters and shoes
Chilling with pop, just listen to the blues
And talking with your mom about my love for her daughter
Suggesting to me that I just oughta
Watch myself (inch by inch)
Watch myself (and use some sense)
So I did (hey) it didn't do a damn thing
But they still complain so now I sing

It's just another case of that old PTA

Buster Rhymes, the mighty infamous
Always misbehaving and mischievous
Causing aggravation, I'll never pause
Pushing out spit balls through plastic straws (in class)
Until I got caught at last
For lighting up the courtyard grass
Hey teacher, teacher don't try to flex
Buster Rhymes is about to get a complex
Hey, yo, in class, kicked it to this girl Cheryl (word)
The teacher tried to throw me a referral (no, no, no)
But not with detention, no, nor with suspension
All trials wicked and wild, they carry ill styles
Teacher jets to Nynex to talk to my mommy
When she gets home, she's going to wail the body
I hate this relationship to mom and teacher
When she reaches home, hey yo, she knows how to reach ya
OK of today, I am the new school prey
Between my mom, my teacher, and my dad
Hey, yo

It's just another case of that old PTA

Yo, teachers hate me, the girls don't date me
Because I'm C. Brown, class clown
Yet in still, sometimes I chill, yo
Depending on the day and how I feel
Sometimes I'd leave an apple that's rotten and brown
Nowhere to be found
Thumbtacks on seats, five days a week

A riot in the lunchroom, I got ta get some sleep
But I didn't do it (you did it)
I'm suspended (you was with it)
And now it's time to pay for the crime that I never got caught
Like Judge Wapner (Bam, take him to court)
A room of teachers, parents, and preachers
A principal and one kid dressed in sneakers
Case of Brown versus the Board, "Order Order"
Yo, twelve versus one is a slaughter
So I pleaded my case (ahh) face-to-face (ahh)
It was a waste and everyone was in place
Pronounced me guilty, you have 364 days
Of detention to serve, some nerve
I felt dissed, good grief I'm pissed
The head of the board said, "Case dismissed"
As I walk out the room, I heard them say
(Ay ya) (Oh man oh man)

It's just another case of that old PTA

Lifer's Group

The Real Deal

This is Maxwell Melvins, aka 66064
V.P. of the Lifer's Group, help keep our membership low
Now we're gonna give you the real deal

I wake up every morning in the face of a cop
Because I used to take the nine and go (POP POP POP)
So now I'm in prison and yo it's like apartheid
Modernized slavery, straight to the genocide
See some punk locked up to get beat down
Raped down, 'til his booty is broke down
Without a sound, the way he was found
Was in a night gown and his booty was blood bound

Mortified, of AIDS he died
I seen a brother do a suicide because his mother died
Lost all his pride, and couldn't run and hide
I was horrified, can you even visualize
Locked and stocked, no boots to knock
With every female cop cold sweatin' my jock
But as soon as you push up, they put you in lock-up
It's like a set-up, and jimmy is fed up

This is the real deal

Since '75 to 1990
The Lifer's Group's always been behind me
'Cause doin' this time is hard on my mind
Cryin' wasted tears for doin' these years
So man in the blue, what must I do
Bein' behind bars for breakin' two laws
When I came to prison, I was scared as hell
A brother came to me and said I looked very swell
He said I remind him of a fag he sold
For a pack of cigarettes and a Tootsie Roll
My heart was poundin' my blood was cold
But bein' a fag wasn't in my soul
I dropped my lock in a sock
And beat the fucker down the cell block
Five C.O.s to me to the hole
Said, "Knowledge born, WE'RE IN CONTROL"

This is the real deal, suckers

Bein' incarcerated isn't no joke
The strong survive and the weak get broke
Just like a bone if they can't hold their own
And stand strong, they won't last long
In jail because a cell is hell
The system smells and the food tastes stale
So don't be dumb and come, motherfuck crime
'Cause once you cross that line, you're gonna do time
Until they give you a date
But 'til then, you belong to the state

Countin' my days, the many ways
That my mind has phased, it's just a haze
Of black, to be exact, it's hard to keep track
Life and death go together forever and ever
Got a letter, parole board refused
Said I ain't paid my dues, I got the blues

Still, this is the real deal

Oof, another blow from the truth
A nap in the penitentiary, for half a century
Look through the bars, see muscles in big shirts
Give you a week, and you'll be wearin' a wig, jerk
Thought it was funny, well chuckle while your knees buckle
Suddenly the woman inside you unfolds
Hmm, somebody plays with your butt hole
Queer in a year, give up the gear, when you're here
Plus them new shoes, 'cause brother, it's bad news
If you try to play rough dude
Watch ya fess y'all, when ya step in the mess hall
Grab a seat to eat, oops you got beat
'Cause it's a hard life without no sharp knife
You gotta have might to fight, just to live your life
Wanna relax here, but they say, "Nah G"
'Cause on your spare time, you'll be doin' laundry

(Break)

Six in the morning, all I hear is a bell
I thought it was a dream, but no, I'm in jail
Committed a crime and boy, did I fail
21–7 they got me locked in a cell
Prisoner, convict, I will destroy ya
Notorious bank robber, I'm comin' for ya
Too bad, too evil, and I will deceive ya
Inside a penitentiary there is no equal
No wrong, no right, and I'll kill with a knife
Ya wanna come to prison boy, I might take your life
You're just a vice in my style, so ya better think twice
'Cause I'm annoyed, irritated, and here for a fight

Everytime I walk around, I see another brother with life
You're just a dumb little idiot and you can't see the light
So keep out the system, stay a man, and be free
If not, young brother, you come here with me

The real deal (*break*)

I got banged up, stitched up, shut up, word up
I'm fed up, I'm doin' time in lock-up
In the hole, handcuffed to a toilet bowl
I took a fall by the wall, indeed I had to crawl
And when I got up, I tried to make collect calls
To the crib, 'cause I'm doin' a bid
But I wanna leave a message to all the young kids
Black out, I'm strapped, and I don't smoke crack
Dope fiends, Dr. King had a dream
That we would grow up and work together as a team
Crooks, lock 'em up by the book
I'm not buggin' and muggin', sellin' drugs is forbidden
Young, dumb punks, don't come to Rahway Prison
'Cause the drugs is the enemy, believe me, I'm talkin'
Jail is hell and a cell is a coffin
Made of steel
This is the real deal

That's how it is in here, man

M.C. Hammer

Here Comes the Hammer

CHORUS: Uh-oh uh-oh uh-oh uh-oh uh-oh uh-oh
Here comes the Hammer
Uh-oh uh-oh uh-oh uh-oh uh-oh uh-oh
Here comes the Hammer

This—this is a mission that I'm on
Taking out the weak on the microphone
I'm hyped
So, don't talk about the hard-hitting Hammer when you can't
    even walk
On the stage
After me
And if ya do, yo, I got a 'tastrophe
Happens just like that
I rock 'em all from white to black
Oh-oh-oh! Bust it

Here comes the Hammer
Uh-oh uh-oh uh-oh uh-oh uh-oh uh-oh
Here comes the Hammer

Huh-oh huh-oh huh-oh Huh-oh huh-oh huh-oh
Huh-oh huh-oh huh-oh Huh-oh huh-oh huh-oh

"Naw, naw"
Is what I said
When I came to see your show
I looked and it was dead
Dead
You know like a body in the ground will your show ever grow?
Let me know
If not, then close your mouth because your show ain't hot
It needs work
Like a car in a wreck
They call me Hammer, you've got to earn my respect
Oh-oh-oh! Yeah

Here comes the Hammer
Uh-oh uh-oh uh-oh uh-oh uh-oh uh-oh
Here comes the Hammer

Huh-oh huh-oh huh-oh Huh-oh huh-oh huh-oh
Huh-oh huh-oh huh-oh Huh-oh huh-oh huh-oh

Let's make it smooth—Rrruh
Let's make it smooth—Rrruh
Let's make it smooth—Rrruh
Let's make it smooth—Rrruh

I don't hesitate
Or wait
Before the bell rings I'm out the gate
And rolling out for mine
Working so hard for such a long time
And life—is here and gone
So, hail to the Hammer
While I'm watching the throne
Not a king, just feelin' hyped
You dance to the music while I'm on the mike
Oh-oh-oh! Here we go

Here comes the Hammer
Uh-oh uh-oh uh-oh uh-oh uh-oh uh-oh
Here comes the Hammer

Huh-oh huh-oh huh-oh Huh-oh huh-oh huh-oh
Huh-oh huh-oh huh-oh Huh-oh huh-oh huh-oh

Let's make it smooth—Rrruh
Let's make it smooth—Rrruh
Let's make it smooth—Rrruh
Let's make it smooth—Rrruh
Bust it!

A minute or two
And I'm rolling
A whole new style that the people are holding
On—to, I move I groove I rap you're through
You're so plain
Just plain
Your ego's so big that you missed the whole train
And game

My friend, the people wanted more that's why the Hammer's in
Oh-oh-oh! Yeah

Here comes the Hammer
Uh-oh uh-oh uh-oh uh-oh uh-oh uh-oh
Here comes the Hammer

Huh-oh huh-oh huh-oh Huh-oh huh-oh huh-oh
Huh-oh huh-oh huh-oh Huh-oh huh-oh huh-oh

Let's make it smooth—Rrruh
Let's make it smooth—Rrruh
Let's make it smooth—Rrruh
Let's make it smooth—Rrruh

Check me out
Move on the floor and get hyped
You came to get with it and this is your night
Yeah, let 'em know
The cool, the hard, the fly, ho
We're in here
And it's pumping
Hammer's in the speaker and you know the base is pumping loud
And low
It's about that time, so here we go
Oh-oh-oh!
Bust it!

Here comes the Hammer
Uh-oh uh-oh uh-oh uh-oh uh-oh uh-oh
Here comes the Hammer

Huh-oh huh-oh huh-oh Huh-oh huh-oh huh-oh
Huh-oh huh-oh huh-oh Huh-oh huh-oh huh-oh

Let's make it smooth—Rrruh
Let's make it smooth—Rrruh
Let's make it smooth—Rrruh
Let's make it smooth—Rrruh
Bust it!

M.C. Hammer

U Can't Touch This

U can't touch this
U can't touch this
U can't touch this
U can't touch this

My-my-my-my (U can't touch this) music hits me
So hard
Makes me say, "oh my Lord
Thank you for blessing me
With a mind to rhyme and two hyped feet"
It feels good
When you know you're down
A superdope homeboy from the Oaktown
And I'm known
As such
And this is a beat—uh!
U can't touch

I told you homeboy
U can't touch this
Yeah, that's how we livin' and you know
U can't touch this
Look in my eyes, man
U can't touch this
Yo, let me bust the funky lyrics
U can't touch this

Fresh new kicks
And pants
You got it like that now you know you wanna dance
So move
Out of your seat
And get a fly girl and catch this beat

While it's rolling
Hold on
Pump a little bit and let 'em know it's going on
Like that
Like that
Cold on a mission so fall on back
Let 'em know
That you're too much
And this is a beat
They can't touch

Yo! I told you
U can't touch this
Why you standing there, man?
U can't touch this
Yo, sound the bells, school is in, sucker
U can't touch this
Give me a song
Or rhythm
Making 'em sweat
That's what I'm giving 'em
Now they know
You talk about the Hammer, you're talking about a show
That's hyped
And tight
Singers are sweating so pass them a wipe or a tape
To learn
What it is going to take in the '90s to burn
The charts
Legit
Either work hard or you might as well quit

That's the word, because you know
U can't touch this
U can't touch this

Break it down.

Stop . . . Hammer time

Go with the flow
It is said
That if you can't groove to this
Then you probably are dead
So wave
Your hands in the air
Bust a few moves, run your fingers through your hair
This is it
For a winner
Dance to this an' you're gonna get thinner
Move
Slide your rump
Just for a minute, let's all do the bump
Bump bump bump

Yeah, U can't touch this
Look man, U can't touch this
You better get hyped, boy 'cause you know ya can't
U can't touch this
Ring the bell, school's back in
Break it down

Stop. Hammer time

U can't touch this
U can't touch this
U can't touch this
U can't touch this
Break it down

Stop. Hammer time

Every time you see me
The Hammer's just so hyped
I'm dope on the floor
And I'm magic on the mike
Now why would I ever
Stop doing this?
When others making records

That just don't hit
I've toured around the world
From London to the Bay
It's Hammer, go Hammer, M.C. Hammer, Yo Hammer
And the rest can go and play
Can't touch this

U can't touch this
U can't touch this
U can't touch this
Yeah, U can't touch this
I told you, U can't touch this
Too hype, can't touch this
Yo, we outta here, can't touch this

M. c. Lyte

I Cram to Understand U (Sam)

I used to be in love with this guy named Sam
I don't know why 'cause he had the head like that of a clam
But you couldn't tell me nothing 'cause Sam was number one
'Cause to me, oh my Gosh, he was one in a million
I shoulda knew the consequences right from the start
That he use me for my money and then break my heart
But like a fool in love, I fell for his game
But I got mine so I show no shame
In Empire he winked his eye and then he kept walking
All of those who live in Brooklyn know just what I'm talking
The roller disco where we all used to go
And just to have some fun back in 1981
You know the place, Empire Boulevard
Is where I first saw the nigga and he tried to play hard
But I knew the deal 'cause I knew his brother Jerry
And Sam, he just broke up with his girlfriend Terry
So Jerry introduced Sam and I that night

He said, "Hello my name is Sam"
I said, "Hi my name is Lyte"
We dip and we dap and we chit and we chat
About this and that, from sneakers to hats
He said, "Look, I'm in the mood for love
Simply because you're near me
(Let's go) to my house
Lay back and get nice
Watch television, a Riunite on ice"
I said, "A slow down, I know you wanna shake me down
But I'm not one of the girls to go ripping round"

Just like a test
J-Just like a test
Just like a test
I cram to understand U

Next month I finally went to his house
I walked into the door, there was a girl on the couch
I said, "A who's the frog
The bump on the log
You chump, you punk
How could you do me wrong
Singing sad songs about your love was so strong"
You said, "Wait Lyte
You're confused, the girl is my cousin"
Your brother agreed but later said that she wasn't

Just like a test
J-Just like a test
Just like a test
I cram to understand U

Forgotten next month, we went to the deuce
Well, I thought it kinda strange that you had lots of juice
You knew the dopes, the pushers, the addicts, everybody
Ask you how you met them
You said you met 'em at a party
Then these girls tried to tell me you were selling the stuff
I said, "It's not your business so shut the fuck up"

They said, "Oh, ok Lyte, think what you wanna think
But it's gonna be some shit when your man becomes a bum"
I said, "Look, go bust a move, I don't even know you
To put it Lyte, I really don't care to"
They got kinda mad and sort of offended
They said, "We only looking out for yo' best interest"
I said, "Thanks but no thanks" in an aggravated tone
When I wanna find out I find out on my own

Just like a test
J-Just like a test
Just like a test
I cram to understand U

Then my cousin said she saw you with this lady named C
I'm clawing my thoughts, I wonder who she could be
You're spending all your time with her
And not a second with me
They say you spend your money on her
And you're with her night and day
Her name starts with a C and ends with a K
I strain my brain looking for a name to fit this spelling
But I just couldn't do it 'cause my heart kept yelling
Burning, begging for affection from you, Sam
But just like a test I cram to understand U
Thought I knew you well enough to call you a man

Just like a test
J-Just like a test
Just like a test
I cram to understand U

Then it came time, you started looking kinda thin
I asked you why you said, "Exercise, trying stay slim"
I bought it, even though I knew it was a lie
'Cause it really didn't matter, you were still looking fly
But oh no, oh no
You started asking me for money
Butter me up, beg me, and called me your honey
So I gave you two yards

And then I gave you one more
You picked up your jacket and you flew out the door
You came back an hour later
And you asked me for a quarter
I said, "I only got a twenty"
You said, "give me that then"
I said, "Nope, I'll tell you now
You better stop slobbing
Find you a job or you better start robbing"
So I stepped off with a giant step
Picked up my belongings and I just left
So now I see you in Empire every Sunday
Juicing the girls up for some money and a lay
But every time I see you doing it
I just ruin it
Tell them how ya on crack
Smoke, sniff, or chewing it
And as for this girl Miss C, oh well
I was shocked as hell
When I heard, Samuel
When your homeboys told me
I almost went wack
That the girl you was addicted to, her name was crack!

Just like a test
J-Just like a test
Just like a test
I cram to understand U

M.C. sm00th

Smooth & Legit

Sometimes all it takes is a sip of Moet
To make me pick up my pen and then my mind gets wet
And then I inject the rhyme that you select

So your mind do protect
Because I'm well kept
Some say I will juice
When my mind gets loose
With the rhymes I produce
But I will induce pain
Still it remains the same
Smooth's the name
I'm a V.I.P. with an M.B.A.
Very bright attitude
A body I will include
Nor shall I exclude
That I will soothe
But now I will prove
That I am Smooth
So give attention
Where it's deserved
So when I get old
My rhymes you will preserve
Like candy
So sweet, I taste
Mouth watering with no time to waste
I never been conceited but I knew what was up
Five-foot-three, built to a tee
Anxious for reality, the best in actuality
So get off my tip 'cause I'm Smooth
And definitely legit
I ain't having it
'Cause I'm Smooth and definitely legit

Yo, it doesn't matter
If I scatter
I serve my rhymes on a silver platter
So sit down
And listen closely
As I again start to boast, see
But then mostly
I play it pro, see
'Cause I'm the S, the M, the double O-T
To the H, see

Will you peep my new strategy?
Yeah, I weigh 140
But that's not much
'Cause it's pound for pound
But then punch for punch
The tip I'm on, yeah it's Smooth
Now I'm on and ready to prove
The time I invest it will be blessed
'Cause I pray every night but then I brush with Crest
I'm not from the East but I am from the West
The S plus my J
Yeah, I am strong and I am on my way
So yo, get off my tip
'Cause I'm Smooth and definitely legit
I ain't having it
'Cause I'm smooth and definitely legit

I never worry about a man
I got my own
And him I do own
And that is prone
I state that clearly on the m-i-c phone
Yeah the mike you must smoke like a pipe
And when I'm done
You'll know I'm not quite
Through but true
I thought you knew that the rhyme is mine
Just like time is mine
And when I'm on the mike, yeah, it's all divine
Until ya find
That it'll all combine
New Jacks I'm gonna play
With your mind
'Cause you're a New Jack, ya like to be exact
Ya just react to the crowd
Yeah, the pack
When I'm on the stage
Believe that
If your head aches, Smooth will relieve that
Well, are you pissed?

Well, come get some of this
So you could get dissed and like I said, I don't miss
'Cause I'm crisp like a dollar bill
Oh yeah, a meal
More filled as I hit and instill
'Cause I'm B.A.D.
Yeah, that's me
I'm just as bad
As I could be
But I'm mostly sexy
But I'm built to a tee
'Cause I'm Smooth
An equipped cutie
No, I'm not picky, are you ready for a quicky?
A battle, naw, it won't be quick
'Cause after this, you'll all be on a dis tip
So what, do you want some of this?
'Cause I'm 'a tell you exactly where to find me
I'm the queen of 1990
My rhymes are clear but also thrive, see
'Cause I'm taking charge
Living large
So don't barge
On my time when I start to motivate
And on your mind, yeah, I think I'll demonstrate
'Cause I could be teacher
Or like a preacher
Sit on down as I start to deceit ya
'Cause your mind's equipped for one thing
But not for the dope rhymes Smooth sings
So, yo, get off my tip
'Cause I'm Smooth and definitely legit
I ain't havin' it
'Cause I'm Smooth and definitely legit

Main Source

Just a Friendly Game of Baseball

Awwww shit, another young brother hit
I better go over to my man's crib and get the pump
'Cause to the cops, shooting brothers is like playing baseball
And they're never in a slump
I guess when they shoot up a crew, it's a grand slam
And when it's one, it's a home run
But I'm 'a be ready with a wild pitch
My finger got a bad twitch plus I wanna switch
Sides and step up to the batter's box
Fuck red and white, I got on black sox
But let 'em shoot a person from the white sox, what's the call?
Foul ball
Babe Ruth would've make a good cop but he didn't
Instead he was a bigot, dig it
My life is valuable and I protect it like a gem
Instead of cops shooting me, I'm going out shooting them
And let 'em cough up blood like phlegm
It's grim, but dead is my antonym
And legally they can't take a fall
Yo, check it out, it's just a friendly game of baseball

R.B.I.—real bad injury
But don't get happy, you're in jail for a century
Just as bad as being shot in the groin
To see who'll shoot you, they'll flip a coin
And watch you run for the stretch
But you don't know the man is at home waiting to make the
    catch
So the outfielder guns you down
You're out, off to the dugout, underground
I know a cop that's savage, his pockets stay green like cabbage
'Cause he has a good batting average
No questions, just pulls out the flamer

And his excuses get lamer
Once a brother tried to take a lead
But they shot him in his face saying he was trying to steal a base
And people watch the news for coverage on the game
And got the nerve to complain
They need to get themselves a front row seat
Or save the baseline for a beat
'Cause hellivision just ain't designed for precision y'all
It's just a friendly game of baseball

A brother caught on but I don't know where the brother went
The umpires are the government
I guess they kicked him out the game and replaced him with a
     pinch hitter
And the scam, he was quitter
So the cops usually torment, I mean tournament
Win 'em, I was saying
You can't let the umpires hear you speaking bad
Or like the other kid, you won't be playing
'Cause they'll beat you 'til your ass drop
A walking gun with a shell in his hand is their mascot
When you run around, let it be noted
Step lightly, the bases are loaded
My man got out from three strikes, in the skull
But the knife he was carrying was dull
Instead of innings, we have endings
What a fine way to win things
And hot dog vendors have fun
Selling you the cat, rat, and dog on a bun
And when you ask, "What is all of this called?"
It's just a friendly game of baseball

"You low-lifes.
You take that! And that! And that!
I'm here to protect and serve
And that's exactly what I'm gonna do."

Main Source

Lookin' at the Front Door

We fight every night, now that's not kosher
I reminisce with bliss of when we was closer
And wake up to be greeted by an argument again
You act like you're ten
So immature, I try to concentrate on a cure
And keep lookin' at the front door
Thinkin' if I were to evacuate
You'd probably be straighter than straight
And wouldn't have so much hate
'Cause you don't know the pain I feel when I see you smilin'
And when I roll up you start wilin'
So I front like everything's hunky-dory
But it's a whole different story
You don't like the fact that I'm me
I don't put on a show
When it comes time for you to have company
And your friends don't understand your choice of man
They speak proper while my speech is from a garbage can
But regardless, you shouldn't have to be so raw
I'm lookin' at the front door

I'm lookin' at the front door
Baby, I'm lookin' at the front door
I'm lookin' at the front door

And when you're with your friends, I glide to the side
Until the spotlight is mine and never sabotage a good time
But when they're not around, the fights commence
I'm the one you're against and it doesn't make sense
'Cause I'm the one that you claim to love for life
But all I get is gray hairs and strife
And I can play some ole stuck-up rapper role
And get foul every time you lose control

But that's not my order of operations
So I should win an award for lots of patience
'Cause that's all a fella can have
With a girl who's shootin' up his world like Shaft
And I don't think that I can take it anymore
I'm lookin' at the front door

My friends always tell me how I'm lucky to possess
The best looking girl in the whole U.S.
But every time you scream, you blow your finesse
Tryin' to dis the Profess—
Or twenty-four hours of acting sore
Sometimes I wish you'd come down with lockjaw
So I don't have to take in the breakin'
You treat me like a burnt piece of bacon
It seems like just two years
Back when we were bonded and not pierced
But now I keep itchin' to jet
Sittin' in the chair just to stare, set to sprint
Yo, sweetheart, you better take a hint
I say it now like I said it before
I'm lookin' at the front door

MelloW Man AcE

Mentirosa

Ain't got nobody (baby)

(Baby) (When I come home)
Check this out, baby, *tenemos tremendo lio*
Last night you didn't go
A la casa de tu tio
(I'm getting tired)
Resulte ser, hey, you were at a party
Higher than the sky

Emborrachaba de Baccardi
(No I wasn't) I bet you didn't know
Que conocia al cantinero
(What?)
He told me you was drinking
And wasting my *dinero*
Talking about come and enjoy
What a woman gives a *hombre*
(But first of all, *sí*, I have to know your *nombre*)
Now I really want to ask you
Que si es verdad (Would I lie?)
And please, *por favor*
Tell me *la verdad*
Because I really need to know, yeah
Necesito entender
If you're gonna be a player
Or be my *mujer*
'Cause right now you're just a liar
A straight *mentirosa*
(Who me?)
Today you tell me something
Y mañana otra cosa

Ain't got nobody (Baby)
(Baby) (When I come home)
(Lord knows you gotta change)

I remember the day
Que tu me decia
Time and time again
Que tu me queria (I do)
And at the time, hey
Yo te creia
Porque no sabia
That you were a *relambia*
Yo with *fulanito y menganito*
Joseito y Fernandito
Larry and Joey
Y Vinnie's brother *Chico* (Uh-huh)
Mucho quefletera

That's a straight skeezer
Si quiere un pedacito (baby)
Go her way 'cause she's a pleaser
But I'll tell ya straight up
Porque brother *me di de cuenta*
That on Main Street
Her *cuerpo estaba a la venta*
Now get some *el que quiera*
Get some *cualquira*
Hey yo, she don't care, man
She's a *tremenda fiera*
Yeah, you're hot to trot
And out to get what I got
Pero ya que te conozco
What I got, she gets not
'Cause you're just a *mentirosa*
Con tu lengua venemosa
Today you tell me something
Y mañana otra cosa
(Lord knows you got to change, baby)

Girl, I can't believe you
You know my mother's talking about me
My friends are talking about me
Not me, about you
(About me?)
You ain't nothing but a skeezer
(A skeezer? Don't be calling me no skeezer)
Tremenda fletora mami, sí (uh-huh)
La verdad (*eso es lo que te cries*)
I bet you go to church and you're scared to confess
(No I do confess baby, I do confess, yeah)
Do you tell the truth though?
(Yeah I do) Yeah right (Do you?)
Yeah, you're nothing but a skeezer
You know what, I got some other stories to say about you
It goes like this (Baby)

Un dia estaba en tu casa y
Ring! There goes the phone

Rocojiste y dijiste
(Call me back, I'm not alone)
El queria tu direccion
Yeah, just your address
Y antes que colgaste
And before you hung up
(Give me your address)
¡Ay Alabeo! ¡Que Descarada!
Is what ran through my mind
So I said, "let's go out tonight"
She said ("we go out all the time")
¡Alabeo! man, *ella no sabia*
De yo, I knew her plan
De que iba a salir
With that other man
So I told the girl in Spanish
I said, "Hey, *ya me voy*"
(*¿Pero porque?*)
'Cause you ain't treating me
Like I'm some sucker toy
'Cause who needs you anyway?
(I need you)
Con tu lengua venemosa
(*No te vayas meno, no te vayas te necesito*)
Today you tell me something
Y mañana otra cosa
Mentirosa
Ain't got nobody

Monie Love
Monie in the Middle

Brother, what is with you?
You can't take a hint?
I need to shove a splint between your eyes

For you to see you and me were never meant to be
Your homeboy likes me, I like him to
Get out the picture
I get your point but I'm not rolling with the punch
I scrunched up the letter you wrote me in lunch
In fifth period, I paid no notice to your motion
My work is on the table
My pen's in locomotion
Every time I turn around, you're looking in my face
I try to ignore you
The bell rings, I race out the room, zoom
To another room, sit down, what d'ya know?
The lover's in town
The other brother (who?)
The one I wish to talk to
Sitting three seats back and I'm 'a walk over to him
And give him the letter I wrote
Because my feelings towards him are brewing, ya know?

Monie in the middle (where's she at?) in the middle, yo
Monie's in the middle (where that at?) in the middle
Monie in the middle (where's she at?) in the middle
Go, Mo Mo what is she? Monie in the middle

In seventh the knucklehad walks in and sits down beside me
I said, "Yo, why you try'na ride me?"
Day in, day out, I can't seem to get you off my back
What do you think that I should do about that?
In fact it's embarrassing, what a baffoon
You even follow me in the ladies' bathroom
Give me a break, I can't take it, the stakes are too high
Besides, there goes the other brother
I'm not Keith Sweat, so don't sweat me
The other brother's smooth approach is what gets me
He intrigues the Mo, you know
So I suggest the course, toward me you blow
You're wasting time pursuing Monie
'Cause she's pursuing the lover only
And as my mother dear, she told me
Go for what you know Mo, yo

Monie in the middle (where's she at?) in the middle, yo
Monie's in the middle (where that at?) in the middle
Monie in the middle (where's she at?) in the middle
Go, Mo Mo what is she? Monie in the middle

Bringing matters to a close and everybody knows
That I'm no longer in the middle
I've made my decision precisely, precision is a must
For me to solve another riddle
Stepping to a brand new rhythm ism-skisms
Nope I'm not with 'em, I give him
My undivided attention, you know what I'm saying?
No type of games I'm playing when

Monie in the middle (where's she at?) in the middle, yo
Monie's in the middle (where that at?) in the middle
Monie in the middle (where's she at?) in the middle
Go, Mo Mo what is she? Monie in the middle

Naughty By Nature

Ghetto Bastard

Some get a little and some get none
Some catch a bad one
And some leave the job half done
I was one who never had and always mad
Never knew my dad, motherfuck the fag
Well anyway, I did pick-ups, flipped then clipped up
Seen many stick-ups 'cause niggers had the trigger hiccups
I couldn't get a job, nappy hair was not allowed,
My mother couldn't afford us all, she had to throw me out
I walked the strip with just a clip, who wanna hit?
They got 'em quick, I had to eat, this money's good as spent
I threw in braids, I wasn't paid enough
I kept 'em long 'cause I couldn't afford a haircut

I got laughed at, I got chumped, I got dissed
I got upset, I gotta tech and a banana clip
Was down ta throw the lead ta any dealin' tackhead
I still'll been broke so a lotta good it would 'a did
Or done, if not for bad luck I wouldn't have none
Why did I have to live the life of such a bad one,
Why when I was a kid and played I was the sad one
And always wanted ta live like this or that one

Everything's gonna be all right (all right)

A ghetto bastard, born next to the projects
Livin' in the slums wit bums askin' now why, Treach
Do I have ta be like this?
Mama said I'm priceless
So why am I worthless? starvin' is just what bein' nice gets
Sometimes I wish I could afford a pistol then though
To stop the hell, I would 'a ended things a while ago
I ain't have jack but a black hat and napsack
War scars, stolen cars and a black jack
Drop that and now you want me to rap and give
Say somethin' positive, well positive ain't where I live
I live right around the corner from West Hell
Two blocks from South Shit and once in a jail cell
The sun never shined on my side of the street, see?
And only once or twice a week I would speak
I walked alone, my state of mind was home sweet home
I couldn't keep a girl, they wanted kids wit cars and chrome
Some life if you ain't wear gold, your style was old
And you got more juice and dough for every bottle sold
Hell no, I say there's gotta be a better way
But hey, never gamble in a game that you can't play
I'm showin' and flowin' and goin' and owin' no one and not now
How will I do it? How will I make it?
I won't, that's how (why me, huh)

Everything's gonna be all right (all right)

My third year into adulthood and still a knucklehead
I'm better off dead (huh) that's what my neighbor said

I don't do jack but fight and lighten up the street at night
Play hide and seek wit a machete, sexin' Freedy's wife
Some say I'm all and all nothin' but a dog now
I answer that wit a fuck you and a bow wow
'Cause I done been through more shit within the last week
Than a fly floatin' in doo-doo on the concrete
I've been a deadbeat, dead to the world and dead wrong
Since I was born that's my life, oh you don't know the song?
So don't say jack and please don't say you understand
All that man ta man talk can walk, damn
If you ain't live it, you couldn't feel it so kill it, skillet
And all that talkin' 'bout it won't help it out, now will it
In Illtown, good luck, got stuck up props, got shot
Don't worry, got hit by a flurry and his punk ass dropped
But I'm the one who has been labeled as an outcast
That teaches fools, I'm the misfit that'll outlast
But that's full with the bull, smack 'em backwards
That's what ya get for fuckin' wit a ghetto bastard
If you ain't never been to the ghetto
Don't ever come to the ghetto
'Cause you wouldn't understand the ghetto
So stay the fuck outta the ghetto

Everything's gonna be all right (all right)

Why me? Why me?

Naughty By Nature

O.P.P.

Arm me wit harmony . . .
Dave drop a load on 'em . . .

(Hmmm) O.P.P. how can I explain it?
I'll take it frame by frame it

To have y'all all jump and shout and sayin' it
O is for "Other," P is for "People," scratch your temple
The last P, well that's not that simple (huh)
It's sort of like a, well, another way to call a cat a kitten
It's five little letters that are missin', yeah
You get it on occasion if the other party isn't gamin'
It seems I gotta start the explainin'—bust it
You ever had a girl and met her on a nice hello
Then got her name and number then left feelin' real mellow
You get home, wait a day, she's what you wanna know about
Then you call up and it's her girlfriend's or her cousin's house
It's not a front, a F to the R to the O to the N to the T
It's just her boyfriend's at her house
Oh, that's why she's scary

It's O.P.P. time, other peoples' p—you get it?
There's no room for relationships, it's just room to hit it!
How many brothers out there know just what I'm gettin' at
Who think it's wrong 'cause I was splittin' and co-hittin' that
Well if you do, that's O.P.P. and you're not down wit it
But if you don't, here's your membership

Ya down wit O.P.P. (Yeah, you know me)
Ya down wit O.P.P. (Yeah, you know me)
Ya down wit O.P.P. (Yeah, you know me)
Who's down wit O.P.P.? (Every last homie)
Ya down wit O.P.P. (Yeah, you know me)
Ya down wit O.P.P. (Yeah, you know me)
Ya down wit O.P.P. (Yeah, you know me)
Who's down wit O.P.P. (All the homies)

Now for the ladies, O.P.P. means something gifted
The first two letters the same but the last is something different
It's the longest, loveliest, lean, I call it the leanes'
It's another five letter word rhymin' with cleanes' and meanes'
I won't get into that, I'll do it ahh . . . sort of properly
I'll say the last P hmmmm, stands for Property
Now ladies here comes a kiss (*kiss*) blow a kiss back to me (*kiss*)
Now tell me exactly
Have you ever known a brother to have another like a girl or wife

And you just had to stomp her toes 'cause he looked just that nice
You looked at him, he looked at you and you knew right away
He had someone but he was goin' to be yours anyway
You couldn't be seen wit him at all and still you didn't care
'Cause in a room behind a door, no one but y'all are there
When y'all are finished, y'all could leave and y'all all know
Then y'all could throw that skeleton bone right in the closet door
Now don't be shy 'cause if you're down, I want your hands up
    high
Say O.P.P. (O.P.P.) I like it said wit pride
Now when you do it, do it well and make sure that it counts
You're now down with a discount

Ya down wit O.P.P. ((Yeah, you know me)
Ya down wit O.P.P. (Yeah, you know me)
Ya down wit O.P.P. (Yeah, you know me)
Who's down wit O.P.P. (Every last lady)
Ya down wit O.P.P. (Yeah, you know me)
Ya down wit O.P.P. (Yeah, you know me)
Ya down wit O.P.P. (Yeah, you know me)
Who's down wit O.P.P. (All the ladies)

A scab tried to O.P.P. me
I had a girl and she knew that
Matter of fact her and my girl was partners that
Had a fallout, disagreement, yeah an argument
She tried to do me so we did it in my apartment—bust it
That wasn't the thing, it must have been the way she hit the
    ceilin'
'Cause after that she kept on comin' back and catchin' feelin's
I said, "Let's go, my girl is comin' so ya gotta leave"
She said, "Oh no I love you Treach," I said, "Now child, please
You gotsta leave, come grab your coat right now, ya gotta go"
I said, "Now look, you choose the stairs or choose this damn
    window
This was fling, a little thing you shouldn't of brought your heart
'Cause you knew I was O.P.P. hell, right from the very start"
Come on, come on, now let me tell you what it's all about
When you get down, you can't go 'round runnin' off at the
    mouth

That's rule number one in this O.P.P. establishment
You keep your mouth shut and it won't get back to her or him
Exciting isn't it, a special kind of business
Many of you will catch the same sort of O.P.P. visit with
Him or her for sure, I'm goin' to admit it
When O.P.P. comes, damn, Skippy I'm wit it

Ya down wit O.P.P. (Yeah, you know me)
Ya down wit O.P.P. (Yeah, you know me)
Ya down wit O.P.P. (Yeah, you know me)
Who's down wit O.P.P. (This whole party)
Ya down wit O.P.P. (Yeah, you know me)
Ya down wit O.P.P. (Yeah, you know me)
Ya down wit O.P.P. (Yeah, you know me)
Who's down wit O.P.P. (This whole party)

NicE & sm00th

Funky for You

Hey yo—
Dizzy Gillespie plays the sax
Me, myself, I love to max
Redbone booties, I out to wax
Stick up kids is out to tax

Spring again, and I'm feeling fine
Pass me an ice-cold glass of wine
So I can get mellow
Lay back and let my girl play the cello
Hello
I hate Jell-0
Let me be me, relax in my tepee
And watch a Hardy Boy mystery

Greg N-I-C-E

I'm nitro, and I'm hype so don't ever believe that you can
    deceive me
Seen many visions of love and splendor
I'm the real thing, not like a pretender
I rock rhymes over beats on the real tip
Stay real strong and hang on like a vise grip
Use my mind to control all my body parts
Got an early start, plus I'm very smart
Type of man that the girls wanna read about
Indeed I proceed to rock the house without a doubt
Stepping up next, no further ado
Smooth B is gonna make it real funky for you

I'm gonna make it real funky for you
I'm gonna make it real funky for you
I'm gonna make it real funky for you
I'm gonna make it real funky for you

Smooth B

Notorious, glorious, knowledge is infinite
I live in a fortress, I'm so astronomical
Yet on a physical plane
My body's just a shell, in control is my brain
I strain to gain spirituality
So I can finally be in unity
Harmony with the
All eye-seeing Supreme Being
Knower of histories and mysteries
I'm mystic, also stylistic
Not materialistic, simplistic
Humble, while others tumble, stumble
Smooth B, not bumble rumble
No that's not likely
That's with my old school daze like Spike Lee
Smooth B, my rhymes get better with time
I should get an endorsement for creating fresh lines
And as I grow older, lyrics get hyper
'Cause I'm a dominant black Pied Piper

Spreading peace and love throughout my travels
And take time to read and unravel
Day to day problems and then solve them
I can see clearly now as I revolve around suckers
Who perpetrate heroes
But I'm no sandwich
More like a Manwich
Or maybe like a meal
Which is much more real
Than Clark Kent or the Man of Steel
Teddy Tedd, a hip-hop ambassador
Keeping you on the floor, giving you more and more
His cuts exquisite
What is it, a blizzard?
The musical wizard, you should come visit
The man in the back without further ado
Teddy Tedd is gonna make it real funky for you

I'm gonna make it real funky for you
I'm gonna make it real funky for you
I'm gonna make it real funky for you
I'm gonna make it real funky for you

Nikki D

Daddy's Little Girl

Daddy's little girl, but not the girl that Daddy knew
Daddy never had a clue of what his little girl would do
A drifter, swift to open up and get with ya
A pocket full of dreams, as for my love, forget ya
I never concentrated on the fact that I'm loved
Scheme for scheme and things that would lead me to a pipe
    dream
Picture it yes, I'm Daddy's little girl
I never asked for nothing, now it's a string of pearls

My chances are thin, could I win with a substance
A princess with a smile but my sweetness was sort of grim
I never thought the feeling that I had to be wild
'Cause in my mind, I was a mature child
But I couldn't hurt Daddy, I played the role
But on the sneak tip, I was massaging his soul
Nikki had to be free, you see I had to be me
For life just wouldn't flow through correctly
For Daddy's little girl

What Daddy don't know won't hurt him
But I'm Daddy's little girl
(What Daddy don't know won't hurt him)
Daddy's little girl (What Daddy don't know won't hurt him)
Daddy's little girl (What Daddy don't know)

Daddy always tucked me in bed and kissed me goodnight
Said, "Nikki sleep tight," then turn off the light
And when he goes away on a business trip
I flip, lose my grip, party time all
I tell the girls, split the duty, one go pick up the booze
My other half move your ass and go spread the news
The party went on, lasted all night long
Song after song (to the break of dawn)
Then watch some nasty porns in the morn
My body got warm, hmm, from getting freaky with Vaughn
Sexin' like crazy, my body amaze me
By takin' a chance
With a man that didn't faze me
A night so hectic, a bit unexpected
Before I made love, I should have been protected
'Cause now I'm in a jam with this careless punk
And in about three months, my stomach will be plump
Trouble yes, I'm in the hot seat now
Tell my pops? No way, no how
It will break his heart, wreck his whole world
To have to grow up quick, Daddy's little girl

(What Daddy don't know won't hurt him)
But I'm Daddy's little girl

(What Daddy don't know won't hurt him)
Daddy's little girl (What Daddy don't know won't hurt him)
Daddy's little girl (What Daddy don't know)

Neighbors asked could he trust me, yeah Daddy loves me
'Cause I could feel it in his arms strong when he hugs me
But there comes a time when this angel must spread her wings
So I bow my head and get deep into the swing of things
Sort of raunchy, I must be 'cause Mama knew
Every time I skip school, Mama sat home and sang the blues
Now I regret the day that Daddy let me out to play
But I'm a woman now so let's keep it this way
I'm Daddy's little girl

(What Daddy don't know won't hurt him)
But I'm Daddy's little girl
(What Daddy don't know won't hurt him)
Daddy's little girl (What Daddy don't know won't hurt him)
Daddy's little girl (What Daddy don't know)

N W A

Fuck tha Police

Right about now, NWA Court is in full effect
Judge Dre presidin'
In the case of NWA versus the police department
The prosecuting attorneys are M.C. Ren, Ice Cube, and Eazy
     motherfuckin' E
Order, order order
Ice Cube, take the motherfuckin' stand
Do you swear to tell the truth, the whole truth and nothin' but
     the truth, so help yo' black ass?
"You're goddamned right!"
Why dontcha tell everybody what the fuck you gotta say

Fuck tha police comin' straight from the underground
A young nigger got it bad 'cause I'm brown
And not the other color
Some police think
They have the authority to kill a minority
Fuck that shit 'cause I ain't the one
For a punk motherfucker with a badge and a gun
To be beaten on and thrown in jail
We can go toe to toe in the middle of a cell
Fuckin' with me 'cause I'm a teenager
With a little bit of gold and a pager
Searchin' my car, lookin' for the product
Thinkin' every nigger is sellin' narcotics
You'd rather see me in the pen
Than me and Lorenzo rollin' in a Benz-o
Beat up police, out of shape
And when I'm finished, bring the yellow tape
To tape off the scene of the slaughter
Still gettin' swoll' off bread and water
I don't know if they fags or what
Search a nigger down and grabbin' his nuts
And on the other hand
Without a gun, they can't get none
But don't let it be a black and a white one
'Cause they'll slam ya down to the street top
Black police showin' out for the white cop
Ice Cube will swarm
On any motherfucker in a blue uniform
Just 'cause I'm from the C-P-T
Punk police are afraid of me, huh
A young nigger on the warpath
And when I finish, it's gonna be a bloodbath
Of cops dyin' in L.A.
Yo, Dre, I got something to say

Fuck tha police!
Fuck tha police!
Fuck tha police!
Fuck tha police!

Sample Scene One:
Pull your goddamn ass over right now
Aw, shit, and what the fuck you pullin' me over for?
'Cause I feel like it, just sit your ass on the curb and shut the
    fuck up
Man, fuck this shit
All right smartass, I'm takin' your black ass to jail

M.C. Ren, will you please give your testimony to the jury about
    this fucked up incident?

Fuck tha police and Ren said it with authority
Because the niggers on the street is a majority
A gang—that's wit whoever I'm steppin'
And a motherfuckin' weapon is kept in
A stand-by for the so-called law
Wishin' Ren was a nigger that they never saw
Lights all flashin' behind me
But they're scared of a nigger so they mace me to blind me
But that shit don't work, I just laugh
Because it gives 'em a hint not to step in my path
To police, I'm sayin', "Fuck you punk"
Readin' my rights and shit—it's all junk
Pullin' out a silly club so you stand
With a fake-assed badge and a gun in your hand
But take off the gun so you can see what's up
And we'll go at it, punk, and I'm 'a fuck you up
Make you think I'm 'a kick your ass
But drop your gat and Ren's gonna blast
I'm sneaky as fuck when it comes to crime
But I'm 'a smoke 'em now and not next time
Smoke any mutherfucker that sweats me
Or any asshole that threatens me
I'm a sniper with a hell of a scope
Takin' out a cop or two that can't cope with me
The motherfuckin' villain that's mad
With potential to get bad as fuck
So I'm 'a turn it around
Put in my clip, yo
And this is the sound

Yeah, somethin' like that
But it all depends on the size of the gat
Takin' out a police would make my day
But a nigger like Ren don't give a fuck to say

Fuck the police!
Fuck tha police!
Fuck tha police!
Fuck tha police!

Yo, man, whatchya need?
Police, open now (Oh shit), we have a warrant for Eazy E's arrest
Oh shit
Get down and put your hands up where I can see 'em!
Man, what did I do?
Just shut the fuck up and get yo' motherfuckin' ass on the floor
But I didn't do shit
Man, just shut the fuck up

Eazy E, why don't you step up to the stand and tell the jury how
    you feel about this bullshit?

I'm tired of the motherfuckin' jackin'
Sweatin' my gang while I'm chillin' in the shack an'
Shinin' the light in my face and for what?
Maybe it's because I kick so much butt
I kick ass, or maybe it's 'cause I blast
On a stupid-assed nigger when I'm playin' with the trigger
Of an Uzi or an AK
'Cause the police always got somethin' stupid to say
They put up my picture with silence
'Cause my identity by itself causes violence
The E with the criminal behavior
Yeah, I'm a gangster, but still I got flavor
Without a gun and a badge, what do you got?
A sucker in a uniform waitin' to get shot
By me or another nigger
And with a gat, it don't matter if he's smaller or bigger
(Size don't mean shit, he's from the old school, fool)
And as you all know, E's here to rule

Whenever I'm rollin', keep lookin' in the mirror
And ears on cue, yo, so I can hear a
Dumb motherfucker with a gun
And if I'm rollin' off the eight, he'll be the one
That I take out and then get away
While I'm drivin' off laughin', this is what I'll say

Fuck tha police!
Fuck tha police!
Fuck tha police!
Fuck tha police!

The verdict:
The jury has found you guilty of being a red-neck, white-bread,
    chicken-shit motherfucker
"That's a lie! That's a goddamn lie!"
Get him out of here!
"I want justice!"
Get him the fuck out my face
"I want justice!"
Out right now!
"Fuck you, you black motherfuckerrrrrrrr!"

Fuck tha police!
Fuck tha police!
Fuck tha police!

100 Miles and Runnin'

(You don't really think you're gonna get away, do you?
We haven't spotted them yet, but they're somewhere in the
    immediate vicinity)

A hundred miles and runnin'
M.C. Ren I hold the gun an'

You want me to kill the motherfucker and it's done in
Since I'm stereotyped to kill and destruct
Is one of the main reasons I don't give a fuck
The chances are usually not good
Since I first put my hands on a hot hood
Gettin' jacked by the you-know-who
With any black and white the capacity is two
We're not alone, we're three more brothers on the street brothers
Now we're on the dime 'cause we're not stupid motherfuckers
They're out to take our heads for what we said in the past
Point-blank they can kiss my black ass
I didn't stutter when I said, "Fuck tha police"
Because it's hard for a nigga to get peace
Now it's broken and can't be fixed
'Cause police and little black niggas don't mix so
Now I'm creepin' through the fall
Runnin' like a team now, see I'm not a slack-jaw
So for now I'm packin' and gunnin'
Hold it in the air 'cause M.C. Ren has a hundred miles and
     runnin'

(In pursuit, four fugitives on the run
FBI sources tell us that the four are headed a hundred miles to
     their home base, Compton)

Lend me your motherfuckin' ear
So I can tell you why
I'm runnin' with my brothers, headed for the home base
With a steady pace that my face has just re-raced
The road ahead goes on and on
The shit is gettin' longer than the motherfuckin' marathon
Runnin' on but never runnin' out
Stayin' wired and if I get tired, I can still go out
Hitchhikin' if that's what I got to
But nobody's pickin' up a nigga with a attitude
Confused, yo but Dre's a nigga with nothin' to lose
One of the few who's been accused and abused
Of the crime of poisonin' young minds
But you don't know shit til you been in my shoes
And Dre is back from the C-P-T

Droppin' some shit that's D-O-P-E
So fuck the P-O-L-I-C-E
And any motherfucker that disagrees
Suckers runnin' hard, hard and fast
Because I'm a nigga known for havin' a notorious past
My mind was slick, my temper was too quick
Now the FBI's all over my dick
Get runnin' just to find the gun that started to clock
That's when the E jumped off the startin' block
A hundred miles from home and yo it's a long stretch
A little sprintin' motherfucker that they won't catch
Yeah, back to Compton again
Yo, it's either that or the Federal pen
Cause niggas been runnin' since the beginning of time
Takin' a minute to tell you what's on my motherfuckin' mind
Runnin' like I just don't care
Compton's fifty miles but yo, I'm 'a get there
Archin' my back and on a straight rock
Just like Carl Lewis, I'm blowin' the fuck out
From city to city I'm a menace as I pass by
Rippin' up shit just so you can remember I'm
A straight up nigga that's runnin' and gunnin' and comin'
Straight at yo' ass
A hundred miles and runnin'

(This one goes out to the four brothers from Compton
You're almost there, but the FBI has a little message for you:
"Nowhere to run to, baby, nowhere to hide"
Good luck brothers)

Runnin' like a nigga I hate to lose
Show me on the news but I hate to be abused
I knew it was a set-up, so now I'm gonna get up
Even if the FBI wants me to shut up
But I've got 10,000 niggas strong
They got everybody singin' my "Fuck tha police" song
And while they treat my group like dirt
Their whole fuckin' family is wearin' our t-shirts
So I'm a run til I can't run no more
'Cause it's time for M.C. Ren to settle the score

I got a urge to kick down doors
At my grave like a slave even if the Ren calls
Clouds are dark and brothers are hidin'
Dick-tricklin' silly motherfucker are ridin'
We started with five and yo, one couldn't take it
So now there's four 'cause the fifth couldn't make it
The number's even, now I'm leavin'
We're never gettin' took by a bitch with a weave in
Her and the troops are right behind me
But they're so fuckin' stupid, they'll never find me
One more mile to go through the dark streets
Runnin' like a motherfucker on my own two feet
But you know I never stumble or lag last
I'm almost home so I better haul ass
Tearin' up everything in sight
It's a little crazy motherfucker dodging a searchlight
Now let's chase, the shit is done and
Four motherfuckers goin' crazy with
A hundred miles and runnin'

(Stop! Stop! Stop! Stop!)

Surprise, niggas!

N W A

Straight Outta Compton

You're now about to witness the strength of street knowledge

Straight Outta Compton!
Crazy motherfucker named Ice Cube
From the gang called Niggers with Attitudes
When I'm called off
I got a sawed-off
Squeeze the trigger

And bodies are hauled off
You too, boy, if you fuck with me
The police are gonna have to come and get me
Off yo' ass
That's how I'm goin' out
But a punk motherfucker that's showin' how
Niggers fuck 'em up
They wanna rumble
Makes a man cook 'em in a pot like gumbo
Goin' off on a motherfucker like that
With a gat that's pointed at yo' ass
So give it up smooth
Ain't no tellin' when I'm down for a jack move
Here's a murder rap to keep ya dancin'
With a crime record like Charles Manson
AK-47 is the tool
Don't make me act the motherfuckin' fool
Me and you could go toe-to-toe, no maybe
I'm knockin' niggers out the box daily
Yo, weekly, monthly, and yearly
Until then, dumb motherfuckers see clearly
That I'm down, with the capital C-P-T
Boy, you can't fuck with me
So when I'm in your neighborhood
Ya better duck
Cause Ice Cube is crazy as fuck
As I leave, believe I'm stompin'
But when I come back, boy
I'm comin' Straight Outta Compton

Straight Outta Compton
Straight Outta Compton

Yo, Ren (What's up?), tell 'em where ya from
Straight Outta Compton
Another crazy-assed nigger
For punks I smoke, yo, my rep gets bigger
I'm a bad motherfucker and you know this
But the pussy-assed niggers won't show this

But I don't give a fuck
I'm 'a make my snatch
If not from the records
From jackin' a crowd
It's like burglary
The definition is jackin'
But when I'm legally armed
It's called packin'
Shoot a motherfucker in a minute
I find a good piece of pussy
And go up in it
So if you at a show in the front row
I'm 'a call you a bitch or a dirty-ass ho
You probably get mad like a bitch is supposed to
But that shows me, slut, you're talkin' pro's to
A crazy motherfucker from the street
Attitude legit 'cause I'm tearin' up shit
M.C. Ren, controls are automatic
For any dumb motherfucker it starts static
Not a right hand 'cause I'm the hand itself
Every time I pull a AK off the shelf
Security is maximum and that's the law
R-E-N spells Ren but I'm raw
See, 'cause I'm the motherfuckin' villain
The definition is clear
You're the witness of a killin'
That's takin' place without a clue
And once you're on the scope
Ya ass is through
Look, you might take it as a trip
But a nigger like Ren is on the gangster tip
Straight Outta Compton

Straight Outta Compton
Straight Outta Compton

Eazy is his name and the boy's comin'
Straight Outta Compton
Is a brother that'll smother your mother

And make your sister think I love her
Dangerous motherfucker raisin' hell
And if I ever get caught
I make bail
See, I don't give a fuck
That's the problem
I see a motherfuckin' cop, I don't dodge him
But I'm smart
Lay low, creep a while
And when I see a punk pass
I smile
To me it's kinda funny, the attitude
Show a nigger drivin'
But don't know where the fuck he's goin'
Just rollin'
Lookin' for the one they call Eazy
But here's a flash
They never sees me
Ruthless, never seen, like a shadow in the dark
Except when I unload
You see a spark can jump over a hesitation
And hear the scream of the one
Who got the last penetration
Give a little gust of wind
And I'm jettin'
But leave a memory
No one'll be forgotten
So what about the bitch who got shot
Fuck her
You think I give a damn about a bitch?
I ain't a sucker
This is the autobiography of the E
And if ya ever fuck with me
You'll get taken
By a stupid dope brother
Who will smother
Word to the motherfucker
Straight Outta Compton

Damn! That shit was dope!

paris
Break the Grip of Shame

Enter into a new realm, a new dimension,
Pay close attention
And witness knowledge born on the microphone
For the people that I call my own
Remember back when good rap was just a cool dance hit
Even though it wasn't sayin' shit
Well them days is gone, I don't play that
Pick the punk and I'll say like, "wack"
Stick with the sick style for the serious
Hip-hop lovers can't get enough of this
Black tracks on wax are so smooth
You can't help but to start to move
This is a callin', a plea for unity
Black is back, uplift, and be free
Keep pushin', the movement moves on
So strong, now

With a raised fist, I resist
I don't burn, so don't ya dare riff
Or step to me, I'm strong and Black and proud
And for the bullshit, I ain't down
Life in the city's already rough enough
Without some young sucker runnin' up
You don't know me, so don't step
I'll roll to the right and then bust your lip
Paris is my name, I don't sleep
I drop science and keep the peace
Here to bust this for better justice
Another dope Scarface release
This is a serious style for the gifted
Pro-Black radical raps upliftin'
Still growin', the powers so strong
You can't stop it, now—

All right, let's start some more shit
Straight up on the movement tip
With forces strong as Allah's my third eye
Black is back and P-Dog'll never die
Who says that you can't do this
Can't be wise or be for the movement
Games I won't have so don't you play none
You'll see why when I'm gone
Skinheads end up dead 'cause I don't play
Brothers swarm under the form of Scarface
Round up, Roll out, we'll roll 'em up like Rolos
I'll stomp sixteen solos
Straight for the jugular, hope that I don't swarm
And bust a cap by night so
You just keep your place 'cause I won't stop
I'll keep pushin' that movement rock when I

paris
The Devil Made Me Do It

This is a warnin', another cut to move on
Another beat that's so strong
Hold on and I'll get wicked and then some
Stir up shit as the wit gets wisdom
P-Dog comin' up, I'm straight loc'd
Pro-Black and it ain't no joke
Comin' straight from the mob that broke shit last time
Now I'm back with a brand new sick grind
So Black check time and tempo
Revolution ain't never been simple
Followin' the path of Mao and Fanon
Just build your brain and we'll soon make progress
Paid your dues, don't snooze or lose
They came with the master plan and got you

So know who's opposed to the dominant dark-skinned
Food for thought is a law for the brotherman

(The Devil Made Me Do It)

P-Dog with a gift from heaven
Tempo 116.7
Keeps you locked in time with the program
When I get wild, I'll pile on dope jams
Then spit on your flag and government
'Cause help the black was a concept never meant
Nigga please, food stamps and free cheese
Can't be the cure for a sick disease
Just the way the devil had planned it
Raped and pillaged everyone on the planet
And give 'em fake gods, at odds with Allah
Love thy enemy and all that hoopla
Hear close the words I wrote
Crack cocaine is genocide of Black folk
Who in their right mind ever could've
Missed this? Damn right when ya think seditious
And I move swiftly, ya can't get with me
The triple six moved quick but missed me
When I came off involved in conscience
So don't ask why next time I start this

(The Devil Made Me Do It)

Now let's get wild, allow me to freestyle
And build and fill your mind up with know-how
And common sense of defense the next time
A pig try to step to this, listen
Never let someone whip on ya
That don't belong to the set ya from, ya
Can't be intrigued by the leads a pig leads
Unless ya don't give a fuck to be free
Keep stompin' on 'em, keep stompin'
Attitude, but I ain't from Compton
I can't be fucked around or muffed around

I can't be held down, check the sound
And keep in tune, on point, on target
The revolution won't be thwarted
Or set back 'cause my man, it's plain to see
Must end the white supremacy
So let the rhythm roll on when I kick this
Brothers gonna work it out with a quickness
And now you know just why a panther went crazy
The Devil Made Me

(*Voiceover*)
Beware the beast-man
For he is the devil's pawn
He kills for sport, or lust, or greed
Yea, he will murder his brother to possess his brother's land
Shun him
For he is the harbinger of death

p. M. Dawn

Comatose

Ask me that question again: who am I, what am I
Look at my face, the eyes don't lie
If I was one with the smooth tongue used for fun
I'd take a look at myself and ask myself why

I got a thread, a thread that I'm holdin' on
For sanity, my mind takes the things that are goin' on
Close to the soul and actually steppin' on
These people are doin' wrong, the list can go on and on

For ages, tangled up through mazes
As lost as a meal that's pushed to a panther
I keep my eyes on those who pass by
They'll look to P.M. Dawn, the quest for the answer

Mercy, mercy me till I see
The end of the human race's Grand Prix
Mr. Red knows I pose a threat
Yeah, I like to see 'em sweat

Dr. Vibe tends to get hypnotic
Reality thinks that Prince B is erotic
The magic wand seems to be misplaced
I can't see it if it's covered in lace

The best way to keep your word is not to give it
I don't make promises 'cause promises die
But those who use hate just won't participate
So that's why I choose to use my eyes

And stay comatose

A positive or negative impression on your brain
Whatever remains, whatever stays the same
Results from an inside view or perspective
Other than that persona snaps from the strain
But what remains to be seen
Is how you choose to use your time
And still the point blank calculation's unclear
Of whether your text can catch these lines
Or toss 'em to the side so you can't realize
Illusions only last 'til the scene is through
Approaching this scenario what would you do
Lose your noodle or try some voodoo
Accept defeat then what's the next phase
Rely on the brave, rely on the cockiest
The secret of any victory lies in
The organization of the nonobvious and the comatose

So they tell me a lot to keep my head straight
But the view's set before us like an unseen crime
I like to watch and watch close to see what they might take
A tick from a tock, a line from a rhyme
A leaf off an elm, a move might yell bold
An unseen realm, but what that realm holds
Is nothin', nothin' that makes sense

They walk with small talk as I watch the consequence
Swell up and overflow into a large brook
Maybe it's the undertow or what the time look
To put together scenes make it all seem clear
A pacified picture is the life being dream
'Til it's tried by the spies that's when they realize
But roses ain't red and the violets ain't blue
But those that are swift will pinpoint the trip
Everyone else'll think it's deja vu
Except the comatose.

p. M. Dawn

To Serenade a Rainbow

I think I wanna fly away

Sitting on top of the setting sun
Trying to capture at age twenty-one
Let's leave it at "beauty's only skin deep"
But love likes to sail when I exhale my lungs

Fine wines, good times
To try to be an angel's pantomime?
"Pot holes in my lawn," that's the ticket
But a different definition than the soul defines

Does an "X" mark the spot on a single heart
When they've more than billions of Cupid's darts
To try to spread love to the multitude
But then there's the feud that tears things apart
Moonbeams condition my dreams
To its current shades of purple and green
I'm convinced that my aura has the same glow

And this produces my affection toward rainbows
Wondering why? Why only my eyes embrace you
'Cause if I was blind, I'd persist to chase you
Through the window I'm watching you smile at me
Now I live for the times when you profile for me
The breeze, the wind
Influxuates my adrenaline
See it's an ode to the fact that you've put your colors on
Now all I gotta do is tell you it's wrong
And counteract my tears with a grin
To balance your feelings in a mind that spins
Is to Serenade a Rainbow
While riding on the tail of the wind

I think I wanna fly away

Loving you is easy 'cause you're beautiful
I don't think so, I think that that's a lot of bull
My heart and soul have completely taken over
I'm sick from one of those love hangovers
I watch the comedy called intellect
Which wraps the nooses around our necks
It seems the unreal's becoming more real
They've taken me down to strawberry fields
Meet me at the tip of Orion's nose
And play me a song that your heart composed
Why, you can blow me away and I can still see blue
Agape compels me to love you
Break me down until you see the sun
I look at you and smile and you ask, "How come?"
Father, I talk to you for peace of mind
A kaleidoscope's prone to make me blind
It's like a fairy tale from the Brothers Grimm
To fall in love from the slightest whim
Is to Serenade a Rainbow
While Riding on the tail of the Wind

I think I wanna fly away
Fly away

Poor righteous Teachers

Rock dis Funky Joint

Time to get funky-new-radical-hip
As I get to the point
ROCK DIS FUNKY JOINT!
Wait a sec
The teacher's gotta check the intellect for stumma-step
Den, den give you it
But, but give you what?
The P, the R, the T, fa often comes to tear shit up
But my style be just enough
To manifest the fabric mathematics, Black be that of Asiatic
Rock the joint, subtract the static
Then as you rocking to my concept
And I gots to stand fa this?
For his wise, civilized, dip-hip-hop rhyme from a Black mind
G kicking it to ya all the time
"I-Salaam-you-laikum" or a peace sign
Represents my way of life and this be that of Islam
I take my time, think before I manifest a rhyme
Sharp and accurate to stop the music on a dime
Knowledge me a capella
Wisdom, G, I'm manifesting
Understanding
Understood
So there's no need fa keep ya guessing
Follow me now, see?
See, I be rocking
The second hand is ticking, still the posse don't be clocking
Controllers of the clock be ticking closer to the point
ROCK DIS FUNKY JOINT!

Sta-stumma-step: the style that I use when
When thoughts flow rather rapidly
P.R.T. Posse backing me

Easy now, star, you know exactly who we are
Poor Righteous Teachers, tribe be P.R.T. for short, now
Now dem want more, hmmmm? Or am I too much for the
    mental?
Proceed, teacher, please, just keep it sorta simple
Like hip-hop, yet complicately I place it
According to the moods of my intellect
Step for step, I step a little closer to the point
ROCK DIS FUNKY JOINT!
But, but I'm your teacher
I teach ya
Rocker when I rock ya
The king, Aquil Fabeem's a different style of hip-hopper
Smooth like a wise word spoken from a prophet
Rough like a slave trying to get away
See, I combine with two kinds of rhyme
Trying ta reach ya
The knowledge of myself makes me a Poor Righteous Teacher
Stop to flip the topic, Islamicly I drop it
My duty be to teach, so keep ya pistol in your pocket
I, Self, Lord and Master, travel faster
As I get closer to the point
ROCK DIS FUNKY JOINT!

Fa-stumma-step, yet
Yet, I'm on top of it, I
I have to get
The styles that you be seeking in the words that I be speakin'
Poor Righteous Teachers' Posse teachin'
Anyone that lacks this style that I be stylin'
Mentally profilin' or should I say I'm
Smooth with the roughness
Just serving justice
Suckers try to suck this, but
But I be scopin'
Never, I'm not sleepin' (because his culture freed him)
G, whose posse ruling? (P.R.T.)
Word, B, it's sorta simple, see
Now look at me, the holy intellectual type
When I write, the spirit always kicks me something hype

I rock the mike, yo, 'cause it's my home, like
Like I'm creating
Man-I-be-festating
Can I say I'm great when there's not another brother greater?
Turn to culture freedom for support
G, manifest the point
ROCK DIS FUNKY JOINT!

But no excuses
Losers never rock dis
Snakes try to stop this
Purified and holy hip-hopness
Listen to the concept
Sweat, tech, techno
Peace be the Lord or feel the sword when I speak
"Ai-Salaam-Alaikum" ("Wa-Alaikum-As-Salaam")
A universal greeting from the people of our kind
Step into the realm of my cipher
Feel the different type of
Coming stumma-slipping-stepping technique
Twelve hundreds mastered by Divine
He's asking me to rock
So now I'm giving him the spot
Style be the lyrics I be kicking
Intelligence be ticking, somewhat symbolic to a bomb
Many brothers rolling, fell a victim
I'm not living with them
Because they didn't know the time
Turn to culture freedom for support
G, manifest the point
ROCK DIS FUNKY JOINT!

public Enemy

Don't Believe the Hype

Don't believe the hype

Back—caught you lookin' for the same thing
It's a new thing—check out this I bring
Uh-oh, the roll below the level
'Cause I'm livin' low
Next to the bass (c'mon)
Turn up the radio
They claim that I'm a criminal
By now I wonder how
Some people never know
The enemy could be their friend, guardian
I'm not a hooligan
I rock the party and
Clear all the madness, I'm not a racist
Preach to teach to all
'Cause some, they never had this
Number one, not born to run
About the gun
I wasn't licensed to have one
The minute they see me, fear me
I'm the epitome—a public enemy
Used, abused, without clues
I refused to blow a fuse
They even had it on the news
Don't believe the hype

Don't believe the hype

Yes—was the start of my last jam
So here it is again, another def jam
But since I gave you all a little something
That we knew you lacked

They still consider me a new jack
All the critics, you can hang 'em
I'll hold the rope
But they hope to the pope
And pray it ain't dope
The follower of Farrakhan
Don't tell me that you understand
Until you hear the man
The book of the new school rap game
Writers treat me like Coltrane, insane
Yes to them, but to me I'm a different kind
We're brothers of the same mind, unblind
Caught in the middle and
Not surrenderin'
I don't rhyme for the sake of riddlin'
Some claim that I'm a smuggler
Some say I never heard of ya
A rap burglar, false media
We don't need it, do we?
It's fake, that's what it be to ya, dig me?
Yo, Terminator X, step up on the stand and show the people
    what time it is, boyyyyy!

Don't believe the hype

Don't believe the hype—it's a sequel
As an equal, can I get this through to you
My 98's boomin' with a trunk of funk
All the jealous punks can't stop the dunk
Comin' from the school of hard knocks
Some perpetrate, they drink Clorox
Attack the Black, because I know they lack exact
The cold facts, and still they try to xerox
The leader of the new school, uncool
Never played the fool, just made the rules
Remember there's a need to get alarmed
Again I said I was a timebomb
In the daytime, radio's scared of me
'Cause I'm mad, 'cause I'm the enemy
They can't come on and play me in prime time

'Cause I know the time, plus I'm gettin' mine
I get on the mix late in the night
They know I'm living' right, so here go the mike, psych
Before I let it go, don't rush my show
You try to reach and grab and get elbowed
Word to Herb, yo if you can't swing this
Learn the words, you might sing this
Just a little bit of the taste of the bass for you
As you get up and dance at the LQ
When some deny it, defy it, I swing bolos
And then they clear the lane, I go solo
The meaning of all of that
Some media is the wack
As you believe it's true
It blows me through the roof
Suckers, liars, get me a shovel
Some writers I know are damn devils
For them I say, "Don't believe the hype"
Yo Chuck, they must be on the pipe, right?
Their pens and pads I'll snatch
'Cause I've had it
I'm not an addict, fiendin' for static
I'll see their tape recorder and grab it
No, you can't have it back, silly rabbit
I'm goin' to my media assassin
Harry Allen, I gotta ask him
Yo Harry, you're a writer, are we that type?

Don't believe the hype
Don't believe the hype

I got Flavor and all those things you know
Yeah boy, part two bum rush the show
Yo Griff, get the green, black, red, and
Gold down, countdown to Armageddon
'88 you wait the S-One's will
Put the left in effect and I still will
Rock the hard jams, treat it like a seminar
Reach the bourgeois, and rock the boulevard
Some say I'm negative

But they're not positive
But what I got to give
The media says this
Red black and green
Know what I mean
Yo, don't believe the hype

public Enemy

Fight the Power

1989, the number, another summer (get down)
Sound of the funky drummer
Music hittin' your heart 'cause I know you got soul
(Brothers and sisters, hey)
Listen if you're missin', y'all
Swingin' while I'm singin' (hey)
Givin' whatcha gettin'
Knowin' what I'm knowin'
While the black band's sweatin'
And the rhythm rhyme's rollin'
Gotta give us what we want (Uh!)
Gotta give us what we need (Hey!)
Our freedom of speech is freedom or death
We got to fight the powers that be
Lemme hear you say

FIGHT THE POWER
We got to fight the powers that be

As the rhythm's designed to bounce
What counts is that the rhyme's
Designed to fill your mind
Now that you've realized the pride's arrived
We got to pump the stuff to make us tough

From the heart
It's a start, a work of art
To revolutionize, make a change, nothin' strange
People people, we are the same
No we're not the same
'Cause we don't know the game
What we need is awareness, we can't get careless
You say what is this?
My beloved, let's get down to business
Mental self-defensive fitness
(Yo) Bum rush the show
You gotta go for what you know
To make everybody see, in order to fight the powers that be
Lemme hear you say

FIGHT THE POWER
We got to fight the powers that be

Elvis was a hero to most
But he never meant shit to me, you see
Straight up racist that sucker was simple and plain
Motherfuck him and John Wayne
'Cause I'm black and I'm proud
I'm ready and hyped plus I'm amped
Most of my heroes don't appear on no stamps
Sample a look back, you look and find
Nothin' but rednecks for 400 years if you check
"Don't Worry Be Happy"
Was a number one jam
Damn, if I say it you can slap me right here
(Get it) Let's get this party started right
Right on, c'mon
What we got to say (Yaaaah!)
Power to the people, no delay
To make everybody see
In order to fight the powers that be

FIGHT THE POWER
We got to fight the powers that be

public Enemy

911 Is a Joke

Hit me!

Going, going, gone
Now I dialed 911 a long time ago
Don't you see how late they're reactin'?
They only come and they come when they wanna
So get the morgue truck, and embalm the goner
They don't care 'cause they stay paid anyway
They teach ya like an ace, they can't be betrayed
I know you stumble with no-use people
If your life is on the line, then you're dead today
Late comin's with the late comin' stretcher
That's a body bag in disguise, y'all I'll betcha
I call 'em body snatchers, quick they come to fetch ya?
With an autopsy ambulance just to dissect ya
They are the kings 'cause they swing amputation
Lose your arms, your legs, to them it's compilation
I can prove it to you, watch the rotation
It all adds up to a fucked-up situation

So get up, 'a get, get, get down
911 is a joke in yo' town
Get up, 'a get, get, get down
Late 911 wears the late crown
Get up, 'a get, get, get down
911 is a joke in yo' town
Get up, 'a get, get, get down
Late 911 wears the late crown

Everyday they don't never come correct
You can ask my man right here with the broken neck
He's a witness to the job never bein' done
He would've been in full effect in '8 911
Was a joke 'cause they always jokin'

They the token to your life when it's croakin'
They need to be in a pawn shop on a
911 is a joke, we don't want 'em
I call a cab 'cause a cab will come quicker
The doctors huddle up and call a flea flicker
The reason that I say that 'cause they flick you off like fleas
They be laughin' at ya while you're crawlin' on your knees
And to the strength so go the length
Thinkin' you are first when you really are tenth
You better wake up and smell the real flavor
'Cause 911 is a fake life saver

So get up, 'a get, get, get down
911 is a joke in yo' town
Get up, 'a get, get, get down
Late 911 wears the late crown
Get up, 'a get, get, get down
911 is a joke in yo' town
Get up, 'a get, get, get down
Late 911 wears the late crown

public Enemy

Welcome to the Terrordome

I got so much trouble on my mind
I refuse to lose
Here's your ticket
Hear the drummer get wicked
The crew to you to push the back to black
Attack, so I sat and japped
Then slapped the Mac(intosh)
Now I'm ready to mike it
(You know I like it) Huh
Hear my favoritism roll, "oh"
Never be a brother like me go solo

Lazer, Anastasia, 'maze ya
Ways to blaze your brain and train ya
The way I'm livin', forgiven
What I'm givin' up
X on the flex
Hit me now
I don't know about later
As for now, I know how to avoid the paranoid
Man I've had it up to here
Gear
I wear got 'em goin' in fear
Rhetoric said
Read just a bit ago
Not quittin' though
Signed the hard rhymer
Work to keep from gettin' jerked
Changin' some ways
To way back in the better days
Raw metaphysically bold
Never followed a code
Still dropped a load
Never question what I am, God knows
'Cause it's comin' from the heart
What I got, better get some
Get on up hustler of culture
Snakebitten
Been spit in the face
But the rhymes keep fittin'
Respects been givin', how's ya livin'
Now I can't protect
A paid off defect
Check the record
An' reckon an intentional wreck
Played
Off as some intellect
Made the call, took the fall
Broke the laws
Not my fault that they're fallin' off
Known as fair
Square

Throughout my years
So I growl at the livin' foul
Black to the bone, my home is your home
But welcome to the terrordome

Subordinate terror
Kickin' off an era
Cold deliverin' pain
My 98 was '87 on a record, yo
So now I go bronco

Crucifixion ain't no fiction
So called chosen, frozen
Apology made to whoever pleases
Still they got me like Jesus
I rather sing
Bring
Think, reminisce
'Bout a brother while I'm in sync
Every brother ain't a brother 'cause a color
Just as well could be undercover
Backstabbed, grabbed a flag
From the back of the lab
Told a Rab, "Get off the rag"
Sad to say, I got sold down the river
Still some quiver when I deliver
Never to say I never knew or had a clue
Word was heard, plus hard on the boulevard
Lies, scandalizin'
Basin'
Traits of hate, who's celebratin' with Satan?
I rope a dope, the evil with righteous bobbin' an' weavin'
An' let the good get even
C'mon down
And welcome to the terrordome

Caught in the race against time
The pit and the pendulum
Check the rhythm and rhymes
While I'm bendin' 'em

Snakes blowin' up the lines of design
Tryin' to blind the science, I'm sendin' 'em
How to fight the power
Cannot run and hide
But it shouldn't be suicide
In a game, a fool without the rules
Got a hell of a nerve to just criticize
Every brother ain't a brother
'Cause a black hand
Squeezed on Malcolm X the man
The shootin' of Huey Newton
From a hand of a nig who pulled the trig

It's weak to speak and blame somebody else
When you destroy yourself
First nothin's worse than a mother's pain
Of a son slain in Bensonhurst
Can't wait for the state to decide the fate
So this jam I dedicate
Places with the racist faces
An example, one of many cases
The Greek weekend speech I speak
From a lesson learned in Virginia (Beach)
I don't smile in the line of fire
I go wildin'
But it's on bass and drums, even violins
Whatcha do, gitcha head ready
Instead of gettin' physically sweaty
When I get mad
I put it down on a pad
Give ya somethin' thatcha never had
Controllin'
Fear of high rollin'
God bless your soul and keep livin'
Never allowed, kickin' it loud
Droppin' a bomb
Brain game, intellectual Vietnam
Move as a team
Never move alone
But welcome to the terrordome

Queen Latifah

Come into My House

Give me body (Don't make me wait)
Welcome into my queendom
Come one, come all
'Cause when it comes to lyrics, I bring them
In spring I sing, in fall I call
Out to all the ones who had a hard day
I've prepared a place on my dance floor
The time is now for you to party
I thought it would be a good chance for
You to move (One Nation Under the Groove)
House music always soothes
So get with the flow, let's go
Yo! can you rock to a house groove tempo?
If so, then shall we let the games begin
What better-off position can you be in
I'm on fire, the flames too hot to douse
The pool is open, come into my house

Don't make me wait
Come into my house
(Don't make me wait)
(Give me body)

Here's a dance step from Al and Kika
Bass and treble flow through the speakers
Ride the rhythm, I know it's gonna reach ya
I'm the Queen Latifah
Now it's time to run through it
Forty-five King (yeah, baby) cue it
Yeah there you go, I told you you could do it
Now did you enjoy it? (that was cool) I knew it
Dance to the beat of the drum, give me some

With the Flavor Unit I come
To say, "ride the grooveline
Don't swing the pipe vine
Listen to the smooth line
Throw away the white line"
It's a house party I'm hostin'
Come and rock with the one who's chosen
You can't turn me inside out
For those who dare to
Come into my house

Don't make me wait
Come into my house
(Don't make me wait)
(Give me body)

It's a new fusion I'm usin'
You ask what is it I'm doin'
Hip-hop house, hip-hop jazz
With a little pizazz
From the Queen, the Queen of Royal Badness
Remember me from "Wrath of My Madness"?
This is my rap that rocks this party
I'm a hijack and jack your body
This is not an erotic interlude
Keep in mind I move multitudes
The Asiatic black woman hard-core beat drummin'
It's hard to keep a good woman down so I keep comin'
Blow for blow I take and I give some
Still I rise and I symbolize wisdom
I hope the lyrical display has you aroused
It's an open invitation
Come into my house

Don't make me wait
Come into my house
(Don't make me wait)
(Give me body)

Queen Latifah

The Evil That Men Do

You asked, I came
So behold the Queen
Let's add a little sense to the scene
I'm livin' positive
Not out here knocked up
But the lines are so dangerous
I oughta be locked up
This rhyme doesn't require prime time
I'm just sharin' thoughts in mind
Back again because I knew you wanted it
From the Latifah with the Queen in front of it
Droppin' bombs, you're up in arms and puzzled
The lines will flow like fluid while you guzzle
You slip, I'll drop you on a BDP-produced track
From KRS to be exact
It's a Flavor Unit quest that today has me speakin'
'Cause it's knowledge I'm seekin'
Enough about myself, I think it's time that I tell you
About the Evil That Men Do

Situations, reality, what a concept
Nothin' ever seems to stay in step
So today here is a message for my sisters and brothers
Here are some things I want to cover
A woman strives for a better life
But who the hell cares
Because she's livin' on welfare
The government can't come up with a decent housin' plan
So she's in no man's land
It's a sucker who tells you you're equal
(You don't need 'em
Johannesburg cries for freedom)

We the people hold these truths to be self-evident
(But there's no response from the president)
Someone's livin' the good life tax-free
'Cause some poor girl can't find
A way to be crack-free
And that's just part of the message
I thought I had to send you
About the Evil That Men Do

Tell me, don't you think it's a shame
When someone can put a quarter in a video game
But when a homeless person approaches you on the street
You can't treat him the same
It's time to teach the deaf, the dumb, the blind
That black on black crime only shackles and binds
You to a doom, a fate worse than death
But there's still time left
To stop puttin' your conscience on cease
And bring about some type of peace
Not only in your heart but also in your mind
It will benefit all mankind
Then there will be one thing
That will never stop you
And it's the Evil That Men Do

rUn - D. M.c.

Faces

In your face all the time
All in your face when I'm kickin' my rhyme
All these faces in front of me
Face to face with Run-D.M.C.

Faces, faces, faces, faces

Knuckleheads in my face for a second
But I move the crowd and I reckon
That a sucker might jump and try to bass
So kill that noise and get out my face, punk
And let a real M.C. collect dollars
The true crew and few come from Hollis, Queens
And by all means necessary
My vocabulary is very extensive, and expensive
So hard it'll put you in intensive care
Proceed with caution
Often suckers get lost in the sauce when
Faces just start speakin' on faces
And leavin' traces of a racist remark
And that sparks a fight day and night, dark and light
Different types of faces

Faces, faces, faces, faces

As we come back on, as we come back on
(All in your face I place this rhyme)
In this groove, your face is doomed
You got punched in your face as soon as you heard this
    tune

I race at a pace with no shoe laces
The race is faces, places, disgraces
Taste the bass of the racial facial
Disgraceful, tasteless, races, faces
Get out my face, don't bass, don't waste my time, my brother
I'm not color blind
I walk the face of the earth
Hey step, face the best and I'll just
Rip, flip or trip, won't shut up or let go
Get out my face so we could go head up
Damn, D, yo yo, they don't understand me
In this land when they always try to ban me
Hyping the stereotype of a face
And that's the problem with the human race

Haste makes waste, don't trace the other places
We're all the same but with different faces

Faces, faces, faces, faces

Faces
Yeah, D
And everywhere I go I see
Faces
Faces
Around, around the world, international faces, yeah
Now bust it

Yo, I took a look in the face of a girlie
The way she looked that day, I must say
Something about the way my Afro's growin'
Well, is it funky? (Yeah) well, OK
Is she jockin' my 'fro or my fame
Do she want me because of my name
I like the ladies sweet and serious
Not those hos that plays the game
On every Tom, Dick, and Harry
Sean, Jerry, John, Nick, Curly, Mo, and Larry
You thinkin' you'll marry, well you're crazy
My baby you won't carry
'Cause I like a girl that's low key
That's how it's gotta be to be with me
And I'll take her to all the exotic places
The name of this jam is called
Faces

So many faces
And everywhere I go I see
Faces
Everywhere you go you see
Faces
International faces, I'm an Afro and I'm outta here

rUn -D. M.c.

It's Like That

Unemployment at a record high
People coming, people going, people want to die
Don't ask me because I don't know why
But it's like that and that's the way it is

People in the world try to make ends meet
You travel by car, train, bus, or feet
I said you got to work hard to want to compete
It's like that and that's the way it is

Money is the key to end all your woes
Your ups, your downs, your highs, and your lows
Won't you tell me last time that love bought your clothes
It's like that and that's the way it is

Bills rise higher every day
We receive much lower pay
I'd rather stay young, go out, and play
It's like that and that's the way it is

War going on across the sea
Street soldiers killing the elderly
Whatever happened to unity
It's like that and that's the way it is

Disillusion is the word
That's used by me when I'm not heard
I just go through life with my glasses blurred
It's like that and that's the way it is

You can see a lot in this life span
Like a bum eating out of a garbage can
You notice one time he was your man
It's like that (what?) and that's the way it is

You should have gone to school
You could have learned a trade
But you laid in the bed
Where the bums have laid
Now all the time you're crying that you're underpaid
It's like that (what?) and that's the way it is

One thing I know is that life is short
So listen up, homeboy, give this a thought
The next time someone's teaching, why don't you get taught
It's like that (what?) and that's the way it is

If you really think about it, times aren't that bad
The one that messes with successes will make you glad
Stop playing, start praying, you won't be sad
It's like that (what?) and that's the way it is

When you feel your failure, sometimes it hurts
For a meaning in life is why you search
Take the bus or the train, drive to school or church
It's like that and that's the way it is

Here's another point in life you should not miss
Do not be a fool who's prejudiced
Because we're all written down on the same list
It's like that and that's the way it is

You know it's like that and that's the way it is
Because it's like that and that's the way it is
You know it's like that and that's the way it is
Because it's like that and that's the way it is

rUn -D. M.c.

My Adidas

My Adidas walk through concert doors
And roamed all over coliseum floors
I stepped on stage at Live Aid

All the people gave and the poor got paid
And out of those speakers, I did speak
I wore my sneakers but I'm not a sneak
My Adidas touched the sands of foreign lands
With mike in hand I cold took command
My Adidas and me, close as can be
We make a mean team, my Adidas and me
We get around together and down forever
And we won't be had when caught in bad weather

My Adidas
My Adidas

My Adidas standing on 2–5th Street
Funky-fresh and yes, cold on my feet
With no shoestrings in 'em, I did not win 'em
I bought 'em off the ave with the black Lee denim
I like to sport them, that's why I bought them
A sucker tried to steal them so I caught him and I fought
    him
And I walk down the street and bop to the beat
With Lee on my leg and Adidas on my feet
And yo, now I'm just standing here, shooting the gift
Me and D and my Adidas standing on 2–5th

My Adidas
My Adidas

Now me and my Adidas do the illest thing
We like to stamp out pimps with diamond rings
We slay all suckers who perpetrate
And lay down law from state to state
We travel on gravel, dirt, road, or street
I wear my Adidas when I rock the beat
On stage, front page, every show I go
It's Adidas on my feet, high top or low

My Adidas
My Adidas

Now the Adidas I possess for one man is rare
Myself, homeboy, got fifty pair
Got blue and black 'cause I like to chill
And yellow and green when it's time to get ill
Got a pair that I wear when I'm playing ball
With the heel inside, make me ten feet tall
My Adidas only brings good news
And they are not used as selling shoes
Wear black and white, white with black stripes
The ones I like to wear when I rock the mike
On the campus of the famous university
We took the beat from the street and put it on TV
My Adidas are seen on the movie screen
Hollywood knows we're good, if you know what I mean
We started in an alley, now we chill in Cali
And I won't trade my Adidas for no beat up Ballys

Salt-n-Pepa

Expression

Oh yeah, Oh yeah
Oh yeah, Oh yeah

You know life is all about expression
You only live once and you're not coming back
So express yourself, yeah

Express yourself
You gotta be you and only you, baby

Express yourself
Let me be me
Express yourself
Don't tell me what I cannot do, baby
Come on and work your body

Now, Jo want to be like Bob
Bob's got it goin' on with no job
And ever'thing Rob got, he got from Robin
And everything she got she got from ho hoppin'
My girl Jilly want to be like Jackie
Fat rope chains and I think that's wick-wacky
Tom and Dick want to be like Harry
Little do they know he's bitin' off Barry
Stan runs a scam but Vinnie's legit
Mercedes coup home troop with no kit
A businessman with a beeper for a reason
Not like Tim because it's in this season

Express yourself
You gotta be you and only you, baby

Yes, I'm Pep and there ain't no body
Like my body
Yes, I'm somebody
No, I'm sorry, I'm 'a rock this Mardi Gras
Until the party ends, friends
Yes, I'm blessed and I know who I am
I express myself on every jam
I'm not a man but I'm in command
Hot damn—I've got an all-girl band
And I wear the gear, yeah, I want to wear too
I don't care, dear, go ahead and stare, ooh
Afraid to be you, livin' in fear
Expression is rare
I dare you

Express yourself
You gotta be you and only you, baby

Yo, excuse us while we rap
(Go ahead, girls, express yourself)
My party's your party, anytime drop in cold
Hip-hoppin', it's always rockin'
Don't you like it when the music
Drop, jump, spread out and stop

Now bring in the go-go, uh-oh
Look at how my butt go
Rock from the left to the right
You wanna step to me, groove me, I know you want to do me
Come on, now fellas, don't fight at my door
They're bum-rushin', they hear the percussion sound
Of my go-go band
I've long ago learned my lesson
It's all about expression
Will the real Salt-N-Pepa please stand and

Express yourself
You gotta be you and only you, baby

Salt-n-Pepa

I'll Take Your Man

Salt-N-Pepa's back and we came to out-rap you
So get out my face before I smack you, ho
Don't you know, can't you understand
If you mess with me, I'll take your man

Uh uh uh uh uh
Well, I'll take your man right out the box
And put him under my padlock
So when you see us together, chillin' in the place
Cold walkin' and sportin' him in your face
Go 'head, roll your eyes, suck your teeth
Keep huffin' and puffin' like a dog in heat
You could call me a crook, a robber, a thief
But I'll be your butcher if you got beef
You know what's up, I ain't no poop out
'Cause Pepa kick butts off dumb young pups
Like you and the rest of your crew
If moms want static, I'll dis her too

So scram, you know who I am, damn, chick
Don't play me close 'cause I'll take your man

I'll take your man whenever I feel like it
This ain't a threat or bet, it's a damn promise
From me to you and your sex life's through
If you get another lover, I'll take him too
All I have to do is say a rhyme or two
And he'll hop and leave you like a kangaroo
I'll make him heel for me, even steal for me
His mother and father he'd kill for me
That's what you get for tryin' to play smart
Now take a hike with that slayed-up heart
Now you don't know if you're comin' or goin'
Look at your face, your jealousy's growin' and showin'
Don't get mad, you don't have the right
I throw below solo but lady like on the mike
Psyche is where I win my battles, huh
I'll handle you like a baby with a rattle
Don't make me prove to you that I can
Either give him up or get slammed
I'll take your man

I'll take your man
That's right, but just for spite
Because you tried to dis me when I was on the mike
But I really don't want 'im
The guy ain't fly, shoot
He can't afford to buy a Fila suit
Runs the same old gear, never had fresh wheels
What he whispered in my ear I can't repeat here
I don't wanna seem to be so damn mean
But you're the hippiest creator I've ever seen
Before I got on the stage, you wished me good luck
Turned around and told your friends I sucked
Well look at you now, you ain't got nobody
Searchin' for love in a fifth of Bacardi
You look bad, girl, you lookin' like you're dyin'
Ain't no use in cryin'
I'll take your man

Yo, Salt, school this fool, I'll take your man
Your fiancé, your husband
You ain't Alice, this ain't Wonderland
And when I say I will, you know I can
Don't mess with me 'cause I'll take your man

I'll take your man any time, at the drop of a dime
'Cause he's rappin' and strappin' so hard on mine
Everywhere I turn, everywhere I look
The brother eyein' me down, he's starin' down my throat
But he's a sucka, sucka? Soft-hearted punk
Goin' skiin' for skeezers, stunts for blunt
So that's why y'all have so many things in common
Him for jus' robbin', you for lap slobbin'
I never ever went out my way to get played
I keep guys like yours held down at bay
You know I can, I got the upper hand, tramp
You don't stand a chance
'Cause I'll take your man

Most girls have guys that's good to go
But yours is slow, he's a freakin' a-hole
The fact still stands, there's no change in plans
Yo, Pepa, your wish is my command
Now you know you know I'll take your
Man—check him out
Ya see what I mean?
He's leadin' the pack as the fella's scream
Go Sandy, get busy
Go Sandy, get busy
It's so easy to make 'em fall for me, Heather
No man can resist Salt-N-Pepa
Because we're perfect from head to toe
It's not speculation, your man says so
Revenge is sweet but payback's a trip, girlfriend
You won't know which is which
But I'll tell you this, don't try to answer this jam
Because if you do then I'll take your
Then I'll take your

And we'll take your
Man

Sch00ly d

Saturday Night

It was Saturday night
And I was feeling kinda sporty
Went to the barn
Caught me a forty
Got kinda high
And, uh, kinda drunk
So I had to beat up this little punk
Forgot my key
Had to ring my bell
My mama came down
She said, "Who the hell?"
Wait, mama, wait, it's me, your little son
Before I knew it, my mom pulled a gun
"I know who you are, but who the hell is that?"
I turned around, man, this bitch was fat
I really don't know how she got into the car
I musta picked her up when I left the bar
You know how I'm the only man
I wanted to chill
But you know how mothers are
She wanted to ill
We waited a little while, then we snuck upstairs
Step by step with a hint of fear
We got into my room, girl started to scream
My mom busted in, what a messed-up scene
Shirt ripped off, drawers down to my knees
Wait, mama, wait, mama, wait, wait please

Put back your gun and put down the broom
My mom messed up the room
The big fat girl went, "No respect"
She jumped up, had to put the bitch in check
Ya come a little closer and you will get shot
I'm sober anyway, I don't need no—hah-hah
You know what I mean?
It's one of those wild Saturday nights, y'all
You know what I mean?
Saturday nights is wild, man, yeah

It was Saturday night
And I was feelin' kinda funny
Gold around my neck
And pockets full of money
Stepped, went to the corner, man, and who did I see
But this superfine baby, lookin' back at me
I said, "Fly lady, man, you got a big butt"
Bitch turned around, all she said was, "What?"
"My name's Schooly School, baby, ah, what is yours?"
Before I know it, up come my boys
Noisy as hell and drunk as shit
Say, "Yo, Schooly School, what time is it?"
Looked a little closer and I knew it was a gag
What I thought was a girl was nuthin' but a fag
Yeah, another wild, wild Saturday night
You know what I mean?
Those Saturday nights keep gettin' wilder and wilder

Everybody rappin'
But they don't know how
Shoulda seen the boy
Rappin' to the cow
He rapped so hard that the nigger saw smoke
He lit up a cheeba and they both took a toke
The cow got high and the boy got by
Hey, don't come in my face and ask me why
Cheeba, cheeba, y'all
Yes, that cheeba cheeba makin' him feel like that
Cheeba cheeba y'all

Oh, some call it cheeba cheeba
Some call it weed
It's the killer, it's the thriller
it's the thing that you need
So cheeba cheeba ya'll

Little Miss Muffet
Sat on her tuffet
Smokin'a J 'n' scratchin' a itch
Along came a spider and sat down beside her
And said, "Yo, what's up with that bitch?"

But then down the road
Came Mary and her lamb
Smokin' a lacy in each and every hand
The poor little spider, he couldn't score any
They was two dollar bitches and he only had a penny
Cheeba cheeba y'all, yeah
Cheeba cheeba, y'all

Well let me tell you a little tale
About Peter the Pimp
Sucker M.C. tryin' to cop a lick
Rode around town in a couple of cars
Got gagged by the man tryin' to stick up a bar
The judge said, "Boy, yo, what was on your mind"
He said, "Hey, cheeba cheeba, cocaine and some wine"
The judge said, "Boy, relax and have a beer
You won't be doin' shit for the next ten years"
Cheeba cheeba, y'all
Yes that cheeba cheeba
Cheeba cheeba, y'all

Some call it cheeba, some call it weed
It's a killer, it's a thriller, it's the thing that ya need
Say cheeba cheeba, y'all
Yeah you know
Me and my man Cool Money
My man M&M
We're most chillin', you know what I mean

My name happens to be Schooly D
If you didn't guess by now, you know
Only Schooly D'll make some crazy-ass shit like this
I get back
Take it away, Cool

Roxanne Shante

Brothers Ain't Shit

Brothers ain't shit
They're lookin' for the next big ass they can stick
But this here chick's not on your dick
Pullin' your cars up close by the sidewalk
And got the nerve to get mad if I don't talk
Steady schemin' on how they wanna stick it from the back
A young motherfucker sellin' crack
Go home and go to bed, son
You just comin' from the barbershop and tryin' to get your head done?
Take your ass downtown on 10th Avenue
Because a sister like me is not havin' you
Play her, go around tellin' other brothers that you laid her
So I guess I'll see your ass later

Some brothers approach you while you're shoppin'
Their girl's not around so they're going' ho hoppin'
From one girl to another
You turn your head for a minute, he's tryin' to kick it to your
    mother
Stop smilin', I know all you wanna do is hit
And I really don't give a shit
They get mad 'cause I always look serious
So they slam on my motherfuckin' period
I'm not impressed by the jewelry and the mink, dummy
Why don't you put some of your money in the bank, sonny
And if I hurt your feelings, I meant to

'Cause these here pants, huh, ya can't get into
Matter of fact, I'm tookin'
So you brothers in the jeep can keep lookin' but I ain't hookin'
Yes, I'm giving you the slip
All you can do is trick
Word
'Cause brothers ain't shit

I'm on my way to the mall with a couple of friends
Some niggers pull up in a blue Benz
A kid named Mark with dark glasses
Talkin' about, "Yo, y'all got some real fat asses"
I kept walkin', Tracy stopped and started talkin'
With all these motherfuckers hawkin' with that dumb-lookin' grin
Bitch gets in the car that was carryin' three men
I know the whole game well
They spend a little money, you end up at a hotel
Well, that's how they planned it
She didn't wanna screw so they left her ass stranded
That's what she gets for wilin'
Cold left the dumb bitch somewhere out in Long Island
Next time she'll act decent
And her moms won't have to come get her ass from a precinct
Remember, Shanté told you
Drugs is not the only thing a girl can say no to
You gotta watch every move that you make on the street
Word up, 'cause talk ain't that cheap
It may become a bad habit
You see a brother with a little bit of dough, you wanna grab it
I get approached by a man sometimes
I throw a fit
Word
'Cause brothers ain't shit

Brothers ain't shit
So don't honk your horn, keep rollin'
No, I don't wanna ride
'Cause the shit might be stolen
Anyway, I know your number
Ya got a "gas, grass or ass" sticker on your bumper

Go ahead and say I'm stuck up
'Cause I ain't doin' nothin' that will make my rep fucked up
'Cause it happens to the best of us
Fuck the rest of us
Niggers keep testin' us
A man could make you wanna kill him
Or late at night
Make you wanna thrill him
He'll give you money, you can even be fly
But he still has to cheat and you wanna know why
That's the dog in him—woof woof
That makes him get up in the middle of the night and go "poof"
You say, "Yo, yo, where you goin'?"
He's cheatin' and he's skeezin' and you're not even knowin'
But this is what they usually do
Suck on the thing and they make ya go "whoo"
And then he hits the door
And for the rest of the night, you don't see him no more
He's got shit at your house, here's what you do
You should do some voodoo
Make his dick small
Make him see spiders on the wall
Then make him throw a fit
Why? 'Cause brothers ain't shit
Brothers ain't shit

Roxanne Shanté

Have a Nice Day

Some people call me Shanny, some people call me Rox
Those who try to I just knocks them out the box
'Cause I'm Shanté an' y'all know the routine
An' here we go again so all hail the queen
I left for a while but it was worth the wait
Because it gave me just enough time to create

A funky rhythm that's guaranteed to move the world
Have the party people screamin' now, "Go on girl"
It's like Diana Ross, I'm the boss
An' those who disapprove you can go for yours
But to think a girl like me, ha, is easy to take
Treat me like Nell Carter, give me a break
'Cause I'm a super female that's called Shanté
And like Hurricane Annie I'll blow you away
Whenever I'm in a battle, yo, I don't play
So you best go about your way
An' have a nice day

A lot of M.C.s today really know how to please
But I gave birth to most of them M.C.s
So when it comes around to the month of May
Send me your royalty check for Mother's Day
Because, yo, ya know, ya can't deal with this
I'm Shanté, the microphone grand mistress
I pioneered like Lola Falana
With a name that stands big like Madonna
Speaking of Madonna, some girls on the mike
Rap like virgins and get real tight
But I get loose with the rhymes I produce
That's why I'm queen of the crew with the juice
'Cause I'm a super female that's called Shanté
And like Hurricane Annie I'll blow you away
Whenever I'm in a battle, yo, I don't play
So you best go about your way
And have a nice day

Shanté—the baddest around
And a name like that can't be broken down
As supreme highness or mighty noble topic exponent
An' any title for a girl you can't believe I own
'Cause to me there ain't none fresher
For me to rock—my pleasure
I'll pick up the microphone and start rockin'
Say the funky rhymes that have the people clockin'
Me, the S-h-a-n-t-é
Good lookin', never tooken' female M.C.

I'm five foot four, maybe a little bigger, brown skin complexion
With the nice figure
Yes, the super female that's called Shanté
And like Hurricane Annie, I'll blow you away
Whenever I'm in a battle, yo
I don't play
So you best go about your way
An' have a nice day

You may remember the voice from a few years ago
When I first came out and dissed UTFO
I chilled for a while, I put down my pen
But now some suckers from the Bronx got me started again
Now I'm not out to dis the whole Boogie Down
Just a featherweight crew from that part of town
Ya made a little record and then you start frontin'
Tried to blank the Juice Crew but ain't hear nuthin'
Now KRS-One, you should go on vacation
With a name soundin' like a wack radio station
And as for Scott La Rock, you should be ashamed
When T La Rock said "It's yours"
He didn't mean his name
So step back poppin' all that junk
Or else BDP will stand for brokin down punks
'Cause I'm an all-star, just like Julius Irving
And Roxanne Shanté is only good for steady servin'
I'm Shanté, I'm-I'm Shanté
I'm Shanté, I'm and your rhymes rh-rhymes are dead

Shazzy

Giggahoe

When I first met you, my eyes were filled with wonder
My heart filled with joy from the spell that I was under
Ya cracked a smile so delectable

That I could eat it
Eyes so full of mischief
That I could read it
Your face told me a story that I really didn't wanna know
Marks and shattered hearts as you
Were runnin' like a Giggahoe
You were proud of your life, I don't blame you
But how many times did the girlies inflame you?
I saw your face when you were pissin' the hot coals
You tried to hide but you were burnin' the toilet bowls
And one-by-one, three down and only two to go
One's already pregnant
The other one's a silly ho
I was a fool for the love in my own mind
Try'na see a love in you that I couldn't find
I gave ya all 'n' all ya did was take
I tried to love but all ya love was fake
'N' you were faker than a fortune cookie
Or a fairy tale
More artificial than a Lee press-on nail
You'd 'a played me out like a priest at a peep-show
Ya ran the game but you were runnin' like a Giggahoe

You scalliwag, battle-axin' pickaninny, pocket-scratchin' Ebenezer
Penny-pincher, nickels for dimes, pennies for clinchin', rags
For clothes and naps for hair
All you want is the poonani
I can't get over you, you got some nerve

You used to go off days, lovin' and leavin' and comin' home
And I used to wait like a puppy for a milkbone
Once you control me, you knew all my deepest fears
I said, "Hold up, I will cry no more tears"
Ya had a mind that was childlike
Ya didn't get your way
And you were wildlike, violent outbreak once and only once, ya
    see
The time you played fly, ya tried to mush me
Are you crazy, you dog, you need a muzzle
That's why I stepped back and I swung on ya with a shovel

I ain't livin' like a low-budget look-a-like
I got a lot of love to give, that's just too hype
Ya shoulda knew what ya had but ya didn't know
'Cause all ya ever wanted to be was a Giggahoe

You nigga-nappin', corny-snappin', booga-pickin', butt-be-kickin'
No tooth, big-lip breathin', night-funk lovin'-mother
Starvin'-marvin' eatin' out of garbage cans wearin' holey
Drawers and a bra strap, tryin' to call yourself a man?
Mack daddyin' on the corner and talkin' about . . .

Somethin' a rest up, lay, and slobber down
Ya had a woman in me but ya also run around
I hate to say it but our love went wrong
Hate to admit it, but my love was strong
We had a good thing but you were too naive to know it
Oops—but you're the macho one, ya can't show it
I was two steps ahead of your game, so now it's your loss
Took my walkin' papers from you and I stepped off
Oh, but you're the winner
You're on a love streak
And all the letters I wrote—well, you can read 'em and weep
And remember me
And remember my face and all the words that I said
Because I won't leave a trace
And anywhere that I go, believe it won't be too far
'Cause ya know who I am and ya know who you are
So believe it and now that I'm gettin' paid
I still chill in the park but not on the arcade
No need in wonderin'
'Cause ya already know
Don't even step to me now
'Cause you're a Giggahoe

Suck my butt with a thousand crazy straws, you stanky smelly bum
You're really somethin' and ain't about nothin', you been
Havin' three-day-old drawers crawlin' around the room
Smellin' up the place, all the time, everytime I walk in here
Ya ain't got no monies to pay the bills, you big square head
Lunch-box carryin' wearin' old Pumas from 1972, wearin' your

Big Salvation Army wardrobe, ain't got no kind of clothes
Always comin' to me, steppin' to every female you can
Bumpin' em up, knockin' em up, hos, non-hos, you name it
Disease-carryin', disease-breedin' Giggahoe . . .

Sir mix-a-Lot

My Hooptie

My Hooptie rollin'
Tail pipe draggin'
Heat don't work
And my girl keeps naggin'

'69 Buick
Deuce keeps rollin'
One hubcap
'Cause three got stolen

Bumper shook loose
Chrome keeps scrapin'
Mis-match tires
And my whitewalls flakin'

Hit Mickey D's
Maharaji starts to bug
He ate a quarter pounder
Threw the pickles on my rug

Runnin', movin'
Tab's expired
Girlies try to dis
And say my car looks tired

Hit my brakes
Out-slid Skittles

Tinted back window
With the bubble in the middle

Whose car is it?
Posse won't say
We all play it off
When you look our way

Rollin' four deep
Tires smoke up the block
Gotta roll this bucket
'Cause my Benz is in the shop

My Hooptie
My Hooptie
Now let's roll!

Four-door nightmare
Trunk lock stuck
Big dice on the mirror
Grill like a truck

Lifters tickin'
Accelerator stickin'
Somethin' on my left
Front wheel keeps clickin'

Picked up the girlies
Now we eight deep
Car's barely movin'
But now we got heat

Made a left turn
As I watched in fright
My ex-girlfriend
Shot out my headlight

She was standin' in the road
So I smashed her toes
Mash my pedal
Boom, down she goes

Boy, I ain't lyin'
Long hairs flyin'

We flipped the skeez off
Dumb girl starts cryin'

Baby called the cops
Now I'm gettin' nervous
The cops see a beeper
And the suckers might serve us

Hit a side street
And what do we find
Some young punk
Droppin' me a flip-off sign

Put the deuce in reverse
And started to curse
Another sucker on the southside
About to get hurt

Homey got scared
So I got on
Yeah, my group got paid
But my group's still strong

Posse move north
Headin' for the CD
Ridin' real fast
So the cops don't see me

Mis-match tires
Got my boys uptight
Two Vogues on the left
Uniroyal on the right

Hooptie bouncin'
Runnin' on leaded
This is what I sport
When you call me big-headed

A pot-hole crusher
Red-light rusher
Musher of a brotha
'Cause I'm plowin' over suckers

In a Hooptie

It's a three-ton monster
Econo-box stomper
Snatch your girlie
If you don't, I'll romp her

Dinosaur rush
Lookin' like Shaft
Some get bold
But some get smashed

Cops say the car smokes
But I won't listen
It's a '69 deuce
So the hell with emission

Rollin' in Tacoma
I could get burned . . .
Betta make a U-turn

Spotted this freak
With immense posterior
Tryin' to roll smooth
Through the Hilltop area

Brothas start lettin' off
Kickin' that racket
Thinkin' I'm a rock star
Slingin' them packets

I ain't with that
So I smooth eject
Hit I-5
With the dope cassette

Playin' that tuff crew
Hard-core dope . . . huh?
The tape deck broke

Damn, what's next?
Brotha's in Gortex
Tryin' to find a spot
Where we could hunt for sex
Found a little club

Called the MCO . . .
Military, competition, you know

I ain't really fazed
'Cause I pop much game
Rolled up tough
'Cause I got much fame

How ya doin', baby?
My name is Mix-A-Lot
Mix-A-Lot got a Benz, boy
Quit smokin' that rock

I got dissed but
It ain't no thang
Runnin' that game
With the home-made slang

Baby got ished
Bremelo gip
Keep laughin' at the car
And you might get clipped

By a Hooptie

Runnin' outta gas
Stuck in traffic
Far left lane
Throwin' up much static

Input, output
Carburetor fulla soot
What'cha want me to do, Mix?
Push, Freak, push

Sputta, sputta
Rollin' over guttas
Cars dipped low
With hard-core brothas

Tank on E
Pulled in the Arco
Cops on tip
For Colombian cargo

We fit a stereotype
That's what he said
Big long car
Four big black heads

Cops keep jockin'
Grabbin' like 'gators
'Bout a stereotype
I'm lookin' nothin' like Noriega

Cops took my wallet
Looked at my license
His partner said . . .
"Damn, they all look like Tyson"

Yes, I'm legit
So they gotta let me go
This bucket ain't rollin' in snow

It's my Hooptie

Sir Mix-a-Lot

National Anthem

(as "The Star-Spangled Banner" is sung in the background)
I'm livin' like hell in a world of death
Protectors of the people wear bullet-proof vests
Your little nephew, flipped him an Uzi
Shot 'em up then—"Who me?"
Locked in a trap by Republican villains
Pinstripe suits, experts at killin'
Civil war but some want out
Trapped in a box called the ghetto, we shout
Heading for the strip because the squares ain't hip
Sell a couple of keys, make the homeboys trip
The President is a dope man's friend

The government's strong but the dope got in
Punish the accused, but the trial was short
A black man dogged in an all-white court
The jury's dismissed, prosecutor says, "Can him"
Now I'm ashamed of my National Anthem

The Pentagon had a plan for a rescue
They said, "Intelligence never makes a miscue"
The thirty-first was the date of death
Lieutenant Colonel Higgins, you know the rest
No negotiations with the terrorist force
But Iran still buzzing off of Oliver North
The Ayatollah's dead, but the heart's not gone
The burning of the flag and Iran goes on
Anti-American, we're loved by few
We pay big money to the ones that do
The Christian militia, they give us big knowledge
But the Pentagon messed up and wouldn't acknowledge
Ollie took orders from the number-one man
But the crap hit the fan and superiors ran
Democrats tripped, the committee said, "Can him"
Now I'm ashamed of my National Anthem

Am I Communist? No, but my brain ain't slow
Not long ago, Mix-A-Lot was poor
Never helped out by the ones with clout
I was mad at the world because I felt left out
Stealing hubcaps, stereos, anything to get paid
I realize I'm a modern-day slave
Posse downtown, the sight was set
I saw my homeboy's mother with a buggy and a bag
People walked by, laughing at poverty
I looked in her face and I soon saw me
College-educated but you can't get a job
The American Dream once again got robbed
Vietnam vets on the streets, that's a shame
Fighting for the man and the man play games
Dogged by the hippies, dope-smoking critics
You blame it on the soldier, but your government did it

My National Anthem
My National Anthem

You gonna teach me now about the care and feeding of
    politicians?
Bolivia, Colombia, the C.I.A.
Any similarities, I won't say
But the dope gets in, uncut like P-Funk
Heading over borders in scent-free trunks
Coffee over dope but the dog don't sniff it
Remember that lady that was broke, she's with it
Started with a key, clocked seven Gs
Then got another shipment, pure D
Heading for Portland, the money was better
Rolling in a Porsche and a cashmere sweater
Crime, revenge, I'm telling you this
The people that laughed are the people that know
Her community complained, calling the police
But where was the community when she was in the street
Dope's coming in and it's killing at random
Now I'm ashamed of my National Anthem

My National Anthem
My National Anthem
My National Anthem
I'm ashamed of my National Anthem
("*The Star-Spangled Banner*" *concludes*)

Slick Rick

Treat Her Like a Prostitute

Here's an oldie but goodie
Hit it
Excuse me

What?
Can I have your attention?
Mm-hmm
There's just a few things that I've got to mention (Uh-huh)
There's girlies out here that seem appealing
But they all come in your life and cold hurt your feelings
I'm telling you
As Rick is my name
I wouldn't trust no girl unless she feels the same
Treat 'em like a prostitute (Do what?)
Don't treat no girlie well until you're sure of the scoop
'Cause all they do is they hurt and trample
Listen up close, here comes my first example

Now ya been with your girlfriend for quite a while
Plans for the future, she's having your child
Celebrate with friends drinking cans and quarts
Telling all your friends about your family thoughts
One friend was drunk so he starts to act wild
He tells the truth about the kid
It's not your child
Acting like a jerk and on his face was a smirk
He said, "Your wife went berserk while you was hard at work"
And she led him on and tried to please him
She didn't waste time, she didn't try to tease him

Treat 'em like a prostitute (Do what?)
Don't treat no girlie well until you're sure of the scoop
'Cause all they do is they hurt and trample
Listen up close, here comes my second example

It's your wife
You buy the tramp jewels and clothes
You get sentimental and bring home a rose
Give her everything 'cause you swear she's worth it
All your friends tell you, "The bitch don't deserve it"
Love is blind, so there goes your wealth
Until one day, you see things for yourself
Came home from work early, Mr. Loverman

You had a card and some candy in your right hand
There's the mailman, he was short yet stout
He went inside your house and didn't come back out
Bust it
Just a friendly stop, come on, is it?
The mailman comes and he pays your wife a visit?
The thought alone makes your temperature boil
You say to yourself, she might still be loyal
You open up your door and stand in a trance
You see the mailman's bag and the mailman's pants
Came home to party
At work had a hard day
Look around your house and you say, "Where the hell are they?"
Run upstairs up to your bedroom
You look inside your room, you see something brewin'
Cover your mouth because you almost choke
You see the mailman's dick way up your wife's throat

Treat 'em like a prostitute (Mm-hmm)
Don't treat no girlie well until you're sure of the scoop
'Cause all they do is they hurt and trample
Listen up close, here comes my last example

Now your girl, she don't like to have sex a lot
And today she's ready and she's hot, hot, hot
As you open up the door she says, "Get on the floor"
She wants to try things she's never tried before
She takes off your drawers and works you over
She calls you Twinkles
And you call her Rover
Next thing you know, the ho starts to ill
She says, "I love you, Harold" and your name is Will
That's not the half 'til you start to ride her
Take off your rubber and there's one more inside her
It's not yours—who can it be?
I think it was a slick rapper, his name is M.C. Ricky

Treat 'em like a prostitute
Don't treat no girlie well, treat no girlie well
Treat no girlie well, until you're sure of the scoop

sPecial eD
I'm the Magnificent

I am the magnificent!
I'm the magnificent with the sensational style
And I can go on and on for like a mile, a minute
I get in it like a car and drive
And if the record is a smash, I can still survive
'Cause I'm the man of steel on the wheel that you're steerin'
Or rather playin' on the record that you're hearin'
You might not understand what I'm sayin' at first
So Action Love, put it in reverse

I'm just conversin' with you, person
This is just a conversation
I'm Special Ed, with the special presentation, hey
I like to play, so for me it's recreation
It's not just a job, it's an adventure
If worse comes to worse, I've got your thirst quencher
But ya gotta buy it, don't even try it
I don't rhyme for free, no matter how dry it gets
I collect my money in sets
One before the show and again when I jet
So I get mine, and I'm 'a get more
'Cause I'm financially secure and I'm sure
So I don't need your tips or advice
'Cause I'm too nice for that, you rat
I can't stand mice, I'm like a cat, kinda frisky
Battling is risky business
You might acquire dizziness, just like whisky
Isn't this enough?
Oh, you think you're tough, cookie
I think you better call your bookie
'Cause you can bet your life, I'm gonna play you like hooky
On a Friday, this is my day
When I was through, I heard you say, "Why they dis me like that?"

I shoulda repent
Somebody shoulda said that Special Ed was the magnificent

I am the magnificent!
I'm the magnificent, dynamite, super dope, outta sight
Special Ed with my trusty pal
Action Love, the run we shall
Continue to win, yet this is not a game
But I'm 'a play you if say you claim to be better
I hate rumors and I give tumors
And our jammies get Grammys
Yet I'm not an actor, it's just a factor that we're famous
Don't blame us for nothin'
Action Love is cuttin', I'm on the rhyme
Skin your teeth and it's your beef that I'll grind
Like a butcher, I'll put you on a table
And let my D.J. cut ya
But you're such a little sucker
I might not even touch ya
I betcha whatcha want is just attention
Your mother and your father shoulda used some prevention
Look at all the time and the money they spent
And now ya wanna die against I—the magnificent?
I am the magnificent!
I'm the magnificent with the sensational style
And I can go on and on for like a mile a minute
'Cause I get in it like a car and drive
And if the record is a smash, I can still survive
I'm the man of steel on the wheel that you're steerin'
Or rather playin' on the record that you're hearin'
You might not understand what I'm singin' at first
So Action Love, put it in reverse

I am the magnificent

Jimmy Spicer

Money (Dollar Bill, Y'all)

Yo, man, them boys is dope
Word
Scratchmaster T (Oh man), Supertrooper (Word)—the posse is
    definitely in effect
Word (word), that's a good record, man
Yo, yo, yo, hold up, m—, yo, can I get a dollar, man?
A dollar?
Anyone got a dollar?
Yeah
You want a dollar?
This is Bill, man, I ain't got no change
I'm kinda thirsty
I don't got no change
OK, I'll give you a dollar, you want a dollar?
Well let me hear the record at least
You want a dollar?
First the record
Psyche, I'll tell you what—dollar bill, y'all
This is by Jimmy Spicer
This record is dope, this is about cash money
Dollar bill, y'all, check it out

Dollar bill, y'all
Dollar bill, y'all
Dollar dollar dollar dollar dollar bill, y'all
Dollar bill, y'all
Dollar bill, y'all
Dollar dollar dollar dollar dollar bill, y'all

Money puts ya home on the range
Money puts the boogie in the stock exchange
Ya make money on your nine to five
To earn your livin' so you survive

It takes money to pay your rent and to eat
Without money, you're hungry on the street
It takes money money
Cash money money
Ah, to the bill

So ya steal some money
Ya go to jail
And then ya turn around, need somethin' for bail
But then ya need a dime to call your lawyer
To plead innocence and say they never say ya
But before your lawyer can get ya free
He asks how will ya pay his fee
But ya have no money, you're in a jam
Your lawyer says to throw the man in the slammer

It takes money money (Dollar bill y'all, dollar bill, y'all)
Cash money (Dollar dollar dollar dollar dollar bill, y'all)
To the bill
It takes money money
That's right, cash money
To the bill, to the B-I-double-L bill
Hit it

Dollar bill, y'all
Dollar bill, y'all
Dollar dollar dollar dollar dollar bill, y'all
Dollar bill, y'all
Dollar bill, y'all
Dollar dollar dollar dollar dollar bill, y'all

It takes money to buy that TV set
It takes money to place a casino bet
It takes money to buy that radio
And money for gas so your car will go
It takes money for you to buy a house
It takes money for a trap to catch a mouse
It takes money to take a vacation trip
And cruise the ocean on a luxury ship
It takes money money money

It takes money to get interest from the bank
It takes money from an army to buy a tank
It takes money to pay your doctor bill
And your psychiatrist, if you're actin' ill
It takes money money money

Dollar bill, y'all
Dollar bill, y'all
Dollar dollar dollar dollar dollar bill, y'all
Dollar bill, y'all
Dollar bill, y'all
Dollar dollar dollar dollar dollar bill, y'all

Well, if you got kids, then ya know
The more you stay, the more they grow
They go from two to four, in a two
But don't think that the growin' is through
They go from four to six and what they wear
They have you spendin' money like a millionaire
They go from eight, nine, and then to ten
Your baby has you spendin' money again
With all your money now gone, your rent's now due
And now your landlord is houndin' you
But you go to lay down and rest your head
But the bill collector done took your bed
It takes money money
Cash money money
To the bill

Dollar bill, y'all
Dollar bill, y'all
Dollar dollar dollar dollar dollar bill, y'all
Dollar bill, y'all
Dollar bill, y'all
Dollar dollar dollar dollar dollar bill, y'all

When ya got ones, fives, and tens
Then sometimes you got friends
But when ya only got pennies, nickels, and dimes
Then you only got friends some of the time
So you make a million dollars to pay your tax

To keep the IRS off you back
Uncle Sam got his, I got mine's
And now I got friends all the time
It takes money money
Cash money, that's right
It takes money money
Cash money money
To the bill, to the B-I-double-L bill
Hit it

spoonie gee

Spoonin' Rap

Ya say, "One for the trouble, two for the time"
Come on y'all, let's rock the . . .

Yes yes, y'all
Freak freak, y'all
Funky beats, y'all
Then ya rock 'n' roll
Then ya roll 'n' rock
And then ya rockin' to the beat that just don't wantcha to stop
'Cause I'm the S to the P double O-N-Y
The one M.C. who ya can't deny
'Cause I'm the baby-maker, I'm the woman taker
I'm the cold-crushin' lover, the heartbreaker
So come on fly girls, please don't stop
'Cause I'm M.C. Spoonie Gee, wanna hit the top
And young ladies, rock on

I was drivin' down the street on a stormy night
Up ahead there was a terrible fright
There was a big fine lady, she was crossin' the street
She had a box with the disco beat
So I hit my brakes but they're not all there

I missed the young lady by only a hair
And then I took a mere look, I said, "la-di-da-di"
A big fine girl, she had a helluva body
Then she looked at me and then she started switchin'
So I took all my keys out of the ignition
Got out the car and kept my mouth shut
'Cause my twenty-twenty vision was right on her butt
I caught up with her I said, "Ya look so fine
I swear to god, I wish you was mine"
She said, "Hey, boy, you're Spoonie Gee"
"That's right, honey, how do you know me?"
She said, "Spoonie Gee, you're all the same
And everybody who disco know your name"
I said, "Come on baby, it's not too far
We gonna take a little walk to my car"
Once we got to the car, we sat in the seat
And then the box was rockin' to the funky beat
And then I looked at her and pushed the seat back
Turned off her box and put on my eight-track
And then I started rappin' without no pause
'Cause my mind was just gettin' in those drawers
And then I got in the star
We started to do it to the beat
And started doin' like this
Started doin' the freak
Yes, yes, y'all
Freak freak, y'all
'Cause I'm M.C. Spoonie Gee, I wanna be known
As a major politician of the microphone
'Cause I'm a man's threat and I'm a woman's pimp
And I'm known as the men's joy
And I'm a man who fights on the microphone
And who all the people enjoy, y'all
Yes yes, y'all
Freak freak, y'all
Ya don't stop
Keep on

See I was breakin' and a-freakin' at a disco place
I met a fine girl, she had a pretty face

And then she took me home, ya say, "The very same night?"
The girl was on and she was outta sight
But then I got the girl for three hours straight
But I hadda go to work so I couldn't be late
I said, "Where's your man?" she said, "He's in jail"
I said, "Come on, baby, 'cause you're tellin' a tale"
'Cause if he comes at me and then he wants to fight
Ya see, I'm gonna get the man good, I'm gonna get 'im right
See I'm 'a roll my bell and keep the bullets still
And when I shoot my shot, I'm gonna shoots to kill
'Cause I'm the Spoonie-Spoon, I don't mess around
I drop a man where he stand right into the ground
You see from Africa to France, say, to Germany
Because ya can't get a man tryin' to mess with me
'Cause I'm a smooth talker, I'm the midnight stalker
I'm the image of the man they call the J.D. Walker
If you're gonna be my girl, just come along
And just clap your hands to my funky song
I don't drink, I don't smoke, I don't gamble neither
And most people call me a woman pleaser
'Cause I keep their phone numbers on a shelf
I go to make love and then I keep it to myself
So no one's gonna know what I'm doin' to you
Not your sister, brother, niece, nor your mother, father, too
And take that, y'all
And don't stop
Ya keep on and on and on and on
Like hot butter on, say what, the popcorn
Young ladies, rock on
Fly guys, what a big surprise
'Cause I'm M.C. Spoonie Gee, don't take no mess
From the north to south or from the east to west
'Cause everybody knows M.C. Spoonie Gee's the best
Young ladies, rock on, y'all
Rock rock, y'all, ya don't stop
Keep on to the shill shot
And then ya rock 'n' roll
And then ya roll 'n' rock
And then ya rock to the beat that just don't wantcha to stop
'Cause I'm the S to the P double O-N-Y Gee

I'm talkin' about me, M.C. Spoonie Gee
Rock on, y'all
Ya don't stop
Keep on to the shill shot
Rock on and on and on and on
Like hot butter on, say what, the popcorn
Don't stop the funky beat 'til the break of dawn
Young ladies, young ladies

'Cause I'm the cool-crushin' lover, goes on to supreme
And when it comes to fine girls, I'm like a lovin' machine
It comes to makin' love, I do the best I can
'Cause I'm known from coast to coast as the sixty-minute man
It comes to makin' face, I got the macho class
I have all the fly girls shakin' their ass
So for all you fly girls who wanna be loved
Check me out 'cause I'm the highest above
I'm gonna call you up and give you an invitation
So you can see the way Spoonie Gee rocks the nation
One time for the mike, y'all
Freak freak, y'all
Funky freaks, y'all
Ya go hip hop a hip hip a hop
And then ya rockin' to the hip and then ya rockin' the hop
And then ya on and on and on and on and on
The beat don't stop until the freaks are gone
And rock on, y'all, ya don't stop
Keep on to the shill shot
If when ya suckers sucker dudes commit a crime
Ya wanna do bad but don't the time
I say ya wanna be dissed and then ya wanna be a crook
Ya find a old lady, take her pocketbook
And then ya steal your mother's pocket money on the sly
You can run but you can't hide
When the cops crashed through, your face turned pale
I'm 'a tell you a little story about the jail
'Cause see in jail there's a game and it's called survival
And they run it down to ya on your first arrival
They tell ya what ya can and cannot do
But if ya go to jail, watch yours for crew

'Cause when ya go in the shower, he's pullin' his meat
He's lookin' at you and sayin' ya look real sweet
And at first there was one then ten walked in
Now how in the hell did you expect to win?
I said ya better look alive not like ya take dope
And please, my brother, don't drop the soap
And if ya get out the bathroom and you're alive
Just remember only a man can survive
In jail, of course, cause when you're doin' fifteen years
Got no thought, ya just have a walk
Never gets no bend
Your mind will turn the corner
Yes yes, y'all
Freak freak, y'all
Ya don't stop
Keep on to shill shot
Like a lime to a lemon and a lemon to a lime
I keep the funkiest beat to say I pass the time
And like lemon and lime and like a lime to a lemon
A M.C. could attract all the women
'Cause I'm Spoonie Gee and I wanna be known
As a major politician of the microphone
Yes yes, y'all
Freak freak, y'all
So just clap your hands
And just stomp your feet
And just rock to the rhythm of the funky beat
To the funky funky funky funky beat
The beat that makes ya get up
On past your feet
Young ladies, rock on, y'all
Rock on, y'all
'Til the break of dawn
I said, ya do the spank on the Patty Duke
Either one ya want, ya gotta get up to
To the rock rock and ya don't stop
Ya see, I jumped the turnstyle for a summer day
And then I seen the guy and then I fled away
And then he pulled his gun but he did not shoot
So come on everybody, let's pay the due

'Cause I'm livin' well and I'm ready to dance
Come on girl, let me show my romance
I'll let ya see the way, how I rock the mike
'Cause I know damn well that I could rock all night
Yes yes, y'all
Freak freak, y'all
Ya don't stop, keep on, y'all
Ya go rock 'n' roll, and then ya roll 'n' rock

Stereo M.C.s

I'm a Believer

I'm a believer

Funk'll fill your life
Funk'll free your soul
Get into the rhythm
Let your body take control

Now—I'm comin' back again
Hittin' the stage like a veteran
Wild oats enrapturin'
U.K. to U.S.A. and then back again
Down the windy roads to tha studio
I dedicate myself to ya audio
Traditional steerin' like Bleriot
So pin back your ears 'cause here we go
Like a crossword puzzle you can't figure out
Buried treasure, you can't dig it out
Without a map to show ya its whereabouts
If we get together, we can work it out
If ya seek y'll find so I begin
In the wilderness riskin' life and limb
And when my hair grows, I take a trim
I count on my fingers from one to ten

When things get me down I have a pressure valve
I let off steam, never throw in the towel
'Cause I'm naturally mad, bad, wicked, and pow
But to the grace of oneness I'll bow
'Cause I'm a believer

Funk'll fill your life
Funk'll free your soul
Get into the rhythm
Let your body take control

Well I ain't one of those who wanna be
A picture of somethin' that I never be
Your own identity's the true form
Fashion disappears but we still go on
From Lavendar Hill we're makin' music
Showin' ya all how to use it
I fire out a newey like one of Cupid's darts
And tear up the place with a rhyme from the heart
If you don't think I'm serious, try me
Some show doubt 'cause I'm a limey
Think all I can say is "gor blimey"
Well on the front line's where you find me
So if ya ain't with it, it's time you were
Send out your spirit and cause a stir
I never lose faith, I'm a hundred proof sure
'Cause I'm a believer
I'm a believer
Man, I'm a believer

Funk'll fill your life
Funk'll free your soul
Get into the rhythm
Let your body take control

I'm a soul survivor, a soul reviver
And I prescribe a dose of stereo fibre
For you rhythm rider, goin' side by side
Bona fide tiger with nothin' to hide
Away, no delay, jus' time to say

The tides are turnin' and there's no other way
From the path of the guidin' light
I won't budge
The ink is flowin' but my words don't smudge
Don't let my brain go dead from hunger
Feed with experience and get stronger
Otherwise you just wander and wander
And the seven deadly sins gonna put you under
For good, my friend, for ever, old bud
Am I makin' myself understood?
Should I fall, I feel no fear
'Cause I'm a believer
I'm a believer
I'm a believer

Funk'll fill your life
Funk'll free your soul
Get into the rhythm
Let your body take control

StetSaSonic

A.F.R.I.C.A.

A-F-R-I-C-A, ANGOLA, SOWETO, ZIMBABWE
TANZANIA, ZAMBIA, MOZAMBIQUE, AND BOTSWANA
SO LET US SPEAK! ABOUT THE MOTHERLAND!

I know this girl whose name is Lola
She lives in a country called Angola
Her president's name is Dos Santos
And a man named Savimbi playin' him too close
She says, "Hey, brother, my country's in a war, we are
Fightin' rebels backed by Pretoria"
Upon hearin' this, I was pretty upset, you know what?
I went and told the STET and the STET said

Yo . . . is Lola's last name Falana?
No, well my cousin lives in Botswana
Are they in war too?
Is a heel on a shoe? My man, they know apartheid like I know
    you
The president is Masire, the capital Gaborone
Where the fight for freedom is a universal tone
So are you with it? I'm in beyond a shadow of doubt
So let's spell it on, spell it on, spell it on out

A-F-R-I-C-A, ANGOLA, SOWETO, ZIMBABWE
TANZANIA, ZAMBIA, MOZAMBIQUE, AND BOTSWANA
SO LET US SPEAK! ABOUT THE MOTHERLAND!

Free South Africa!

I've seen the TV report and I watched it all week
That Samora Machel of Mozambique
Was killed in a crash that couldn't be explained
Yo D., I wanna break! Yo, brother, refrain!
Kenneth Kaunda's in Zambia, I'm in America
SWAPO's in Namibia, Nyerere's in Tanzania
Mugabe's in Harare, Jesse just came back
From the homeland, the green and the black!
So let's spell it out!

A-F-R-I-C-A, ANGOLA, SOWETO, ZIMBABWE
TANZANIA, ZAMBIA, MOZAMBIQUE, AND BOTSWANA
SO LET US SPEAK! ABOUT THE MOTHERLAND!

Apartheid, it's nothing less than conspicuous
Anti-black and pro-ridiculous
Feel it in ya heart 'cause it's so for real
But in the mind it develops and becomes the deal
As the struggle survives, South Africans rely
On us and U-N-I-T-Y
Thinkin' back as a slave, bonded in those chains
The thoughts of being free was never the same
Some committed suicide 'cause times was harsh
And the ones who survived, they got brainwashed

From lightning and thunder hails the storm
We can never forget 'cause the struggle lives on
Release the chains or history will burst
Mandela, Mugabe, he's first, freedom's power
This here is Africa's hour, the unforgotten people in our

A-F-R-I-C-A, ANGOLA, SOWETO, ZIMBABWE
TANZANIA, ZAMBIA, MOZAMBIQUE, AND BOTSWANA
SO LET US SPEAK! ABOUT THE MOTHERLAND!
South Africa no free, neither are we

Those are our brothers and sisters across the sea
I'm speaking for the STET and we make a plea
To fight apartheid, everybody
To fight against the wicked and help Mugabe
To fight apartheid and assist Nyerere
Support the MK and the ANC
We wanna see Nelson and Winnie free
You don't know, you need to study
And when you do, we're sure you'll agree
They need help but so do we
Them with their government
Us with mentality

A-F-R-I-C-A, ANGOLA, SOWETO, ZIMBABWE
TANZANIA, ZAMBIA, MOZAMBIQUE, AND BOTSWANA
SO LET US SPEAK! ABOUT THE MOTHERLAND!

StetSaSonic

Talkin' All That Jazz

Well, here's how it started
Heard you on the radio
Talkin' 'bout rap
Sayin' all that crap

About how we sample
Give an example
Think we'll let you get away with that?
You criticize our method
Of how we make records
You said it wasn't art
So now we're gonna rip you apart
Stop, check it out my man
This is the music of a hip-hop band
Jazz—well you can call it that
But this jazz contains a new format
Point—when you misjudged us
Speculated, created a fuss
You've made the same mistake politicians have
Talkin' all that jazz

Talk, well I heard talk is cheap
But like beauty, talk is just skin deep
And when you lie and you talk a lot
People tell you to step off a lot
You see, you misunderstood, a sample's just a tactic
It's a portion of my method, a tool in fact
It's only of importance when I make it a priority
And what we sample is loved by the majority
But you're a minority in terms of thought
Narrow-minded and poorly taught
About hip hop fame or the silly game
To erase my music, so no one can use it
You step on us and we'll step on you
Can't have your cake and eat it too
Talkin' all that jazz

Lies, that's when you hide the truth
That's when you talk more jazz than proof
And when you lie and address somethin' you don't know
It's so wack that it's bound to show
When you lie about me and the band we get angry
Whip out a pen and start writin' again
And the things we write are always true, sucker

Get a grip 'cause I'm talkin' 'bout you
Seems to me that you have a problem
So we can see what we can do to solve them
Think rap is a fad, you must be mad
'Cause we're so bad, we get respect you never had
Tell the truth, James Brown was old
'Til Eric and Rak' came out with "I Got Soul"
Rap brings back old R&B and if we would not
People could have forgot
We want to make this perfectly clear
We're talented and strong and have no fear
Of those who choose to judge but lack pizzazz
Talkin' all that jazz

Now, we're not tryin' to be a boss to you
We just wanna get across to you
That if you're talkin' jazz, the situation is a no-win
You might even get hurt, my friend
Stetsasonic, the hip-hop band
And like Sly and the Family Stone, we will stand
Up for the music we live and play
And for the song we sing today
For now, let us set the record straight
And later on we'll have a forum and a formal debate
But it's important to remember though
What you reap is what you sow
Talkin' all that jazz

sub Sonic 2

Unsung Heroes of Hip Hop

Hip Hop is not a musical mode noted for modesty
Not the place for self-effacement or honesty
Face it, rappers, the basic format is

To tell us you're bad as if that really matters
To bitch and pitch your third degrees
Towards the nameless, faceless sucker M.C.s
Well, do you really want to base a career
On a '84 Run-D.M.C. idea?
But wait a second, hold up the lesson
Er . . . time for a small confession
Forgive me Father, for I have sinned
Gone with the wind, run with the trend
I've tended to say that I'm the best M.C.
Now I wanna know what my penance will be
Fifty recitations of "Rebel Without A Pause"
Thirty "It's Yours" and twenty "Yes, yes, y'alls"?
Nope, the Steel's punishment is more severe
I gotta give some praise elsewhere
Though, yes, it's under duress, I guess it's best
Not to 'fess and bless nevertheless

The Unsung Heroes of Hip Hop (say it loud, yeah!)
The Unsung Heroes of Hip Hop (say it loud, yeah!)
The Unsung Heroes of Hip Hop (say it loud, yeah!)
The Unsung Heroes of Hip Hop (say it loud, yeah!)

There was a man who one day in 1970
Took his place amidst hip hop's heavenly bodies
The stars who made the music shine
And sadly he may have been wearing flares at the time
Late '80s, he was back on the street
When a crew of two ladies made "It's My Beat"
In fact it was his beat, hidden in the rhythm
But as yet, I regret, respect was not given
Of course, I'm talking about the Funky Drummer
As time went on, he was taxed by all comers
It was the dope beat when Public Enemy used it
Miss Williams' "Sleep Talk" simply improved it
But now, more and more, again and again
It's there on every single record in the Top Ten
And when the Kylie Minogue "Funky Drummer" track comes
You wish the guy had never taken up the drums, but

He's still an Unsung Hero of Hip Hop (say it loud, yeah!)
The Unsung Heroes of Hip Hop (say it loud, yeah!)
The Unsung Heroes of Hip Hop (say it loud, yeah!)
The Unsung Heroes of Hip Hop (say it loud, yeah!)

Time to talk about a hardcore keyboard buff
Who played rock and jazz and even classical stuff
He rocked it and jazzed it and treated it nasty
Until it all sounded like the theme from "Taxi"
The man had a tune he called "Mardi Gras"
And the music he used was, like la-di-da
But when the b-boys bought it and busted the break
All their eyes lit up to spell "Take, take, take"
You know what it is—there's a snare and a kick
And a sound like a doorbell that's mentally sick
Everybody was on it, from D.M.C. to Mantronix
Ruthjoy was ruthless, took it like Subsonic
Two did, but we took another track
Bob James is the name, but who's the drummer in the back?
The boy was bad and his tag is Steve Gadd
M.C.s give thanks for the hits we've had through

The Unsung Heroes of Hip Hop (say it loud, yeah!)
The Unsung Heroes of Hip Hop (say it loud, yeah!)
The Unsung Heroes of Hip Hop (say it loud, yeah!)
The Unsung Heroes of Hip Hop (say it loud, yeah!)

Now as a young M.C. starting to pay my dues
I should praise some of the players whose playing we use
But it's not a mistake when their names go unquoted
Even "Ultimate Breaks" will only tell you who wrote it
Go check a D.J. from the old school
He may know the band, but who manned the drum stool?
To all the artists that I never knew
This part is for you, because my heart is true
You have my admiration, you have my regard
You have my commiseration when times are hard
You have my love, my awe, my dreams, my pride, my hope
But do you have my royalties? Er, nope

Well, that's show biz
Sometimes you just have to step out of the way and let the new
    talent come on through
Peace to the Unsung Heroes of Hip Hop

Sugar hill Gang

Rapper's Delight

I said a hip hop
The hippie the hippie
To the hip hip hop, a you don't stop the rock it
To the bang bang boogie, say up jumped the boogie
To the rhythm of the boogie, the beat

Now what you hear is not a test—I'm rappin' to the beat
And me, the groove, and my friends are gonna try to move your
    feet
See I am Wonder Mike and I like to say hello
To the black, to the white, the red, and the brown, the purple
    and yellow
But first I gotta bang bang the boogie to the boogie
Say up jump the boogie to the bang bang boogie
Let's rock, you don't stop
Rock the riddle that will make your body rock
Well so far you've heard my voice but I brought two friends along
And next on the mike is my man Hank
Come on, Hank, sing that song

Check it out, I'm the C-A-S-AN-the-O-V-A
And the rest is F-L-Y
Ya see I go by the code of the doctor of the mix
And these reasons I'll tell ya why
Ya see I'm six foot one and I'm tons of fun
And I dress to a T

Ya see I got more clothes than Muhammad Ali and I dress so
    viciously
I got bodyguards, I got two big cars
That definitely ain't the wack
I got a Lincoln Continental and a sunroof Cadillac
So after school, I take a dip in the pool
Which really is on the wall
I got a color TV so I can see
The Knicks play basketball
Hear me talkin' 'bout checkbooks, credit cards
More money than a sucker could ever spend
But I wouldn't give a sucker or a bum from the Rucker
Not a dime 'til I made it again
Everybody go, "Hotel motel, watcha gonna do today" (Say what?)
'Cause I'm 'a get a fly girl
Gonna get some spank 'n'
Drive off in a def OJ
Everybody go, "Hotel motel Holiday Inn"
Say if your girl starts actin' up, then you take her friend
Master G, my mellow
It's on you so what you gonna do
Well it's on 'n' on 'n' on on 'n' on
The beat don't stop until the break of dawn
I said M-A-S, T-E-R, a G with a double E
I said I go by the unforgettable name
Of the man they call the Master Gee
Well, my name is known all over the world
By all the foxy ladies and the pretty girls
I'm goin' down in history
As the baddest rapper there ever could be
Now I'm feelin' the highs and ya feelin' the lows
The beat starts gettin' into your toes
Ya start poppin' ya fingers and stompin' your feet
And movin' your body while you're sittin' in your seat
And then damn—ya start doin' the freak
I said damn, right outta your seat
Then ya throw your hands high in the air
Ya rockin' to the rhythm, shake your derriere
Ya rockin' to the beat without a care
With the sureshot M.C.s for the affair

Now, I'm not as tall as the rest of the gang
But I rap to the beat just the same
I got a little face and a pair of brown eyes
All I'm here to do, ladies, is hypnotize
Singin' on 'n' 'n' on 'n' on on 'n' on
The beat don't stop until the break of dawn
Singin' on 'n' 'n' on 'n' on on 'n' on
Like a hot buttered a pop da pop da pop dibbie dibbie
Pop da pop pop, ya don't dare stop
Come alive y'all, gimme what ya got
I guess by now you can take a hunch
And find that I am the baby of the bunch
But that's okay, I still keep in stride
'Cause all I'm here to do is just wiggle your behind
Singin' on 'n' 'n' on 'n' on 'n' on
The beat don't stop until the break of dawn
Singin' on 'n' 'n' on 'n' on on 'n' on
Rock rock, y'all, throw it on the floor
I'm gonna freak ya here, I'm gonna freak ya there
I'm gonna move you outta this atmosphere
'Cause I'm one of a kind and I'll shock your mind
I'll put T-N-T in your behind
I said 1-2-3-4, come on, girls, get on the floor
A-come alive, y'all, a-gimme what ya got
'Cause I'm guaranteed to make you rock
I said 1-2-3-4, tell me, Wonder Mike, what are you waiting for?

I said a hip hop
The hippie to the hippie
The hip hip hop, a you don't stop the rock it
To the bang bang the boogie, say up jumped the boogie
To the rhythm of the boogie the beat
Skiddlee beebop a we rock a scoobie doo
And guess what, America, we love you
'Cause ya rocked and a rolled with so much soul
You could rock till you're a hundred and one years old
I don't mean to brag, I don't mean to boast
But we like hot butter on our breakfast toast
Rock it up, Baby Bubbah
Baby Bubbah to the boogie da bang bang da boogie

To the beat beat, it's so unique
Come on everybody and dance to the beat

A hip hop
The hippie the hippie to the
Hip hip hop, a you don't stop rock it
Rock it out Baby Bubbah to the boogie da bang bang
The boogie to the boogie, da beat
I said, I can't wait 'til the end of the week
When I'm rappin' to the rhythm of a groovy beat
And attempt to raise your body heat
Just blow your mind so that you can't speak
And do a thing 'bout a rock and shuffle your feet
And let it change up to a dance called the freak
And when ya finally do come in to your rhythmic beat
Rest a little while so ya don't get weak
I know a man named Hank
He has more rhymes than a serious bank
So come on Hank sing that song
To the rhythm of the boogie, da bang bang da bong

Well, I'm Imp the Dimp, the ladies' pimp
The women fight for my delight
But I'm the grandmaster with the three M.C.s
That shock the house for the young ladies
And when you come inside, into the front
You do the freak, spank, and do the bump
And when the sucker M.C.s try to prove a point
We're a treacherous trio, we're the serious joint
A from sun to sun and from day to day
I sit down and write a brand new rhyme
Because they say that miracles never cease
I've created a devastating masterpiece
I'm gonna rock the mike 'til you can't resist
Everybody, I say it goes like this
Well I was comin' home late one dark afternoon
A reporter stopped me for a interview
She said she's heard stories and she's heard fables
That I'm vicious on the mike and the turntable
This young reporter I did adore

So I rocked some vicious rhymes like I never did before
She said, "Damn, fly guy, I'm in love with you
The Casanova legend must have been true"
I said, "By the way, baby, what's your name?"
Said, "I go by the name of Lois Lane
And you could be my boyfriend, you surely can
Just let me quit my boyfriend called Superman"
I said, "He's a fairy, I do suppose
Flyin' through the air in pantyhose
He may be very sexy or even cute
But he looks like a sucker in a blue and red suit"
I said, "You need a man who's got finesse
And his whole name across his chest
He may be able to fly all through the night
But can he rock a party 'til the early light?
He can't satisfy you with his little worm
But I can bust you out with my super sperm"
I go do it, I go do it, I go do it, do it, do it
An' I'm here an' I'm there, I'm Big Bang Hank, I'm everywhere
Just throw your hands up in the air
And party hardy like you just don't care
Let's do it, don't stop, y'all, a tick a tock, y'all, you don't stop
Go hotel, motel, what you gonna do today (Say what?)
I'm gonna get a fly girl, gonna get some spank, drive off in a def
    OJ
Everybody go "Hotel, motel, Holiday Inn"
You say if your girl starts actin' up, then you take her friend
I say skip, dive, what can I say
I can't fit 'em all inside my OJ
So I just take half and bust them out
I give the rest to Master Gee so he could shock the house
It was twelve o'clock one Friday night
I was rockin' to the beat and feelin' all right
Everybody was dancin' on the floor
Doin' all the things they never did before
And then this fly fly girl with a sexy lean
She came into the bar, she came into the scene
She traveled deeper inside the room
All the fellas checked out her white Sasoons
She came up to the table, looked into my eyes

Then she turned around and shook her behind
So I said to myself, it's time for me to release
My vicious rhyme I call my masterpiece
And now people in the house, this is just for you
A little rap to make you boogaloo
Now the group ya hear is called Phase Two
And let me tell ya somethin', we're a helluva crew
Once a week, we're on the street
Just to cut in the jams and look at your feet
For you to party, ya got to have the moves
So we'll get right down and get you a groove
For you to dance, ya got to be hot
So we'll get right down and make ya rock
Now the system's on and the girls are there
Ya definitely have a rockin' affair
But let me tell ya somethin', there's still one fact
And to have a party, ya got to have a rap
So when the party's over, you're makin' it home
And tryin' to sleep before the break of dawn
And while ya sleepin', ya start to dream
And thinkin' how ya danced on the disco scene
My name appears in your mind
Yeah, a name you know that was right on time
It was Phase Two just a doin' a do
Rockin' ya down 'cause ya know we could
To the rhythm of the beat that makes ya freak
Come alive girls, get on your feet
To the rhythm of the beat to the beat the beat
To the double beat beat that it makes ya freak
To the rhythm of the beat that says ya go on
On 'n' on into the break of dawn
Now I got a man comin' on right now
He's guaranteed to throw down
He goes by the name of Wonder Mike
Come on Wonder Mike, do what ya like

I say a can of beer that's sweeter than honey
Like a millionaire that has no money
Like a rainy day that is not wet
Like a gamblin' fiend that does not bet

Like Dracula without his fangs
Like the boogie to the boogie without the boogie bang
Like collard greens that don't taste good
Like a tree that's not made out of wood
Like goin' up and not comin' down
Is just like the beat without the sound, no sound
To the beat beat, ya do the freak
Everybody just rock and dance to the beat
Have you ever went over a friend's house to eat
And the food just ain't no good?
I mean the macaroni's soggy, the peas are mushed
And the chicken tastes like wood
So you try to play it off like you think you can
By saying that you're full
And then your friend says, "Momma, he's just being polite
He ain't finished, uh-uh, that's bull"
So your heart starts pumpin' and you think of a lie
And you say that you already ate
And your friend says, "Man, there's plenty of food"
So you pile some more on your plate
While the stinky food's steamin', your mind starts to dreamin'
Of the moment that it's time to leave
And then you look at your plate and your chicken's slowly rottin'
Into something that looks like cheese
Oh so you say, "That's it, I got to leave this place
I don't care what these people think
I'm just sittin' here makin' myself nauseous
With this ugly food that stinks"
So you bust out the door while it's still closed
Still sick from the food you ate
And then you run to the store for quick relief
From a bottle of Kaopectate
And then you call your friend two weeks later
To see how he has been
And he says, "I understand about the food
Baby Bubbah, but we're still friends"
With a hip hop the hippie to the hippie
The hip hip a hop, a you don't stop the rockin'
To the bang bang boogie
Say up jump the boogie to the rhythm of the boogie the beat

I say, "Hank, can ya rock?"
Can ya rock to the rhythm that just don't stop?
Can ya hip me to the shoobie doo
I said, "Come on, make, the make the people move

I go to the halls and then ring the bell
Because I am the man with the clientele
And if ya ask me why I rock so well
A Big Bang, I got clientele
And from the time I was only six years old
I never forgot what I was told
It was the best advice that I ever had
It came from my wise, dear old dad
He said, "Sit down, punk, I wanna talk to you
And don't say a word until I'm through
Now there's a time to laugh, a time to cry
A time to live, and a time to die
A time to break and a time to chill
To act civilized or act real ill
But whatever ya do in your lifetime
Ya never let a M.C. steal your rhyme"
So from six to six 'til this very day
I'll always remember what he had to say
So when the sucker M.C.s try to chump my style
I let them know that I'm versatile
I got style, finesse, and a little black book
That's filled with rhymes and I know you wanna look
But the thing that separates you from me
And that is called originality
Because my rhymes are on from what you heard
I didn't even bite, not a go—word
And I say a little more, later on tonight
So the sucker M.C.s can bite all night
A tick a tock, y'all, a beat beat, y'all
A let's rock, y'all, ya don't stop
Ya go, "Hotel motel whatcha gonna do today" (Say what?)
Ya say, "I'm gonna get a fly girl, gonna get some spankin'
Drive off in a def OJ"
Everybody go, "Hotel motel Holiday Inn"
Ya say if your girl starts actin' up, then you take her friends

A like that, y'all, to the beat, y'all
Beat beat, y'all, ya don't stop
A Master Gee, my mellow
It's on you so whatcha gonna do

Well like Johnny Carson on the Late Show
A like Frankie Crocker in stereo
Well like the Barkay's singin' "Holy Ghost"
The sounds to throw down, they're played the most
It's like my man Captain Sky
Whose name he earned with his super sperm
We rock and we don't stop
Get off, y'all, I'm here to give you whatcha got
To the beat that it makes you freak
And come alive, girl, get on your feet
A like a Perry Mason without a case
Like Farrah Fawcett without her face
Like the Barkays on the mike
Like gettin' right down for you tonight
Like movin' your body so ya don't know how
Right to the rhythm and throw down
Like comin' alive to the Master Gee
The brother who rocks so viciously
I said the age of one, my life begun
At the age of two I was doin' the do
At the age of three, it was you and me
Rockin' to the sounds of the Master Gee
At the age of four, I was on the floor
Givin' all the freaks what they bargained for
At the age of five I didn't take no jive
With the Master Gee it's all the way live
At the age of six I was a-pickin' up sticks
Rappin' to the beat, my stick was fixed
At the age of seven, I was rockin' in heaven
Dontcha know I went off
I gotta run on down to the beat you see
Gettin' right on down, makin' all the girls
Just take off their clothes to the beat the beat
To the double beat beat that makes you freak

At the age of eight, I was really great
'Cause every night, you see, I had a date
At the age of nine, I was right on time
'Cause every night, I had a party rhyme
Going on 'n' 'n' on 'n' on on 'n' on
The beat don't stop until the break of dawn
A sayin' on 'n' 'n' on 'n' on on 'n' on. . . .
Like a hot-buttered de pop de pop de popcorn . . .

Sway & king Tech

Concrete Jungle

So many concrete buildings
And so many sirens from so many drug dealings
Killings occurring at daylight
You know it seems like
Some might someday will see the light
The streets are still filled with derelicts
Schizophrenics screaming out
Just for the hell of it
This story I'm painting may be grim
But then your chances of surviving are slim
'Cause in the streets, the people
Compete for survival
Every day is a battle that'll make a man liable
To submit and commit rape, perjury, or burglary
And for the things I possess, he might murder me
For money, is it funny
You'll be meeting a fast death
And mugged by a thug after breathing
Your last breath
Never underestimate how far would one go
What do you expect
I'm living in a concrete jungle

You've got the feeling
I'm gonna make it all right
You've got the feeling
I'm gonna make it all right

Sometimes it's a blessing
When a blind man can't see
His situations of poverty
Families crammed in abandoned buildings
Freeways drowning, the sound of children
Cement grass, kids playing in glass
Cars pass by fast, bums harass for cash
On the subtrains, graffiti and names
With nothing to take in vain but the city's pain
Then I came with one aim so I strain
To gain my dreams but so it seems
Ain't nothing changed
So there's Jack on the hill with Jill
No time to chill, the man's got a drug deal
Down for his ducats, said, "fuck it" and
Was in the wind
Went to the corner with Jack Horner
To make his in's
And then there's Jill, tumbled on the wrong deal
With nothing to gain but the pain
Of her sex appeal
Another victim, thirteen years old
Who gives a damn that the girl just sold her soul
To a glass pipe, did it last night
Trying to indulge in the glamour of the fast life
She should have took her
One mule and the forty acres
But she wanted money
Fast cars and a skyscraper
That's the reality, a street mentality
Given was goals in exchange for her morality
I'm forced to wonder how far would one go
But what do you expect
I'm living in a concrete jungle

You've got the feeling
I'm gonna make it all right
You've got the feeling
I'm gonna make it all right

Enemies livin' in the concrete
They invade the paradise
Beware of the parasites
Come in all shapes, forms
Dressed in uniforms
Promising dreams about as real as a unicorn
A preacher says he's gonna take you to
The promised land
But you got to pay the cost into his open hands
Another man says he's looking in
Your best interest
He's just a politician seeking position
Wolves dressed up in sheep's clothing
And we're shaking these men's hands
Without even knowing
So I stop to look past the faces of evil
Thinking if I get by how could I bring the people
I teach them to nourish one thought, one entity
Strive for divinity, it'll bring you serenity
And never underestimate how far would one go
You know what to expect when you living
In a concrete jungle

You've got the feeling
I'm gonna make it all right
You've got the feeling
I'm gonna make it all right

T La Rock

Breakin' Bells

A fresh rhyme in the brain is what I contain
Let it out with a shout and it's bound to stain
A part in your heart, right before I start
Try your best with the rest, I'm thinkin' what I've got
What I've been, I intend to intimidate you
It will be a slam dunk or your said virtue
I'll make your hair curl, head swirl, put you in shock
I possess an element to start you on my jock
When I finish, I'll diminish then I'll laugh in your face
And try to build up your ego, put it in the right place
On the scale of intelligence I score a "10"
It will be a revelation from beginning to end

When it comes to smokin' lyrics and programmin' drum tracks
Production work is just between my brain, I will rack
No matter what the job I'll master, I'll always do it well
My skill now perpetual, I'll only excel
To a pro will I remain superior to all
I'll handle any type, no matter big or small
And for my rappin' capability, I'm never underrated
When it comes to smokin' lyrics, I'm always nominated
As the number-one contender in the hip-hop race
All the predators I'm sorry for so now you must face
The ultimate challenge, of course that's me
Superrapper T La Rock, undisputed M.C.
With my voice so stimulatin', feet so seductive
One can't help but find them so reluctant
To attend the performance of another vocalist
The folks you will find will never rap like this
This this

Breakin' Breakin' Breakin' Breakin' Bells
Breakin' Breakin' Breakin' Breakin' Bells

Breakin' Breakin' Breakin' Breakin' Bells
Breakin' Breakin' Breakin' Breakin' Bells

I'm an intellect, a brain-trained adviser
A true so astute a genius that's wiser
Than Attila the Hun and I've only begun
To display my talent which is second to none
I'm a pro when it comes to the show
I'm capable of movin' the row of people
Who came here tonight to hear me recite
My poetry that's guaranteed to excite
All music lovers

My name is T La Rock, close friends call me Terry
Rate me great and far from ordinary
Though so they highly rate me, others will hate me
Try to deny the fact they're greatly envious
Of a person like me
Whose success within the rap world is permanently
At the top and I will not cop out to others
Who feel that I am a threat
But there is no need for worry until you have met
Superrapper T La Rock fresh out the pack
Movin' at top speed, givin' you no slack
So to all ya competition, ya better keep fishin'
For a way to convey a message to position
You right where you wanna be so you can attack
But remember you're dealin' with a person whose practically
As clever as a fox, deadly as a snake
Like pressure once applied to an egg, I'll break
All over you and I'll dis your face, huh
And just in case you're wonderin'
How can a person like me be so unique
In the art of rappin' to the beat
I won't be discreet
I'll be cool, calm, nonchalant
Plus gentle to me your rhymes and lyrics are simply fundamental

Breakin' Breakin' Breakin' Breakin' Bells

D.J. Louie Lou!
Greg Nice!

3rd BaSS

Product of the Environment

In the heart of the city, you was born and bred
You grew up smart and or you wound up dead
Things moved fast but you knew the scoop
And your savior was a rhyme and a beat in a rap group
A modern day production of the city street
You said I didn't have it, that I couldn't compete
So the sleeper did sleep, but the sleeper should 'a woke up
Now you're in my sight, the Buddha says ya smoke up
That's the element you carry your rhymes on
But that style of rhyme won't let you live long
'Cause a strong song to you is what I sent
'Cause I'm a product of the environment

(There it is, in black and white)
(There it is, in black and white)

On the streets of Far Rockaway, Queens
Sea Girt Boulevard, Beach 17th
Redfern House is where no M.C. would ever go
Is where I did my very first show
Had the crowd, had the rhymes goin', I never 'fessed
His reward was almost a bullet in his chest
And on that stage is where I first learned
Stick out my chest or be a kid and get burned
You're so foolish but I think you knew this
That on the microphone, punk, I can do this
And doin' this is what life meant
'Cause I'm a product of the environment

(There it is, in black and white)
(There it is, in black and white)

Back in the days when kids were mackdaddys
Striped Lee jeans, Playboys, and Caddies
Long Beach, the M.L.K. center
He almost caught a bad one when he tried to enter
I'd wait Bang! Bum rush the back door
Then scatter onto the dance floor
Me and my boys skeezin' the cuties
Never had static 'cause everybody knew me
Local D.J.'s tearin' up the wax
And out on the corner some kid gets taxed
After the party, crack open a forty
Vicked it from the store, yo, the man never caught me
Went up to the arcade, cranked the bass
And then the five-oh chased us from the place
Hopped on the railroad, played the conductor
Everywhere I went I always tucked a
Marker in my jacket, tagged it where I went
'Cause we were just the products of the environment

(There it is, in black and white)
(There it is, in black and white)

I wanna tell you somethin' that gets me kinda mad
It's about my dear old dad
He's tired and worn and works from nine to five
Clockin' thirty Gs a year to survive
But I know kids who in a month or so
Make that money sellin' *lleyo*
Pushin' a drug, I can't understand
Destroyin' a life with a buck in a hand?
Played rotten slum chain local street hero
But if ya ask Serch, you're just a bunch of zeros
Too bad, 'cause when you're older you won't have a cent
'Cause you're a product of the environment

(There it is, in black and white)
(There it is, in black and white)

You hear it in the strength of my voice,
And in the rhythm
Now you know how I was livin'
It happened to me like it happened to Serch
Prime Minister Pete Nice so kick the verse
In Bed-Stuy with my boy Kibwe, hype
Decatur and Kingston on Wednesday night
To the Empire show slammin'
Open for Dana, crew flammin'
Mouth opened wide, all listenin'
Dumb dope with a forty in my system
Unprotected but respected for my own self
'Cause the talent no shade or nothin' else
A time of tension, racially fenced-in
I came off (and all the brothers blessed him)
I left more than a mark, I left a dent
'Cause I'm a product of the environment

3rd BaSS

Steppin' to the A.M.

Ready in the intro, cue up the Serch-light
Prime is to the center stage, I grab the first mike
Projecting the voice with this mike that I'm cuffin'
You ain't my nucca, sucker I'm snuffin'
The word of the third stands true so no panickin'
Man vs. man—you freeze up like a mannequin
Petro, you let go the wax for the new jacks
To dwell upon you're steppin' on the trigger as the tune smacks
Square on the butt, Pete gave me the cue
So I'm 'a put up or shut up until my jam is through
But for now I wanna freak 'em so I'll embark
To spark your mission, posse, 'til way past dark
Don't park, there's no standin', or I'll play the five-oh

You don't stop movin' until the Serch says so
To keep the tribe hoopin', shootin' out to play 'em
Three the hard way'll keep you steppin' to the A.M.

What's the time
What's the time
What time is it?

My mind asks a question, I respond to a silver-domed
     microphone
One step beyond the straights of '88 to the curves of the '90s
I'm universal, I set a line free
Behind me the three the hard way, the jackpot
Awaiting Satan's tryin' to take cheapshots
We groove crowds the three stand proud, the brothers 'round the
     way sit down
And say, "How'd you do this?"
Ludicrous rhythm and rhyme
Anticipated like a bottle of Heinz
Ketchup, no catch-up 'cause you fell behind
I'm steppin' to the A.M., kickin' down swine
Pete Nice skims over lyrics, I pick 'em
Strong and long, you're wrong, I stick 'em
He's the lord with the sword with my cable swingin'
Like the pit of the pendulum, Pete Nice is bringin'
A sunrise with no lies, legitimate and you despise
Envy this M.C.'s magnitude so realize
The M.C. emceed, the D.J. deejayed until the next time
I'll keep you steppin' to the A.M.

What's the time
What's the time
What time is it?

No weight on the felt plate, deep bass for low-rides
Needle-tortured groove, move the record 'til the wax dries
Schoolin' the swine on the strength of my vocab
Put you under, you're a gunner, you're thinkin' that you had
Lyrics to the A.M. but the house needs a swinger

You st-t-t-utter, but I'm a stinger
My rhyme's so potent, I wrote 'em and it's evident
You're just a stunt seekin' a settlement
The lyrical line, the article original
Afflict like a convict, I ain't no criminal
Schemin' on a cable or slobbin' a knob
You played me like a foul ball, how ya livin', Hobbs
Not groovin' to the A.M., the master spoon feedin' out a jumper
You're bumpin' a freak while I'm G'in'
Pete'll let the record spin
Serch'll get his second wind
Motivate the crowd 'til it's steppin' to the A.M.

What's the time
What's the time
What time is it?

I slide swiftly, keep a brother steppin'
Loungin', streppin' my throat
Sweatin' as you get hit with the rhythm
The line sustain like a crane so I lift him
Slow and smooth
Flowin' like fluid, the masses did worship
The lyrics the three did amid all crisis
Droppin' like a guillotine, you're moist
Fearin' the voice of the rhyme fiend
Whose scene is set, Pete Nice is your worst dream fulfilled
You illed, I drilled, I heard a loud scream
My mind is cued so I'll run down a menu
That downgrades the weak as my lyrics tend to
The needs of a shaker, sweatin' to the point of exhaust
So listen to the mission, horse
Blinded by the science, my mind starts flexin',
Sexin' down females to the A.M. perplexin'
A complex reflex
You wonder if we slumber
The three don't sleep, eh, yo, Pete Nice take 'em under
Steppin' to the A.M.
I'm steppin' to the mike
To snatch up and smash up the club until daylight

---

three Times Dope

Greatest Man Alive

E.S.T., the ackniculous wonder
I'm the greatest man alive
E.S.T., the ackniculous wonder
I'm the greatest man alive
E.S.T., the ackniculous wonder
E.S.T., the unusual fellow (oh yeah)

Landscapin' mentally shapin'
Get the gist, don't miss what I'm sayin'
Hilltop bringin' let the bass drop
Soak'n up saps like a household mop
Out 'o' romp stomp so you're no comp
Ya try to rock, we bump, the whole house jump
Gotta bust a sucker or else it get's borin'
Just like you people need ya coffee in the mornin'
And every word is honestly stated
Ya get it, not synthetic or fabricated
Keep ya eyes open, I got ya on a scope
Know it like a poet cause I diddi-do-dope
Fly like a falcon, strong like a stallion
Now all I need is a gold medallion
Providin' small time suckers with info
E.S.T.'s the unusual fellow

("Definitely the best thing that's happened")

Yes it's the E-S, the man ya can't understand
Much funky on ya FM band
The brown-eyed bombshell, rockin' ya well,
Disignitin' all bitin' and frontin' as well
We propel our records to sell
Like a speedy Lamborghini, we're bound to excel
Given the chance to shake ya pants

It's somethin' that you'll never forget
I'll make ya wake up in a cold sweat
Drippin' with the fluid that wets ya when ya do it
Know this like Otis when ya style is bogus
Love to party with a girly with a dope body
Gotta bite my tongue, I'm so high strung
E-S, the name knockin' boots is the game
If ya ain't a queen, I love ya just the same
My name is E.S.tizenizm, col'gettin', bizinizm
Rallyin' the funky dope razzamatizm
Hit ya with the hardness comin' with the clarity
Skyin' over suckers, defyin' all laws of gravity
The style in my hair like a new wave Afro
E.S.T.'s the unusual fellow

("He's too good to be true")

With a ultra-fresh topic for this here recital
With another one of those crazy fresh titles
It'll be shakin' up and it'll be takin' up
Space in the race 'cause the sinista will crank it up
E.S.T. is the one, the so original
The boy so live, should have his name on ya cereal
Instead of Swatch, you wear a sinister watch
Worn by the suckers who be swearin' they clock'n
'Cause ain't nobody takin' my place
Ya know what I mean?
Instead of Guess you wear some E-S jeans
Tight around ya poontang, so when ya shake that thang
Everybody want to shake it again
I feel it shuttin' it up in my bones
Magically moved by the microphone
At first I just twitch then I get that itch and real quick
Ya see me flickin' up the "on" switch
Sweatin' like a dog in front of sell-out crowds
Dippin' em all in the 3-D style
No matter how ya hype up ya twelve inches
They don't get it
They want my album, ya got to deal wit it
Ya could've had yours out but now I took ya

Still ain't got one out 'cause ya chasin' funky hookas
And all the real slimmies jammin' off my flow
E.S.T.'s the unusual fellow

E.S.T., the ackniculous wonder
I'm the greatest man alive

("He's too good to be true
He's—he's tall, he's handsome, he's rich, exciting
Definitely the best thing that's happened")

E.S.T., the ackniculous wonder
I'm the greatest man alive

Tim Dog

Fuck Compton

Oh shit motherfuckers step to the rear and cheer
'Cause Tim Dog is here
Let's get right down to the nitty gritty
And talk about a bullshit city
Talkin' about niggaz from Compton
They're no comp and they truly ain't stompin'
Tim Dog a black man's task
I'm so bad I'll whip Superman's ass
All you suckers that rif on the West Coast
I'll dis and spray your ass like a roach
Ya think you're cool with your curls and your shades
I'll roll thick and you'll be yelling out "Raid!"
One hard brother that lives in New York
Where brothers are hard and we don't have to talk
Shut your mouth before we come out stompin'
Hey, yo Eazy

Fuck Compton

(Why you dissin' Eazy?)
Cause the boy ain't shit
Chew him with tobacco, an' spit him in shit
I crush Ice Cube, I'm cool with Ice T
But N.W.A. ain't shit to me
Dre beatin' on Dee from Pump It Up
Step to the dog and get fucked up
I'm simplistic, imperialistic, idealistic
And I'm kickin' the ballistics
Havin' that gang war
We want to know what you're fightin' for
Fighting over colors?
All that gang shit is for dumb motherfuckers
But you go on thinking you're hard
Come to New York and we'll see who gets robbed
Take your jeri curls, take your black hats
Take your wack lyrics and your bullshit tracks
Now you're mad and you're thinking about stompin'
Well I'm from the South Bronx

Fuck Compton

Tim Dog and I'm the best from the East
And all this Compton shit must cease
So keep your eyes on the prize and
Don't jeopardize my arrive 'cause that's not wise
You really think that you can rhyme
Well come and get some of this loaded tech-nine
Bo bo bo shots are cold gunnin'
And you'll really be a hundred miles and runnin'
You wanna play go ride in a sleigh
I'm so large I fuck Michel le'
In the bathroom we was bonin'
You shoulda heard how the bitch was moanin'
Do Do Do Do Dooo Do Do Do Do Do Do Do
Shut the fuck up bitch, you can't sing
Ya sound like a kid playin' on a swing ("Fuck you")
I'm the man at hand to run the band
That's in command

You know who the fuck I am
Tim Dog, what's my motherfuckin' name
Tim Dog, that's my motherfuckin' game
So whether you think that I'm just a myth
That riff, the lift, the gift, the if, the fifth
The shift, the spliff, that's in control, to hold
To fold, to bold and make an ache and take and fake
Wooh! And I'm still too great.

Fuck Compton!

tone Lōc

Funky Cold Medina

Cold coolin' at a bar, and I'm lookin' for some action
But like Mick Jagger said, "I can't get no satisfaction"
The girls are all around, but none of them want to get with me
My threads are fresh and I'm looking def, yo
What's up with L-O-C?
The girls I saw jockin' at the other end of the bar
Havin' drinks with some no-name chump
When they know that I'm the star
So I got up and strolled over to the other side of the cantina
I asked the guy, "Why you so fly?"
He said, "Funky Cold Medina"

Funky Cold Medina

This brother told me a secret on how to get more chicks
Put a little Medina in your glass
And the girls will come real quick
It's better than any alcohol or aphrodisiac
A couple of sips of this love potion and she'll be on your lap
So I gave some to my dog, when he began to beg

Then he licked his bowl and he looked at me
And did the Wild Thing on my leg
He used to scratch and bite me
Before he was much, much meaner
But now all the poodles run to my house
For the Funky Cold Medina

You know what I'm sayin'? I got every dog in my neighborhood
Breakin' down my door, I got Spuds McKenzie, Alex from
    Stroh's
They won't leave my dog alone with that Medina, pal

I went up to this girl, she said, "Hi, my name is Sheena"
I thought she'd be good to go with a little Funky Cold Medina
She said, "I'd like a drink," I said ok, I'd go get it
Then a couple sips, she cold licked her lips
And I knew that she was with it
So I took her to my crib, and everything went well as planned
But when she got undressed, it was a big old mess
Sheena was a man
So I threw him out, I don't fool around
With no Oscar Meyer weiner
You must be sure that your girl is pure
For the Funky Cold Medina
You know, ain't no playin' with a man
This is the '80s and I'm down with the ladies, ya know?

Break it down

Back in the saddle, lookin' for a little affection
I took a shot as a contestant on the Love Connection
The audience voted and you know they picked a winner
I took my date to the Hilton for Medina and some dinner
She had a few drinks, I'm thinkin' soon what I'll be gettin'
Instead she started talkin' about plans for a weddin'
Said wait, slow down, love, not so fast, says "I'll be seein' ya"
That's why I found you don't play around
With the Funky Cold Medina
Ya know what I'm sayin', that Medina's a monster, y'all
Funky Cold Medina

---

tone Lōc

Wild Thing

Workin' all week, nine to five for my money
So when the weekend comes
I can go get live with the honey
Rollin' down the street
I saw this girl and she was pumpin'
I winked my eye and she got into the ride
Went to a club, it was jumpin'
Introduced myself as Lōc, she said, "You're a liar"
I said, "I got it goin' on baby doll
And I'm on fire"
Took her to the hotel, she said, "You're the king"
So be my queen, if you know what I mean
And let's do the Wild Thing

Shoppin' at the mall, lookin' for some gear to buy
I saw this girl, she cold rocked my world
And I had to adjust my fly
She looked at me and smiled and said
"You got plans for the night?"
I said, "Hopefully if things go well, I'll be with you tonight"
So we journeyed to her house, one thing led to another
A key in the door, I cold hit the floor
Looked up and it was her mother
I didn't know what to say
I was hangin' by a string
She said, "Hey you two, I was once like you
And I liked to do the Wild Thing"

Posse in effect, hangin' out is always hyped
And when me and the crew leave a shindig
With a girl who's just my type
Saw this luscious little frame
I'm ain't lyin' fellows, she was fine

This sweet young miss, cold gave me a kiss
And I knew that she was mine
Took her to the limousine
Still parked outside
I tipped the chauffeur when it was over
And gave her my own ride
Couldn't get her off my jock she stick with me
Like static cling
But that's what happens, when bodies start slappin'
From doing the Wild Thing

Doin' a little show at the local discotheque
This fine young chick was on my jock
So I said, what the heck
She wanted to come on stage
And do a little dance
So I said, "Chill for now but maybe later
You'll get your chance"
So when the show was finished
I took her around the way
And what do you know, she was good to go
Without a word to say
We was all alone and she said, "TONE
Let me tell you one thing
I need fifty dollars to make you holler
I get paid to do the Wild Thing"
Say what?
Yo luv, you must be kiddin'
Yo, Walk you ready?
Let's break on outta here
Hasta la vista, baby

Wild Thing

Too Short

Freaky Tales

These are the tales, the freaky tales
These are the tales that I tell so well
These are the tales, the freaky tales
These are the tales that I tell so well

I met this girl, her name was Joan
She love the way I rock on the microphone
When I met Joan, I took her home
She was just like a doggie, all on my bone

I met another girl, her name was Ann
All she wanted was to freak with a man
When I met Ann, I shook her hand
We ended up freakin' by a garbage can

The next young freak I met was Red
I took her to the house and she gave me head
She liked to freak is all she said
We jumped in the sheets and we broke my bed

There's another girl, her name is Mary
Talk about sex and the girl acts scary
I heard she was freakin' from my homeboy Jerry
Took her to the house and I popped that cherry

Young and tender, sweet Denise
Get her in the bed and the girl's a beast
I tell you homeboy, if you get a piece
She'll only start talkin' 'bout signin' the lease

The next tender, her name was Lori
An X-rated movie wouldn't tell her story
She had a twin sister, her name was Lisa
And just like Lori, she's a real dick-pleaser

My girlfriend's name was Michelle
Her booty was bigger than a tail on a whale
When I freaked Michelle, I freaked her well
Her pussy got hotter than the flames in hell

I g'd this girl, her name was Tammy
I didn't wanna do it 'cause the bitch was flammy
She had a best friend, her name was Jane
I pulled her to the side and split that game

I met a lot of freaks in my life span
Freaked one night with a girl named Pam
The very next day, I saw her with her man
One week passed and I was in her again

I had an old tender, her name's Janine
She was thirty-two and I was only eighteen
She likes to freak, she's just a fiend
It really didn't matter when I saw her in jeans

I wanna big freak, fat and sloppy
I'll kick on back and watch her mop
Two tons of fun, Big Mama Jama
A country girl from Alabama

I met this freak, her name was Beth
Her pussy got wet and it smelled like death
I was tired as hell, I was drippin' sweat
But I was all up in her, tryin' to hold my breath

Bake and shake us
I met this freak in Vegas
She said her name was Donna
She was a built little freak from China

I said I don't pimp or gigolo
I'm havin' so much money I don't need a ho
You can break yourself but you can't break me
You never met a player like Short, baby

I knew a dick-sucker named Betty Jo
Took her to my house and we did it on the floor
The girl got freaky and I'll tell you more
She was down on her knees, beggin' to blow

She's like another freak named Renee
You get her all alone and she'll make your day
Like Burger King, she knows the play
With a freak like Renee, you can have it your way

These are the tales, the freaky tales
These are the tales that I tell so well
These are the tales, the freaky tales
These are the tales that I tell so well

I met this girl, thick as hell
Only sixteen, said her name was Lynell
I took her to my house, I could not wait
Her shit was much tighter than a sentry safe

Let me tell ya this, since we're talkin' young
I met another girl, said her name was Yvonne
Always talkin' 'bout havin' fun
Once again at the cat, I had it goin' on

I'm Sir Too Short, couldn't be no punk
I'm tryin' to get funky like female funk
So when ya see me comin' or see me goin'
I'll keep my money, let the hos keep ho-in'

I once met a sinner, she did it for free
On the Foot Hill Bus Number 43
All the way in the back, she was workin' me
Had my big beat box and I was jammin' the beat

I met this freak named Antoinette
Mack on baby like an ice-cold vet
Everything she had is what I get
'Cause I'm Too Short, baby, I don't play that shit

I met another freak, her name was Rita
Baby thought Too Short just might eat 'er
I told her like this, she could suck my peter
Or either go home 'cause I knew I didn't need 'er

Scratched her name out of my telephone book
Never again took a second look
'Cause the next young freak, her name was Sharon
She kept lookin' while I kept starin'

Baby came through with my homeboy Darren
Her booty was stuffed in the jeans she was wearin'
She never left, he cut out
I know ya all know what I'm talkin' about

There's a freak named Shannon—such a sinner
She smokes that pipe and she's gettin' thinner
Shannon is cool but her mind is gone
One fat rock and it's goin' on

She had another buddy, came by my place
Thick-assed bitch, said her name was Grace
She walked in the door, workin' lace
Ya should 'a seen that look that was on my face

She's like this tender named Belinda
The homeboys call her Belinda the Blender
She gave head like she made it up
She was twenty years old with a big round butt

Had a girl, looked like Olive Oyl
Her father was rich and the girl was spoiled
When she got mad her blood would boil
But I wrapped her all up like aluminum foil

These are the tales, the freaky tales
These are the tales that I tell so well
These are the tales, the freaky tales
These are the tales that I tell so well

Sugar delight
Friday night
It's goin' on
Too Short

Three weeks ago I met this freak
She followed me around like Mary's sheep
I hid around the corner and when she came
I grabbed her by the arm and I asked her name

She said it was Anita, her man's in Santa Rita
I took her to my house and, homeboy, I g'd 'er
Send her on her way the very next day
Playboy Short was ready to play

I bumped into this girl, her name's Roshon
We hit the motel and had it goin' on
Holiday Inn 'til the break of dawn
When I took baby home, I freaked her mom

I knew this tender named Shiree
I took her to my house and let her freak on me
Baby was a fan, she loved my beat
But I wouldn't raise my leg and let her kiss my feet

I met this freak named Yolanda
Rode baby doll like a brand new Honda
I was on top, she was up under
The bed hit the wall and it sounded like thunder

I once had a date with a girl named Kitty
She was so fine with her big fat titty
All night long, she was actin' shitty
So I macked on baby like I was Frank Nitty

There's another girl, her name is Rose
I used to ride baby like brand new vogues
I never saw Rose wearin' clothes
She's a Penthouse Pet ready to pose

I was ridin' down the street when I met Janet
Her booty was bigger than the whole damn planet
Ass everywhere, I just can't stand it
Tried to palm it but I could not manage

I had this freak, her name was Bunny
Said I'm the only man who called her Honey
Everything I did to her was funny
I macked on Bunny and I took her money

Eight tonight, a date with Shirley
She was real short and her hair was curly
If you saw baby, you'd like this girlie
She was so fine, I went to get her early

Shirley was freakin' like a girl named Rachel
Her bite was vicious and it sure was fatal
She liked to kiss all on my navel
Those are her lips on top of my label

I knew another freak, her name was Candy
Real big lips and they came in handy
I smooth got worked and it was so dandy
I hooked the broad up with my homeboy Randy

He did me a favor in return
Gave me a lizard, said her name was Laverne
Baby got tossed then I got on
I grabbed the microphone and started singin' my song

My young homeboy heard me rap
And he said he had way more freaks than that
So I told him like this, "They might be freakin'
But boy ya never had that t.p. treatment"

Too Short

Life Is Too Short

I remember how it all began
I used to sing dirty raps to my East Side fans
Back then I knew ya couldn't stop this rap
No M.C. could rock like that
Then the new style came, the bass got deeper
Ya gave up the mike and bought you a beeper
Do ya wanna rap or sell coke?
Brothers like you ain't never been broke
People wanna say it's just my time
Brothers like me had to work for mine
Eight years on the mike and I'm not jokin'
Sir Too Short comin' straight from Oakland
California, home of the rock
Eight woofers in the trunk, beatin' down the block
Short dog, I'm that rappin' man
I said it before and I'll say it again

Life is too short
Too short
Life is too short

Life is to some people unbearable
Committin' suicide and that's terrible
Was it much too much or nothin' big?
If ya live my life, you'd be fightin' to live
Life is to me my main asset
I be doin' all right and keep it just like that
Chill out at the house and pump that bass
I'm tryin' to get rich as I rock the place
Everybody's got that same old dream
To have big money and fancy things
Drive a brand new Benz, keep your bank right here
Never hear me stutter once because I talk real clear
It's on you, homeboy, watcha gonna do?
You can take my advice and start workin', fool
Or you can close your ears and run your mouth
And one day, homeboy, ya soon find out

Life is too short
Too short
Life is too short

Life is too short, would you agree?
While I'm livin' my life, don't mess with me
It's been a long time, baby, since I first got down
But I still keep makin' these funky sounds
'Cause I don't stop rappin', that's my theme
I make a lot of money, do you know what I mean?
Like this, complicated ya must stay up
Ya asked a simple question boy, don't say "What?"
Ya only live once and ya callin' it hell
Policeman tryin' to take ya to jail
You could give a man time but you don't know
In a matter of time, I'll be runnin' the show
Now another young buck wants to be on top

Makin' big money, slangin' hop
The task force tryin' ta peel your cap
Turn around, homeboy, ya better watch your back

Life is too short
Too short
Life is too short

You can take back all the things you give
But ya can't take back the days you live
Life is to some people who've been on earth
Livin' every single day for what it's worth
I live my life just how I please
Satisfy one person I know, that's me
Work hard for the things I achieve in life
And never rap fake when I'm on the mike
'Cause if a dream is all you got, homeboy
Ya gotta turn that dream into the real McCoy
No time to waste, just get on that case
Ya can't be down 'cause ya need to taste
A good life livin' like a king on a throne
Gettin' everything ya want and tryin' to have all your own
So life
Don't be stupid though
'Cause when ya waste it, you'll know

Life Is
Life Is
All right, that's it

Too Short

Little Girls

Little girls of the world
You're all so sprung
Fifteen, sixteen, and all so young
I thought about two just last night
Grabbed my pen then I started to write
A rap that a cap like a true-blue rap
Not a washed-up almost M.C. sap
Little girls so fresh and I know you are
Wanna take a little ride in my new car
I said you're more than bait
It's more like hell
Ya screw a little girl and end up in jail
Even though she seems she's nineteen
Ya lookin' at her body and it's breakin' your jeans
Well ya know she's not, so don't play dumb
Little girls walkin' 'round tryin' to give me some
But I tell 'em like this, I'm the player Short
Playin' freaks like you is just a sport
Becomin' way too real, well I can never be funny
Niggers like me just want your money
Give it up 'cause I'm no lost cause
Little girl recognize, Too Short's the boss
When they turn sixteen, we all find out
What little girls like that are all about
So you girls out there that fit my rhyme
Ya better think twice before ya jump on mine

Little girl so thick ya might think she's grown
But if ya knew her when she was one ya might leave her alone
She's trouble, homeboy, with a big fat "T"
Little girls like that make old men pee
Then a brother like me might break my neck
Lookin' back sayin', "ooh" 'bout to get in a wreck

'Cause she's always flirtin', might give me a look
Like I put her in the oven and she started to cook
But when I put her on the spot
She could not hang with my so-rough, so-tough Playboy game
I only said two words, somethin' like, "get busy"
Her head started hurtin' and she got real dizzy
Growin' up too fast, all you little girls
Lettin' brothers like me cold crush your world
Shoulda listened to your mama when she told ya so
But ya went and got g'd, now ya want some mo'
Ya ain't payin' me money, talkin' 'bout love
And the other girl is who I'm thinkin' of
Can ya understand, I'm just a man
I wanna come in this world and cold take romance
So just step on back while I walk on by
I might look you down and I might say, "hi"
And if ya come up choosin', I just might laugh
Say, "Little girl, check me out in about two-and-a-half
Years"

I took a little girl to a drive-in show
Jumped in the back and heard, "no no no"
She was only sixteen but the girl was ripe, thirty-six, twenty-four,
    and a thirty-five
I was wastin' time, spittin' lines
Thinkin' 'bout goin' home, go gettin' mine
Baby said, "Stop it," I said, "Drop it"
I tried everything but I could not cop it
I was goin' to the store 'bout a month ago
Met another girl, just loved my show
We talked for a while and it was all about
Havin' big fun later on in her house
She said her pops was gone but her mother was there
And everything's cool 'cause she don't care
So I gave her a ride, kissed her good-bye
I said I'd be back and you all know why
Went to find my thrill up on that hill
I was comin' right back with the power drill
I had fun for a while but it wasn't enough
When it all got good, her pops showed up

He musta walked in the room and said, "Young punk"
'Cause when he walked in the room, he smelled the funk
Then he tried to mash but I don't play
'Cause I was outta that window and on my way
Little girl

Every night you called and said come by
Ya tell me things changed and I know you lie
I came by last week, ya said drive on up
And your pops came out, talkin' all that stuff
Next night we made a date for nine o'clock
And I always wondered why ya walked the block
I saw ya waitin' on the corner when I made the turn
I didn't really think ya got it 'cause it wasn't for Sir
I said, "Ya look so good but ya always do"
I was rushin' to the house for the old one-two
But the ones ain't cool and the twos don't work
Every time I tried, ya kept sayin' it hurt
And then it all came out under all your tears
Seems ya only been alive for fifteen years
Ya coulda fooled me baby with your lies and schemes
Ya said ya worked in the mall and just turned eighteen
When it came down to it, I couldn't go through it
It's all so sad 'cause ya wanted to do it
Little girl, you wanna have some fun
Ya better wait a few years 'cause you're much too young
Stop playin' games, ya might find a guy
Who will like ya for yourself not for all your lies
So I put it like this and I don't play
If I see a young ass, I'm not goin' your way
Young girl

Treacherous three

Put the Boogie in Your Body

CHORUS 1: Get up, get up
Ya got to get down
Get up, get up
Get it, get on down
Get up, get up
Get down, a get down
Get up, get up, get up or get down

Party people listen up close
Haaah, take a drink and give us a toast
Because we're your hosts from coast to coast
We'll rock for the least but give you the most
Now all you party people in the place
Sittin' around with a smile on your face
We know you came here to party
So get on up, then put the boogie in your body
Huh Huh Hah Hah Huh Yeah

Allow me to introduce to you, hah!
The number-one rappin' and rhymin' crew
Special K, Sunshine, and Kool Moe Dee
We're better known as the Treacherous Three
Now all you party people that's not on the floor
You're not gettin' what you bargained for
Ya see ya paid that money so you could party
So get on up and put the boogie in your body
Huh Huh Hah Hah Huh Yeah

To rock—ya need to boogie
To shock—ya need to boogie
To rock or shock, shock or shock
Ya need to boogie
To move—ya need to boogie

To groove—ya need to boogie
And that's what we're here to prove
Ya need to boogie
For sound—ya need to boogie
Around—ya need to boogie
To dance and just get on down
Ya need to boogie

For all the party people, I got an idea
Somethin' that we want all y'all to hear, hah!
We gonna set this party straight
We both got talent, let's combinate

CHORUS 2: Now I got the boogie
You got the body
Put it together and make this a party
We got the highs and we got the bass
But we can't tell who's in the place
So fly girls
Say, "Yeah" ("Yeah")
And fly guys
Say, "Present" ("Present")
And party people
Make some noise and let me know you're here
Let me hear ya say, "Yeah" ("Yeah")
Now clap (*clap*)
Now let me hear ya say, "Party"! ("Party!")
Now get on up and put the boogie in your body

We wanna keep ya movin', keep ya groovin'
To the funky beat
But all we ask of you is to keep provin' that
Ya feel the heat
And if you're not on the floor yet
Then ya can bet that it's up to you
So just put the boogie in your body
And let it work for you

CHORUS 1
Huhhh!

Now all you fly guys on the wall
Get on off and let's have a ball
Because you know you can't rock 'em all
Put the boogie in your body, y'all
Until you need a little Geritol

Now all the fly girls in a chair
Get on up and throw your hands in the air
And rock to the beat like you don't care
'Cause the boogie's in the atmosphere
I said it once and let me make it clear
I said it once and I hope you heard
'Cause my job is to spread the word
'Cause we gonna set this party straight
We both got time, let's combinate

CHORUS 2
Huh Huh Hah Hah Huh Yeah
Ah Ohhhh!

We wanna keep ya movin', keep ya groovin'
To the funky beat
But all we ask of you is to keep provin' that
Ya feel the heat
And if you're not on the floor yet
And you can bet that it's up to you
So just put the boogie in your body
And let it work for you

CHORUS 1

BREAK

Ah-huh-huh, well excuse my cough
But it's Kool Moe Dee and I'm signin' off
Now I got a name game that I wantch'all to play
Better listen good to what I say
Now when I say, "Kool," ya say, "Moe Dee"
When I say my name just repeat it to me

It's Kool (Moe Dee!)
Kool Moe Dee (Kool Moe Dee!)

We're gonna play the game again
In the same old way
Except when I say, "Special"
You say, "K"
It's Special (Kaaay!)
Special K (Special Kaaay!)
Ah-haah, we're gonna play the game again
Just one more time
When I say, "L.A."
Ya say, "Sunshine"
L.A. (Sunshine!)
L.A. Sunshine (L.A. Sunshine!)

Now all you fly guys on the wall
Get on off and let's have a ball
Just join the party and party hearty
And get on up and put the boogie in your body
Huh Huh Hah Hah Huh Yeah
Get on up and put the boogie in your body
Huh hah put the boogie in your body
Huh Huh Hah Hah Huh Yeah

So come on, everybody
So come on, everybody
Come on, come on
Come on, everybody
Get on up and put the boogie in your body
Huh Huh Hah Hah Huh Yeah

Put the boogie in your body
Come on, everybody

A tribe called Quest

Ham 'n' Eggs

I don't eat no ham 'n' eggs
'Cause they're high in cholesterol
Hey, yo, Phife, do ya eat 'em?
No, Tip, do you eat 'em?
Uh-uh, not at all
Again: I don't eat no ham 'n' eggs
'Cause they're high in cholesterol
Jarobi, do ya eat 'em?
Nope
Sha, do ya eat 'em?
Nope
Not at all (hey)

A tisket, a tasket
What's in mama's basket
Some veggie links
And some fish that stinks
Why just the other day
I went to grandma's house
Smelled like she conjured up a mouse
Eggs was fryin'
Ham was smellin'
In ten minutes
She started yellin'
"Come and git it"
And the gettin' looked good
I said, "I shouldn't eat it"
She said, "I think ya should"
But I can't
I'm plagued by vegetarians
No cats and dogs
I'm not a veterinarian
Strictly collard greens

And a occasional steak
Goes on my plate
Asparagus tips looked yummy yummy yummy
Candy yams inside my tummy
A collage of good eats
A snack, some nice treats
Applesauce and some nice red beets
This is what we snack on when we're questin'
No second guessin'

I don't eat no ham 'n' eggs
'Cause they're high in cholesterol
I dig it
Hey, yo, Phife, do ya eat 'em?
No, Tip, do ya eat 'em?
Uh-uh, not at all
Come on again
I don't eat no ham 'n' eggs
'Cause they're high in cholesterol
Jarobi, do ya eat 'em?
No, Sha, do ya eat 'em?
Nope, not at all
Bridge!

Now drop the beat
So I can talk about my favorite tastings
The food that is the everlasting
See I'm not fasting
I'm gobblin'
Like a doggone turkey
Beef jerkeys, slim jims
I eat sometimes
I like lemon and limes
And if not that
I get the roti and the sour sop
Sit back, relax
Listen to some hip hop
Gum drops and gummy bears
Tease my eyes
A sight for sore ones

And so are pies
And other goodies that are filled with goo
Fried apple hoops
Delectable delights
Controls my appetites
Pa says, "Boy, eat right"
But I know what I like
Chicken for lunch
Chicken for my dinner
Chicken chicken chicken
I'm a finger-lickin' winner
When breakfast time comes
I don't recognize
Pig in the pan
Or a pair of roguish eyes
Fancy stewed tomatoes
Home-fried potatoes
Or anything with flair
You cook it, I'm in there
Pay attention to the Tribe
As we impose
This is how it goes

I don't eat no ham 'n' eggs
'Cause they're high in cholesterol
Hey, yo Phife, do ya eat 'em?
Hey, Tip, do ya eat 'em?
Uh-uh, not at all
Come and get 'em!
I don't eat no ham 'n' eggs
'Cause they're high in cholesterol
Yo, Jaro', do ya eat 'em?
No, Sha, do ya eat 'em?
No, not at all (Again, again again)
I don't eat no ham 'n' eggs
'Cause they're high in cholesterol
Afrika, do ya eat 'em?
Nope, Pos, do ya eat 'em?
Hell, yeah, all the time
I don't eat no ham 'n' eggs

'Cause they're high in cholesterol
Hey yo Phife, do ya eat 'em?
Nah, Tip, do ya eat 'em?
Uh-uh, not at all
I don't eat no ham 'n' eggs
'Cause they're high in cholesterol
Yo, Jarobi, do ya eat 'em?
Nope, Sha, do ya eat 'em?
Nope, not at all
I don't eat no ham 'n' eggs
'Cause they're high in cholesterol
Afrika, do ya eat 'em?
Nope, Gary do ya eat 'em?
Yeah, all the time

A tribe called Quest

I Left My Wallet in El Segundo

My mother went away for a month-long trip
Her and some friends on an ocean-liner ship
She made a big mistake by leaving me home
I had to roam so I picked up the phone
Dialed Ali up to see what was going down
Told him I pick him up so we could drive around
Took the Dodge Dart, a '74
My mother left a yard but I needed one more
Shaheed had me covered with a hundred greenbacks
So we left Brooklyn and we made big tracks
Drove down the Belt, got on the Conduit
Came to a toll, we paid and went through it
Had no destination, we was on a quest
Ali laid in the back so he could get rest
Drove down the road for two-days-and-a-half
The sun had just risen on a dusty path
Just then a figure had caught my eye

A man with a sombrero who was four feet high
I pulled over to ask where we was at
His index finger he tipped up his hat
"El Segundo," he said, "my name is Pedro
If you need directions, I'll tell you pronto"
Needed civilization, some sort of reservation
He said a mile south, there's a fast food station
Thanks, señor, as I start up the motor
Ali said, "Damn, Tip, why you drive so far for?"

(Well describe to me what the wallet looks like)

Anyway a gas station we passed
We got gas and went on to get grub
It was a nice little pub in the middle of nowhere
Anywhere would have been better
I ordered enchiladas and I ate 'em
Ali had the fruit punch
When we finished we thought for ways to get back
I had a hunch
Ali said, "Pay for lunch"
So I did it
Pulled out the wallet and I saw this wicked beautiful lady
She was a waitress there
Put the wallet down and stared and stared
To put me back into reality, here's Shaheed:
"Yo, Tip, man, you got what you need?"
I checked for keys and started to step
What do you know, my wallet I forget

Yo, it was a brown wallet, it had props numbers, had my jimmy
    hats I got to get it man

Lord, have mercy
The heat got hotter, Ali starts to curse me
I feel bad but he makes me feel badder
Chit-chit-chatter, car starts to scatter
Breaking on out, we was Northeast bound
Jettin' on down at the speed of sound
Three days coming and three more going

We get back and there was no slack
490 Madison, we're here, Sha
He said, "All right, Tip, see you tomorrow"
Thinking about the past week, the last week
Hands go in my pocket, I can't speak
Hopped in the car and torpe'ed to the shack
Of Shaheed, "We gotta go back" when he said
"Why?" I said, "We gotta go
'Cause I left my wallet in El Segundo"

Yeah, I left my wallet in El Segundo
Left my wallet in El Segundo
Left my wallet in El Segundo
I gotta get, I got-got ta get it

2 - live Crew

Dirty Nursery Rhymes

My mama and your mama was talkin' a little shit
My mama called your mama a bull-dykin'-assed bitch
I know your sister and the bitch ain't shit
She slagged me and all the boys and even sucked our dick

Jack and Jill went up the hill
To have a little fun
Jack got mad, kicked Jill in the ass
'Cause she couldn't make him come

Mama Bear and Papa Bear went for a walk through the forest
Mama Bear asked Papa Bear could he eat her porridge
Papa Bear said, "Shit, bitch, you must think I'm sick
Just get down here on your knees and suck this bad-assed dick"

Abraham Lincoln was a good old man
He hopped out the window with his dick in his hand
He said, "'Scuse me, lady, I'm doin' my duty
So pull down your pants and give me some booty"

There's an old lady who lives in a shoe
Got a house full of kids, don't know what to do
She sucked and fucked all the niggers around
When it's time to pay rent, could none be found

Little Miss Muffet
Sat on a tuffet
With her legs gapped open wide
Up came a spider
Looked up inside 'er
And said, "That pussy's wide"

Little Jack Horner
Sat on a corner
Fuckin' this cutie pie
Stuck in his thumb
Made the bitch come
Said, "Hell of a nigger am I"

Humpty Dumpty fell off the wall
'Cause a ho on the ave was suckin' his balls
All the king's horses and all the king's men
Couldn't put that fat motherfucker back together again

Little Red Ridin' Hood was on her way
To Grandmother's house
But before she got there, she met this man
That turned her hot ass out

Rapunzel, Rapunzel, let down your hair
The dog's on my ass and gettin' near
The hair came loose and fell in the lake
Bitch checked the weave that's in that lake

2 - live Crew

In the Dust

Takin' this shit into the effect mode
Expressin' my feelin's before I explode
About the sufferin' that's on to a black man
By the money-hungry seekin' white man
Fuckin' up our streets with pollution
Then lockin' niggers up for the solution
There they go again, pickin' on the little man
Fuck with the cartel of the white man

Arrest musicians for the things they say
But can't find a crime after it got sprayed
This is America—In God We Trust
We won just this but
Our dick is in the dust

I'm stereotyped, so I fit the description
A nigger has a stigma for pushin' or pimpin'
Police harass me
They use brutality
Without askin' me
A man gets out of his car
And reaches for his license
Cop pulls a gun and cold-iced him
I'm a victim of society
I got societal ills
It's harder to pay bills than pop pills
Ya send a brother off to fight for your country
When asked for ours, we get nothin'
I look for work and get my feelin's hurt
They got my back against the wall
And my dick is in the dirt

Let's talk about this man they call Nino Brown
The black man they call Nino Brown
Ya know, there's a lot of Nino Brown's in every city in the United
    States of America
America has formed a Nino Brown in every city
Basically because we have no way out
Is that what America really wants us to think?
That we don't have a way out?
Here's an example: you have never seen a black man come into
    Miami with pounds and pounds of marijuana, pounds and
    pounds of cocaine
You have never seen a black man drop off a kilo load of cocaine
    out of a plane
You have never seen this
But yet and still it's in our community every day and we're the
    ones goin' to jail for it

The system is designed to lead us astray
So we turn to drugs and guns for pay
It's a sign of the times
I got to get mine
All I live is a life of crime
I came up hard from a ran-down ghetto
Ya talk ya ass off but tell me what a nigger know
All I see is a lot of neighborhood drama
Babies cryin', I'm wonderin' where's the momma
She OD'd and got rushed to trauma
A dealer has to deal to make a fast buck
She was just a patient, what the fuck
His back's against the wall
And his dick is in the dust

2 - live Crew

Me So Horny (As Clean as They Wanna Be)

Sittin' at home
Watchin' Arsenio Hall
So I got my black book
For a freak to call
Picked up the telephone
Then dialed the seven digits
Said, "Yo, this Marquis, baby
Are you down with it?"

I arrived at her house
Knocked on her door
Not havin' no idea of what
The night had in store

I'm like a dog in heat
A freak without warnin'
Not havin' appetite for love
'Cause me so horny

Girls always ask me
Why I bug so much
I say, "What's wrong, baby doll
With being a nut?"
'Cause my nature is risin'
And you shouldn't be mad
I won't tell your momma
If you don't tell your dad

I know he'll be disgusted
When he sees your clothes messed up
Won't your momma sure be mad
If she know you'd just been had

I'm a freak in heat
A dog without warnin'

My appetite is love
'Cause me so horny

You can say I'm desperate
Even call me perverted
When I leave you lost and deserted
I play with your heart
And won't show no shame
I'll be blowin' your mind
'Cause I'm linked to the game

I'm just like that guy
They call Georgie Puddin' Pie
I break the girls' hearts
And I make them cry

I'm a dog in heat
A freak without warnin'
Not havin' appetite for love
'Cause me so horny

2 - live Crew

Me So Horny (As Dirty as They Wanna Be)

"What do we get for ten dollars?"
Everything you want
Everything?
Everything
(Sock it to me)

Oh me so horny
Oh me so horny
Oh me so horny
We love you long time

Sittin' at home
With my dick all hard

So I got my black book
For a freak to call
Picked up the telephone
Then dialed the seven digits
Said, "Yo, this Marquis, baby
Are you down with it?"

I arrived at her house
Knocked on the door
Not havin' no idea of what
The night had in store

I'm like a dog in heat
A freak without warnin'
Not havin' appetite for sex
'Cause me so horny

Oh me so horny
Oh me so horny
Oh me so horny
We love you long time

Girls always ask me
Why I fuck so much
I say, "What's wrong, baby doll
With a quick nut
'Cause you're the one
And you shouldn't be mad
I won't tell your momma
If you don't tell your dad"

I know he'll be disgusted
When he sees your pussy busted
Wouldn't your momma be so mad
If she know I got that ass

I'm a freak in heat
A dog without warnin'
My appetite to sex
'Cause me so horny

Oh me so horny
Oh me so horny

Oh me so horny
We love you long time

You can say I'm desperate
Even call me perverted
But you'll say I'm a dog
When I leave you fucked and deserted
I play with your heart
Just like it's a game
I'll be blowin' your mind
While you're blowin' my brain

I'm just like that man they call
Georgie Puddin' Pie
I fuck all the girls
And I make them cry

I'm like a dog in heat
A freak without warnin'
Not havin' appetite for sex
'Cause me so horny

Oh me so horny
Oh me so horny
Oh me so horny
We love you long time

It's true you were a virgin
Until you met me
I was the first to make you hot
And wet-ty wet-ty
You told your parents that we're goin' out
Never to the movies
Just straight to my house

You said it yourself
You like it like I do
Put your lips on my dick
And suck my asshole, too

I'm like a freak in heat
A dog without warnin'

My appetite to sex
'Cause me so horny

Oh me so horny
Oh me so horny
Oh me so horny
We love you long time

U M C
One to Grow On

Castle on the borderline is surely like this
Approaching of a UMC is purely hypeness
A fact, so I mention it again and again
It's not necessary, those who comprehend my message very clearly
But not along the way of translucent
Throw your hands up for the man who sent
Invaders of my fruit basket, tow a casket
Meaning done away, see the flocks run away
So as a UMC I ask myself who can be the leaders
Resembling the stars that are far
Well it's you Hass G and that's a find
The Koolness in Me at a whim who would freeze Blue Cheese
Spinnin' 360 on a runway Stop! and hear many more than one
      say u-n-i-v-e-r-s-a-l
Go on 'cause we gave them all one thought to grow on

Apprehend my method, my method is apparent
I see clearly this world's transparent
So I reach down deep, deliver salvation to the hands of the weak
The meek, the mild
Then tame the wild
'Cause that's how I'm styled
The wizard of rhymes, my symbol is A-U
In layman's terms, gold, so watch me shine through

A new zoo review coming right at you
And you and you, Kim is coming through
I grow on because my strength is that of two
If rhyme's a boat, the beat must be my crew
A mental ingredient, all of which is alarming
Not harming, better say disarming
Yes I disarm ya, I neutralize your weaponry
To make ya more appropriate to deal with me
And then I give you one to grow on

Grow on this when you're feeling kinda small
Grow on this to get through life ya'll
Grow on this to have fun for the creators
Grew and grew and when the time came play the
Oh flow short now we get to the port of authority
You and I verse the majority
Here's what we're looking at here
At the count of three let's hear the UMC cheer
"UMCn's a new way of bein' "

Grow on this to make your life seem great
Grow on this and take control of your fate
Grow on this until you finally understand
Grew and grew and now the boy's a u-man
Go sit beside the shoreline, think about your woes
Read the whips and waves, identify your foes
Then realize in this instance of existence
There is great resistance to the minds that mixed this
Yes I've made things known but then again I'm on the down low
It's obvious because my methods show
That I rule on three planes of reality
Universally, mystically, conceptually
Then in due time you may find that I'm livin' in the world of my
    design
And I give you one to grow on

Urban dance squad
Living in the Fast Lane

Quest for the ducats and cheques
Tired of fixin' the ends together
Better better climb the ladder
To the top, to the top, to the top
Where big shots make the bucks and call the shots
And budge the status to super, they hold the grudge
'Cause it's goin' your way, beyond the fair play
Obedience to what you say, hey
For your presence, they stay the hell away
A free doorway, things are okay
No matter what they say, that's only hearsay
To choke in the smoke, while you consume a J
Stay ahead of the game, clock the dames
Gain the fame, ready to tame
Some feel the pain, some hail your name
Ducks stay lame, while you're livin'
In the fast lane

Livin' in the fast lane
Livin' in the fast lane
Livin' in the fast lane

Pedal to the metal, goin' fast, fast
Ferrari-level, got the class, class
Yes, cold-clockin' cash 'n' sex
While the mass hold hands up to catch
Relax, no complaints, satisfaction
No red tape—twenty-four-hour action
Meat the bizniz—get the glitz
Get the B., get the B. to unzip the zips
Trippin', trippin'—cold ego trippin'
Shatterin' pride, why they're flippin'
Sippin' 40s, how you're livin'

Value is given, while you're driven
In the fast lane

Livin' in the fast lane

Every day, excellency
Breakin' laws, hey, no penalties
If you do supply the Gs
Authorities make sure they don't seem
Free from the burden of life
Seek other ways to strive
With the scene and reach the untold
That you're bold and it leaves you cold
They build up while you only mold
'Cause it's the dough you hold
So play your head role
Break doors, open another store
Let the green flow and pour
Watch the score of dimes
Same time the snow is snorted up your nose
To a cigar, you're much a closed door
Holdin' a pose and never grow old
A fast lane bro', livin' in
The fast lane

Livin' in the fast lane

Roxanne Roxanne

Yo, EMD
Yeah, what's up man?
There go that girl they call Roxanne
She's all stuck up
Why do you say that?
'Cause she wouldn't give a guy like me no rap

Man, she was walking down the street so I said, "Hello
I'm Kango from UTFO"
And she said, "So"
I said, "So? Baby don'tcha
I can sing, rap, dance in just one show"
'Cause I'm Kango, Mr. Sophisticator
So far's I know, ain't nobody greater
From beginning to end and
To beginning
I never lose because I'm all about winning
But if I was to lose, I wouldn't be upset
'Cause I'm not a gambler, I don't bet
I don't be in no casino
And baby, why ya sheez so
The is I is the grizeat kizang kizzo
I thought she'd be impressed and
Give me devious rap
I thought I had her caught inside my sinister trap
I thought it'd be a piece of cake
But it was nothin' like that
I guess that's why I keep a thinkin', ain't that right, Black?
(*ad lib*)

With a bang-bang brother I fell bad
But I ain't committing suicide with no crab
Calling her a crab is just a figure of speech
She's a apple, a pear, a plum, and a peach
I thought I had it in the palm of my hand
But man oh man, if I was grand
I'd bang Roxanne

Roxanne Roxanne, can't you understand
Roxanne Roxanne, I wanna be your man

Yo Kango! I don't think that you're dense
But you went about the matter with no experience
You should know she doesn't need a guy like you
She needs a guy like me with a high I.Q.
And she'll take to my rap cause my rap's the best
The educated rapper, M.D. will never fess

So when I met her, I wasted no time
But stuck-up Roxanne paid me no mind
She thought my name was Larry
I told her it was Gary
She said she didn't like it so she took to call me Barry
She said she'd love to marry
Her baby she would carry
And if we had a baby, we'd name the baby Harry.
Her mother's name was Mary
Which was really quite contrary
Her face is very hairy
And you could say it's scary
She lives in Mt. Airy, her father's a fairy
His wife's a secretary, his son's in military
They forced him to enlist, I guess it wasn't voluntary
His daughter's name is Sherry
His sons are Tom and Jerry
Jerry had the flu but it was only temporary
Back in January or was it February
But every time I sing this rhyme, it makes me kind of weary
It's only customary to give this commentary
Some say it's rap, some say it's legendary
Keep searchin' all you want, try your local library
You'll never find a rhyme like this in any dictionary
But do you know, after all that
All I've received was a pat on the back
That's what you get, it happened to me
Ain't that right, Mixmaster I-C-E?

Roxanne Roxanne
Roxanne Roxanne

You thought you had her roped
You thought you was cupid
But EMD, yo' rap was plain stupid
I know you're educated but when will you learn
Not all girls want to be involved with bookworms
You gotta be stronger in ways she can't resist
So educated rapper, huh, bust this

Since she's the new girl around the block
I had to let her know I was the Debonair Doc
I said, "I'd like to speak with you, if I can
And if I'm correct here, your name is Roxanne"
She said, "How'd you know my name?"
I said, "It's gettin' around
Right now, baby, you're the talk of the town
Please let me walk you to the corner, my rap will be brief"
She said, "I seen you before, you look like a thief"
I said, "Me? The Doc? A hood? A rock?"
Runnin' 'round the street robbin' people on the block
Naaa, that's not my style, to crime I'm not related
As far as I'm concerned I'm too sophisticated
Then it seems I got through 'cause she cracked a smile
That let me know my rap was worth her while
She said, "You call yourself a doctor?"
I said, "This is true"
She said, "Explain to me really what doctors must do"
I said, "This is very good 'cause I don't say this every day
It's a major medical field the doctor must play"
Dermatology is treatment of the skin
If infected and you see me I'm your number one in
There's anaesthesiology, opthamology, internal medicine, and
     plastic surgery
Orthopedic surgery and pathology, a disease caused by the change
     of the body
She said, "Ooh, that's very unique"
Gave me her number and kissed me on the cheek
She said she had to go but she'd be back by eight
She said call her at nine to arrange a date
Did you take her to the beach?
That's what we planned
But she stood me up, Roxanne Roxanne

Roxanne Roxanne, I wanna be your man
Roxanne Roxanne, and here's our game plan

The beat is here, so we will reveal it
And if you think it's soft, then Roxanne—feel it

Vanilla Ice

Ice Ice Baby

Yo, VIP, let's kick it

Ice Ice Baby, Ice Ice Baby
All right stop, collaborate and listen
Ice is back with my brand new invention
Something grabs a hold of me tightly
Then I flow like a harpoon, daily and nightly
Will it ever stop? Yo—I don't know
Turn off the lights and I'll glow
To the extreme, I rock a mike like a vandal
Light up a stage and wax a chump like a candle

Dance, bum rush the speaker that booms
I'm killing your brain like a poisonous mushroom
Deadly, when I play a dope melody
Anything less than the best is a felony
Love it or leave it, you better gain way
You better hit bull's eye, the kid don't play
If there was a problem, Yo, I'll solve it
Check out the hook while my D.J. revolves it

Ice Ice Baby, Vanilla, Ice Ice Baby, Vanilla
Ice Ice Baby, Vanilla, Ice Ice Baby, Vanilla

Now that the party is jumping
With the bass kicked in, the Vegas are pumping
Quick to the point, to the point no faking
I'm cooking M.C.s like a pound of bacon
Burning them if they're not quick and nimble
I go crazy when I hear a cymbal
And a hi hat with a souped up tempo
I'm on a roll and it's time to go solo
Rolling in my 5.0
With my ragtop down so my hair can blow

The girlies on standby, waving just to say hi
Did you stop? no—I just drove by
Kept on pursuing to the next stop
I busted a left and I'm heading to the next block
That block was dead

Yo—so I continued to A1A Beachfront Ave.
Girls were hot, wearing less than bikinis
Rockman lovers driving Lamborghinis
Jealous 'cause I'm out getting mine
Shay with a gauge and Vanilla with a nine
Reading for the chumps on the wall
The chumps acting ill because they're so full of eight balls
Gunshots ranged out like a bell
I grabbed my nine—all I heard were shells
Falling on the concrete real fast
Jumped in my car, slammed on the gas
Bumper to bumper, the avenue's packed
I'm trying to get away before the jackers jack
Police on the scene, you know what I mean
They passed me up, confronted all the dope fiends
If there was a problem, Yo, I'll solve it
Check out the hook while my D.J. revolves it

Ice Ice Baby, Vanilla, Ice Ice Baby, Vanilla
Ice Ice Baby, Vanilla, Ice Ice Baby, Vanilla

Take heed 'cause I'm a lyrical poet
Miami's on the scene just in case you didn't know it
My town, that created all the bass sound
Enough to shake and kick holes in the ground
'Cause my style's like a chemical spill
Feasible rhymes that you can vision and feel
Conducted and formed, this is a hell of a concept
We make it hype and you want to step with this
Shay plays on the fade, slice like a ninja
Cut like a razor blade so fast, other D.J.s say "damn"
If my rhyming was a drug, I'd sell it by the gram
Keep my composure when it's time to get loose
Magnetized by the mike while I kick my juice

If there was a problem, Yo,—I'll solve it
Check out the hook while my D.J. revolves it

Ice Ice Baby, Vanilla, Ice Ice Baby, Vanilla
Ice Ice Baby, Vanilla, Ice Ice Baby, Vanilla Ice

Yo man—let's get out of here! word to your mother

Ice Ice Baby, too cold, Ice Ice Baby, too cold, too cold
Ice Ice Baby, too cold, too cold, Ice Ice Baby, too cold, too cold

who Am I?

Nickel Slick Nigga

The setting is a cool breeze day
Where it takes place, in the city of L.A.
I'm nine years old to be exact
Checker bellbottoms, brown shirt, with a dusty-ass cap
Goin' to the ABC market, had to get some new biscuits
Two dollars, what a bargain
Proceeding up the street while I'm humming a tune
Uh, first time I witness somebody tryin' a Jack move
If I'm correct it was a Elco tryin' to Jack a '64
Niggas trying to tip-toe and yo, pointin' the gauges
Tryin' to take the brother's *lleyo*
He was what was up, got out the vehicle, and bailed
He just had to run in my direction
But they smoked his ass, now he's next to the sports section
But the nigga drop the *lleyo* on the ground
So then I pick the shit up, ran down, and around the corner
Yo, uh, through nearby alley
Escape through a tiny gate
I WAS A NICKEL SLICK NIGGA
I WAS A NICKEL SLICK NIGGA
I WAS A NICKEL SLICK NIGGA
I WAS A NICKEL SLICK NIGGA

Huffin' and puffin' but I finally got to the pad
My mother ask where I was at
I said, "Yo, I was over Sno's house playin' some marbles"
She believe what I said so I went to my quarters
You see I shared rooms with my cousin who was mentally slow
But he was a big-ass fuck
Six feet five, three hundred pounds or mo', nickname "Big
    Truck"
Took the sack out of my pants, unraveled the product
Told my cousin, "We gotta hustle and bustle to make money
    back"
I make connections, you watch my back
Set up a program called the Lemonade Stand
But I wasn't sellin' drinks
I was sellin' big bands an' bundles an' boulders of dubs, yea
At this time I was gettin' more pub, yo
From this cluck and that cluck and everybody wanna cluck-
    cluck
But me an' Truck, we didn't give a fuck
But the spot got hot, police raid
They took Truck to jail but me, I got away
I WAS A NICKEL SLICK NIGGA
I WAS A NICKEL SLICK NIGGA
I WAS A NICKEL SLICK NIGGA
I WAS A NICKEL SLICK NIGGA

Fo' years pass, now I'm thirteen
Bought me a duster to go undercover
My cousin's jail sentence was almost finished
Now we were back in the streets, in the mix, in it to win it
Pullin' cards, checkin' fools, takin' names down
Now my status for ballin' was set to ground
Other hustlers knew I was doin' my best
'Cause I was a ballin' young-assed nigga from the west
Bought a pimped-out crib in Pomona
Not far from the city so that way I can hit corners
Now who expect this little juvenile punk
Straight ballin' y'all, as they kept on fallin' for it
It was a smooth operation, you see
'Cause I had the look, your whole fuckin' family would love me

Five years swoop, now I'm eighteen
Sold a lot of product so they start callin' me Kokane
At this time, I was bustin' funky rhymes
Hook my shit up with '87 now I'm gettin' mine
Laylaw was in effect and he said, "Let's do this"
Gave my shit to E then I signed with Ruthless
But Truck was left on the spot, hmmm, what I do
Hook the nigga up with that Kokane rock
Now Truck was gettin' paper from the *lleyo*
Me, I'm gettin' paid from my motherfuckin' record sales
So there it is, is a player gettin' bigger
I guess I joined a whole organization of NICKEL SLICK NIGGAS

whodini

Haunted House of Rock

Welcome to the place
Where all the creatures meet
The last building to your left
On the dead-end street
You find skeleton bones
Outside on the pavement
And torture chambers down in the basement
Cobwebs hanging over your head
Music being played
By the Grateful Dead
And spinning on the turntable
Back to back
Was no other than my main man
Wolfman Jack
The M.C. of the night
Rapper to the tunes
Was a Creature from the Black Lagoon
Said the sign on the door

That can't be missed
Please enter but at your own risk
'Cause people were reported going in the haunted house
But never again seen coming out
You ask me if it's true
I'll leave it up to you
Isn't it a fright, I hope I see ya tonight

You send out invitations
For weeks and weeks
We invited in all kinds of creeps
Like Dr. Jekyll and Mr. Hyde
The Addams Family
And the Monster 5
And the Invisible Man
Where could he be?
We know he got inside the party free
One of these days
They're gonna catch him red-handed
Got him sneaking in free
And being a booty bandit
The bartender was cute
But kinda hairy
And Dracula was killing those Bloody Marys
He got drunk as a skunk
He started trouble already
Everybody knew his bark
Was bigger than his bite
It was the only place
For you to be
There was two hundred witches
In the party for free
And all was well
Until the clock struck twelve
Everybody jumped up and
Started raising hell

They were screamin', they was breakin'
Foaming at the mouth

Just minor side effects
Of the haunted house
You had haunted dreams
All in your sleep
You'd be tossing and turning
To the funky beat
Frankenstein was there
With some crazy-looking chick
I think she said her name
Was Voodoo-on-a-Stick
She had a big fat head and
A skinny body
I wouldn't be caught with her alone
Much known at a party
She's always there with the monster crew
I seen everybody there
Except you
Why didn't you come
Weren't you prepared?
Or could it be
That you was scared?
It's just not fair
That you couldn't be there
Because you really missed a lot
I'm telling ya
We really brought the place down at
The Haunted House of Rock

"Jalil, where'd ya go?"
Quiet, man, can't you see I'm trying to sneak outta here?
Word, man, let's break out
This place is crazy
Which way you gonna run, man
This way or that way?
Yo, man, let's just get outta here
It don't make no difference which way we go
Yes it do
Why?
'Cause I don't wanna run over you

x-clan

Funkin' Lesson

"Freedom or death
You shall all be moved
Vainglorious
This is protected by the red, the black, and the green
With a key, sissy"

Abracadabra—Ala baby professor
All hail funkin' lesson
Sweet tongue, grand writer of scrolls
Now behold, let the legend unfold
Born in the cosmos for no timin', space to exist
Vibe in the midst of the chaos
Mortals label me as illogical, mythological
They couldn't comprehend when I brought the word
A stick called verb, a black steel nerve
Teachin' those actors and actresses
Who write a couple of lines on what black is—really
Then they label me a sin
When a brother just speaks what's within
I guess I'm blacker than the shadow
In the darkest alley that they're always scared to go in—Boo!
I wear boots and beads, bags and braids
Stick and scroll, rings and shades
Walk in the light of the moon
But I never been a batman, African, call it black man
Brother extracts the African steps in your movements
Enhance your improvements
Grand Funk—a new home for the phrase
Funkin' lesson, the pathway

Let me tell you about blackness, grits, and cornbread
How can you act this

I exist on a plane where the jar is my brain
I'm livin' to retrieve cells
Antenna, my stick, picture bigger, native licker, figure
The poom of the trigger goes zoom! Not boom
Not a bunch of sissies, but saviors
Braver
The red, black, and green
It's just so much more than red, black, and green
You ask what I mean
But yet the sundial shades and lights of dreams
Watch too late, oops! upside your head
You drop through abyss like lead
Where you goin', what's your speed
What's your pleasure, what's your need?
Trees and branches, roots and seeds
Forwards, backwards, many degrees
Questions, answers, what's the sum?
We have come

"Out of the darkness, in panther's skin comes
Doctors—drivin' pink caddies,
Bearin' the remedy to your existence
Yes it gets blacker with a Nat Turner lick
Martin, Adam, Malcolm, Huey
There's a party at the crossroads"

I return from the stone crib
Bringing verbal milk, a stool, and a bib
Be filled of the black sap from the tri-womb
It flows freely on the tomb
Wheat bread, taste of jam
Come take a stroke to the rhythm of the grand
Verbalizer comin' from the temple of void
Crown from a hat, man from a boy
Onward ride as I talk with Rah
Converse with Horace, create with Ptah
Arrive with Geb, to roar with Bast
Aton, Temu as I ride the raft
Roof of the world I sit
Cross-legged, right over left

Drums of dance, to drums of war
Who knows the score, speak no more
Who watches down with the eyes of black
To the east blackwards
Sissy

YoYo

Dope Femininity

An aggressive intro
Lettin' you know I'm on the battle tip
Appearance is fragile
But I'm packin' power like a battleship
Rip through flesh and bones
Like a Piranha
My D.J. Chilly Chill
Is cuttin' better than Benihana
Needles are illegal
But people are sure to love it
I'm doin' somethin' right
That's why you homiez are dumbin' it
Hands considered
A weapon for wreckin' like a wreckin' ball
It it's bitten, it's copywritten
In other words, I'm checkin' you

On the cross fader
He's as evil as Darth Vader
With the life saver
But his cut's so much greater
The brother is swift
With his right and it's as if
If it was possible
He'd be scratchin' compact discs
There's no comparison

When he's tearin' 'em
He has the chance to glance
So watch quickly as his movements advance
I'm comin' on the I-B-W-C tip
Who's better for an audience than party shit—nothin'
Come on

As I'm speakin', you're weakin'
I'm thinkin', how could ya beat me?
I come out victorious
Even if you try to cheat me
Rough and rugged with Street Knowledge behind me
I-B-W-C is the way to define me
Smooth and slick
As I trick your mentality
Check my lyrics, if you ever wanna battle me
Posse up, I got the Mob behind me
On a record store shelf is where you find me

A poor poetic
Provin' punks are phantasm
Got a lock on the grip
Lock 'em up like a muscle spasm
My music constantly makes money by the minute
I'm in it to win it, so damn it, why don't we begin it
Slayin' and sprayin'
And droppin' rhymes like a prophesy
Distending the reality, there's no stoppin' me
A woman with wisdom
Usin' words to her advantage
Fools gettin' damaged, I hand 'em a bandage
A lyrical bein', free of the mind for those
Who's trapped, stepped up in the zone
Ya better be strapped
Or even scrap or get your manhood taken

Backbones are broke and choke
Neckbones are breakin'
Mikes are sacrificed to the lyrical lord
It's me, the double "Yo," you better watch out for

Keep a lookout
I get took out with the quickness
Watch your back, I get slayed with the swiftness
Dope femininity, livin' like an entity
With friends like the Mob, who the hell needs enemies?

YoYo

Make Way for the Motherload

There's no way you can skip the subject
You move your hips to this 'cause you love it
Admire it, and I'm the one who inspired you
It's the YoYo, listen to the promo
Come on down so you can play the Price Is Right
I get twice as nice, I'm 'a get nice tonight
Get with this, dig the style and the lecture
Feel the texture and you could, see how I could flex
To the slice of life the plans
And pan it left to right and then a close up
I get the most of the styles so focus on
The one who broke the barrier
I'm preparin' ya
Illustratin' many ways of tearing the mike
Rippin' it, put a clip in it
Load the ammo and let it slam when I be kickin' it
Stick it in yer jeep or yer benzo, it's in so
Deep you can bet, YoYo never break a sweat
Quiet is kept but you thought that you had enough
Clown to withstand me, you must go to plan B
I shake away and break away and take away
A brother to fold
So make way for the Motherload

Here's a piece or chunk of the funkiness
You can't understand how a sista came up with this

Style that's so wild
And leaves you shiverin' and danglin'
From the way that I be stranglin'
M.C.s that take their breath away literally
Many step up but they can't get a bit of me
M.C.s dash light like this is their last night
On earth
But they got turned out like a flashlight
Don't consume this, it's toxic and poisonous
There's no need to bring all your girlz to this
'Cause I'll dis ya and fry you in the skillet
Like a piece of pork, I don't care if you're from East New York
I don't flinch or move an inch
Catch this, no bitch, I'm from L.A.
So make way for the monkey wrench
And fit it, your program
I'm swoopin' in the mothership
As if it was a brougham
It's funk that's pumped to the top of the dome
And you can bet your last dollar on the fact that it's on
So admit you were taken by the storm
Of the form of the
Motherload

You had to make way so sit down and take a number
You was 'sleep and so you slumber silently
You can't match me or tie with me
There's a fungus among us so don't try to tongue this phrase
Speak it, try to freak it
It's unique 'cause I got the secret
You peekin' eye for eye as I plan this
Open wide as I try to cram this
Microphone down your throat with forcefulness
You can't afford this so write a report of this
Tell the world how I dissed and dismissed ya
And brought you turbulence
Sorta like a twista
Sistas smother me and cover me and shower me with praises
For the way that I played ya
YoYo's a motha when it comes to the discovery of dopeness

So don't deliver any doses
Any similar to mine, any form, any shape, any tape
With a Street Knowledge label is a caper
Thought about a motha and a brotha who's belligerent
Focused on a female, watch as I deliver it
Del the Homo Sapien and Jinx got the back up of the
    Motherload
Step to the front so I could shove the load of shit you delivered
Up the ass where it came from
Straight to the rectum, that's what you expected from
The Motherload

young Mc

Bust a Move

Bust it

This here's a jam for all the fellas
Try to do what those ladies tell us
Get shot down 'cause you're overzealous
Play hard to get, females get jealous
Okay smarty, go to a party
Girls are scantily clad and showin' body
A chick walks by, you wish you could sex her
But you're standin' on the wall like you was Poindexter
Next day's function, high class luncheon
Food is served and you're stone cold munchin'
Music comes on, people start to dance
But then you ate so much, you nearly split your pants
A girl starts walkin', guys start gawkin'
Sits down next to you and starts talkin'
Says she wants to dance 'cause she likes to groove
So come on, fatso, and just bust a move

Just bust a move

You're on a mission, and you're wishin'
Someone could cure your lonely condition
Lookin' for love in all the wrong places
No fine girls, just ugly faces
From frustration, first inclination
Is to become a monk and leave the situation
But every dark tunnel has a light of hope
So don't hang yourself with a celibate rope
New movies showin', so you're goin'
Could care less about the five you're blowin'
Theater gets dark just to start the show
Then you spot a fine woman sittin' in your row
She's dressed in yellow, she says, "Hello
Come sit next to me, you fine fellow"
You run over there without a second to lose
And what comes next—hey, bust a move

You want it, you got it
You want it, baby, you got it
Just bust a move
You want it, you got it
You want it, baby, you got it

In the city, ladies look pretty
Guys tell jokes so they can seem witty
Tell a funny joke just to get some play
Then you try to make a move and she says, "No way"
Girls are fakin', goodness sake an'
They want a man who brings home the bacon
Got no money and you got no car
Then you got no woman, and there you are
Some girls are sadistic, materialistic
Lookin' for a man makes them opportunistic
They're lyin' on the beach perpetratin' a tan
So that a brother with money can be their man
So on the beach you're strollin'—real high rollin'
Everything you have is yours and not stolen
A girl runs up with somethin' to prove
So don't just stand there, bust a move

You want it, you got it
You want it, baby, you got it
Just bust a move
You want it, you got it
You want it, baby, you got it
Break it down for me, fellas

Your best friend Harry has a brother Larry
In five days from now he's gonna marry
He's hopin' you can make it there if you can
'Cause in the ceremony, you'll be the best man
You say neato, check your libido
And roll to the church in your new tuxedo
The bride walks down just to start the weddin'
And there's one more girl you won't be gettin'
So you start thinkin', then you start blinkin'
A bridesmaid looks and thinks that you're winkin'
She thinks you're kind of cute so she winks back
And now you're feelin' really firm 'cause the girl is stacked
Receptions jumpin', bass is pumpin'
Look at the girl and your heart starts thumpin'
Says she wants to dance to a different groove
Now you know what to do, so you bust a move

You want it, you got it
You want it, baby, you got it
Just bust a move
You want it, you got it
You want it, baby, you got it
Move it, boy

young Mc

Principal's Office

Now, as I get to school, I hear the late bell ringing
Running through the hall, I hear the glee club singing
Get to the office, I can hardly speak
'Cause it's the third late pass that I got this week
So to my first class I run don't walk
All I hear are my sneakers and the scratchin' of chalk
And when I get to the room, I hear the teacher say
"Mr. Young, I'm happy that you could join us today"
I try to sit down so I can take some notes
But I can't read what the kid next to me wrote
And if that wasn't enough to make my morning complete
As I try to get up, I find there's gum on my seat
And with the seat stuck to me, I raise my hand
And say, "Excuse me, but can I go to the bathroom, ma'am"
The teacher got upset and she screamed out, "No
It's off to the principal's office you go"

Twelve o'clock comes with mass hysteria
Everybody rushes down to the cafeteria
Picked up my tray that I had Thursday's lunch
And when I tried the applesauce and I heard it crunch
I'm running up the stairs with a front tooth broken
The nurse just laughed and said, "You must be jokin' "
I looked up at her with a smile on my face
No joke 'cause my front tooth is out of place
So I walk through school with ice on my lip
A nurse's late pass like a gun on my hip
My books are real heavy, I walk and I'm draggin' it
No school lunch next week, I'm brown baggin' it
Forget class, I'm 'a shoot some ball
With the late pass, I've got no trouble at all
But then the nurse walks up and says, "Well, what do you know?
It's off to the principal's office you go"

Recess

Passing notes is my favorite pasttime
I can't wait to find a girl to pass mine to
To express my feeling
Give me a week, me and the girl be dealing
Now one young lady was looking at me
I said, "Hi, my name is Marvin known as Young MC"
But then the bell rang and the teacher came in
And that's when the game of passing notes would begin
I wrote the first note, told her she was fine
And I hoped that the two of us could spend some time
She wrote me back and told me, "You're fine too
I'd love to go on a date and spend some time with you"
So then I sat there reeling and looking at the ceiling
Words can't express the way that I was feeling
Then I thought to myself, the sure way to get her
Is to write another note, oh yes, a love letter
When I finished the note, it was ready to pass
The teacher took it and read it right in front of the class
She read it word by word and line by line
And everybody who was laughing was a friend of mine
Even my girl was laughing, it was too late
No need to write another note 'cause there would be no date
The teacher looked at me and I said, "I know
It's off to the principal's office I go"

Yo, you think this is bad
Wait 'til I get my report card